The Future of Syntax

Also available from Bloomsbury

Pragmatic Particles: Findings from Asian Languages, Jieun Kiaer
Pragmatic Syntax, Jieun Kiaer
English Syntax and Argumentation, Bas Aarts
Theories of Syntax: Concepts and Case Studies, Koenraad Kuiper and Jacqui Nokes
Syntactic Theory, Geoffrey Poole
Emoji Speak: Communication and Behaviours on Social Media, Jieun Kiaer

The Future of Syntax

Asian Perspectives in an AI Age

Jieun Kiaer

BLOOMSBURY ACADEMIC
LONDON • NEW YORK • OXFORD • NEW DELHI • SYDNEY

BLOOMSBURY ACADEMIC

Bloomsbury Publishing Plc, 50 Bedford Square, London, WC1B 3DP, UK
Bloomsbury Publishing Inc, 1385 Broadway, New York, NY 10018, USA
Bloomsbury Publishing Ireland, 29 Earlsfort Terrace, Dublin 2, D02 AY28, Ireland

BLOOMSBURY, BLOOMSBURY ACADEMIC and the Diana logo are trademarks of Bloomsbury Publishing Plc

First published in Great Britain 2024
Paperback edition published 2025

Copyright © Jieun Kiaer, 2024, 2025

Jieun Kiaer has asserted her right under the Copyright, Designs and Patents Act, 1988, to be identified as Author of this work.

For legal purposes the Acknowledgements on p. xii constitute an extension of this copyright page.

Cover design: Elena Durey
Cover images © Ehud Neuhaus/UNSPLASH, and Gareth Harper/UNSPLASH

All rights reserved. No part of this publication may be: i) reproduced or transmitted in any form, electronic or mechanical, including photocopying, recording or by means of any information storage or retrieval system without prior permission in writing from the publishers; or ii) used or reproduced in any way for the training, development or operation of artificial intelligence (AI) technologies, including generative AI technologies. The rights holders expressly reserve this publication from the text and data mining exception as per Article 4(3) of the Digital Single Market Directive (EU) 2019/790.

Bloomsbury Publishing Plc does not have any control over, or responsibility for, any third-party websites referred to or in this book. All internet addresses given in this book were correct at the time of going to press. The author and publisher regret any inconvenience caused if addresses have changed or sites have ceased to exist, but can accept no responsibility for any such changes.

A catalogue record for this book is available from the British Library.

A catalog record for this book is available from the Library of Congress

ISBN: HB: 978-1-3502-5826-6
PB: 978-1-3502-5830-3
ePDF: 978-1-3502-5827-3
eBook: 978-1-3502-5828-0

Typeset by RefineCatch Limited, Bungay, Suffolk

For product safety related questions contact productsafety@bloomsbury.com.

To find out more about our authors and books visit www.bloomsbury.com and sign up for our newsletters.

Contents

List of Figures and Tables	vi
Preface	vii
Acknowledgements	xii
Note on the Text	xiii
1 Challenging the Fundamentals of Linguistic Theory	1
2 The Injustices of Generative Assumptions	21
3 The Injustices of Grammaticality Judgements	41
4 Asian Languages from Asian Perspectives	71
5 The Injustices of Syntactic Terminology and Architecture	105
6 Pragmatic Matters	133
7 The Pragmatic Instinct, Natural Language and AI	145
8 Towards a Sensible Syntax	171
Notes	177
References	181
Index	203

Figures and Tables

Figure

6.1 The 3-E Model   139

Tables

4.1 Languages and their number of search results in descending order   86
7.1 Informal and formal translations into Turkish involving the
     second-person pronouns and associated verbal/adjectival endings   159
7.2 Mistranslations of Kazakh in ChatGPT   160
7.3 Mistranslations of Mongolian in ChatGPT   161

Preface

I must confess that this book took quite some courage for me to write. When I was just finishing my PhD, I spoke with a linguist who was working on language processing. I talked to him about the difficulties in explaining the findings of processing in verb-final languages like Japanese and Korean in current minimalist or other versions of generative grammar. Essentially, I was sharing one of my deepest concerns. He then responded by telling me that I was conflating two things that I shouldn't, namely *competence* and *performance*. At the end of our long discussion, he asked me why I was bothering with such an issue. This encounter took place many years ago, so I may not have remembered his exact words, but his message – which wasn't different from that of many with whom I had spoken before – was this: 'Why do you bother? Nobody cares. Why not do some good experiments, pick up the mainstream theory, and maybe make some tweaks? Then, people will appreciate your work.'

In the years to follow, many people I met and my peers at linguistic conferences said the same thing: 'You're strange. Why do you bother yourself with what nobody else is thinking about?' For a long time, I, too, wanted to avoid the question. I mean, who cares? Why bother? I had convinced myself that I could explore my interests as a simple user or observer of the theory. It's not my problem, after all. What's more, I was interested in how theory and application were relevant to one another but I often questioned whether I belonged. This was truly a difficult time for me.

So, I continued with work, but more so as a Korean linguist. My research then came to focus on applied linguistics, although theoretical linguistics and applied linguistics hardly communicated or collaborated in meaningful ways. This is another big problem, yet I was a bit too put off by theoretical linguistics to try to make any serious attempt at reconciling the two. Then came a time when I was teaching linguistics to my students, who were mostly majoring in Asian languages. This was a turning point for me, as I thought I shouldn't just avoid the problems any longer but face them head on. If the grammar has no learnability implications, then it would be too disheartening for anyone to try to study it. During this time, I recalled studying consumerism as an undergrad, together with linguistics. It was at that moment I realized the important role of pragmatics – the two are linked!

However, deep down, I knew that we needed something beyond what we have now, a more fundamental change to broaden our understanding of human language. It is not a matter of simply repairing things on the surface, but rethinking the very skeleton which underpins our studies.

My journey in linguistics began when I read Chomsky's *Aspects of the Theory of Syntax* (1965) as a third-year student at Seoul National University. I was fascinated by the notion of Universal Grammar and how it could explain the essence of human language, although what interested me the most was its depiction of the creative and ever-innovative nature of language. Thus, I fell in love with this school of 'generative' grammar. Keen to learn more about the mathematical and logical foundation of human languages, I then studied formal semantics for my MA. During this time, however, I started to realize the limits of the generative rules which governed my research. Such rules were (and still are) highly theoretical and complex. Furthermore, they are not well suited to non-English examples. Nevertheless, I pursued a PhD in London which focused on issues around word order variation in Korean – such variation is a linguistic phenomenon which has been labelled as 'scrambling' in generative grammars.

The word 'scrambling' is figurative. It means the following: 'To collect or gather *up* hastily or in disorder [...] To jumble or muddle (something) [...] To make [...] unintelligible by means of a scrambler' (OED Online, 2022a). Note the negative connotations associated with this term. The assumption is that there is a base order from which words are then 'scrambled', thereby resulting in structural variation. This term does a great injustice to the reality of syntax. Cross-linguistically, flexible word order is the norm, yet why is it that the majority of us are made to seem like we are doing something wrong, that we are 'scramblers' deviating from the standard? One might say to just ignore it, that 'it's only a word', but for me, and many others who come from a non-anglophone background, I cannot just ignore it, I cannot dismiss it as 'only a word'. In fact, so much of the terminology used in generative grammars does a disservice to non-English languages around the world (an idea which I explore further in Chapter 2). When analysing non-English languages, why are we made to do so from an English perspective? This was one of my biggest qualms.

When completing my further studies, I could not reconcile my 'native speaker'[1] intuition with theoretical predictions. I was faced with unintuitive explanations for the data which covered the language I have known for all my life. I also found that – during my pursuit of studying word order – many Asian languages (such as Japanese, Turkish, Kazakh and Tamil, to name a few) encountered the same problems. There was a real need to reconcile theory and language in practice. During my research, I discovered operational flaws which cannot be solved by quick fixes, and stumbled upon the chasms that lie between competence and performance. When I then began teaching Korean, my generative syntactic knowledge proved hardly useful; there was no natural link between my linguistic studies and language teaching.

A big part of my job involves teaching linguistics to students who are interested in languages. Throughout my career as a teacher, I have met wonderful linguists in my faculty who are also engaged in the mystery of human language and are eager to share their passion and knowledge; oftentimes, I am deeply impressed at their talent and determination – particularly with my colleagues who study Asian languages (such as Chinese and Japanese) in which they must overcome the hurdles of scripts that they may not have grown up with. To note, two of the definitions of the noun 'linguist' in the *Oxford English Dictionary* state the following: 'A person who is skilled in the learning or use of foreign languages. Also in figurative contexts, an expert in or student of language or (later) linguistics; a person who specialises in the structure or historical development of one or more languages; a philologist' (OED Online, 2022b). Yet even the word linguist itself tends to be used to refer to those who are trained in so-called 'contemporary' linguistics, which is very easily conflated with Chomskyan linguistics.

As for my students, one thing that I have noticed is that when I bring in theory, their eyes glaze over and their brows furrow in confusion. Like me, they have to follow theoretical predictions over their intuitions, leaving them unconvinced, dissatisfied and even disinterested in linguistics. The majority of my students have an Asian language background, and along with those studying an Asian language, they are often disappointed by the seemingly incongruous, and arguably archaic, Anglocentric theory. 'We're discussing an Asian language, so why are we doing syntax from an English perspective and not an Asian one?' It is almost ironic that a field which, for the most part, celebrates different languages and linguistic diversity uses terminology, operations and more, from a primarily English angle. Of course, from a hypothetical deductive perspective – that is to say, a Chomskyan perspective – one should be concerned with foreign languages. However, I think it's important to observe diverse data in use, drawing from languages from around the world. Only then can we really form valuable hypotheses which can be investigated further. Nobody can nor will be able to look at every single language and every piece of data but valid hypotheses need to be drawn from reliable data and sources.

I did not write this book to offer specific suggestions or to argue that other frameworks are wrong. Instead, I ask the community involved in languages and linguistics to re-evaluate our current thinking, with the goal of constructing a better system for our study of language in mind. This system should build bridges between the chasms, prioritize connections over ruptures, and do more justice to the study of language than the system we have now – one that we have had for many decades. Therefore, I propose engaging in a new discourse on the study of language that takes into better account syntax in context and incorporates other perspectives, such as an Asian one.

Times have changed and we are no longer living in Chomsky's 1965. We now inhabit a world rich in multilingual and multicultural diversity, where prescriptive grammars have no real authority in digital and online spheres, and social media plays a vibrant role in our communication. Even emojis, which did not exist sixty years ago, now play big roles in our everyday communication, showing how much our language has changed. Artificial intelligence (AI) is quickly catching up to human languages and in the last five years, since the development of the transformer model and open-AI developed GPT 3, this is even more so the reality. Yet, interestingly, it turns out that AI processing isn't as cost efficient as an ordinary human.

Throughout this book, I explore this aspect, which warrants particular attention. What's more, theoretical linguistics should be able to provide some insight into the reality of human communication, allowing us to see how innate knowledge of language is formed, with works in the emerging field to explore this. It should be noted that while this book intends to introduce and discuss developments in AI related to language and linguistics, as well as syntactic theory over the decades, in an engaging and accessible manner, the very nature of the technology and data means there will be some more technical sections. That said, in each chapter, I will also bring forward some of my own experiences over the past twenty-five years as a researcher and teacher in linguistics, giving snippets of my own personal journey and story.

As much as I have learnt over the years, I have also time and again felt the need to raise the same persistent questions. Why is it then, that we continue to look at a single, complete sentence by an 'ideal, native speaker'? Why do we rely on their grammaticality judgement as the most powerful criterion in explaining human languages? What does an 'ideal speaker' even mean? Should we not instead look at the everyday messy language of people like you and me, wherein great beauty and generative power exist? Contemporary theoretical linguistics has become almost resistant to reality. The fuzzy, unpredictable and unsystematic nature of human language is not duly accounted for by our current framework; when we choose to look at a singular 'grammatical' sentence made by an 'ideal speaker', we encounter the pitfall of oversimplification. In 2022, we can no longer study languages in the same way as in the past. Living in an age of big data, we should be able to predict relatively accurately how humans use language, thereby reconciling theory and 'native speaker' intuitions. It is a grassroots movement in which technology is a useful tool to allow us to more efficiently and accurately spot patterns in data, resulting in conclusions that better reflect reality. The question is now the following: 'How can linguistic theory be more *convincing* in the study of human languages?' We require more sensible approaches that explain the real generative power of human language. As in the words of Ludwig Wittgenstein, 'Don't think, but look!' (1953, §66), which, in line with Jung, implies: 'Don't judge, but perceive!'

It is time to pause, observe, describe and then finally explain. More attention needs to be drawn to observation and description before jumping into explanation. It is time to break the barriers of the norm, to be more diverse and inclusive in our studies. Linguistics is not only for those high up in their ivory towers; even 'lay people' with a passing interest should be able to access it. We need to bridge the gaps between theory and practice, as well as reconcile our black-and-white understanding of inductive/deductive approaches, of competence and performance, and more. This cannot be solved by a simple toolbox update – true modernization is needed.

Acknowledgements

As with all my projects, this book would not have happened without inspiration from colleagues, teachers, and my own students. I am very grateful to my students who never stop questioning the Eurocentric nature of the field and constantly challenge the status quo. Their dissatisfaction about using the current prevalent frameworks to explain Asian languages made me search for alternative explanations and gave me the courage to write this book.

I am especially thankful to Amena Nebres, Dr Simon Barnes-Sadler, Marc Yeo and Louise Hossien for their wonderful assistance with data collection and editorial work. They provided me with great insight and feedback. I am also grateful to Dr Juba Nait Saada for aiding me to understand the development of AI.

I am also thankful to Morwenna Scott and Laura Gallon for their support.

Lastly, I would not have begun this trajectory without the love and support of my family and friends.

Note on the Text

Why this book?

In this book, I invite linguists from all fields – theoretical, applied/empirical, contemporary and traditional – to reconsider the future of syntax. Chomsky's *Syntactic Structures*, published in 1957, brought about a significant shift in contemporary linguistics. Sixty-six years have passed since then, and while the basic architectural assumptions remain the same, the technical complexity has increased significantly over time. This complexity has reached a point where no one outside of generative linguistics can understand what's going on. It would be acceptable to have a complex tool if it were effective. However, in my experience, this tool doesn't seem to work well for most languages besides English and some Western European languages.

As an Asian linguist who works in syntax and pragmatics, hence, I often feel disconnected from current trends in linguistics. Many Asian linguists would agree that there is an almost unbridgeable gap between 'Chomskyan' theories and the data gathered from Asian languages. This gap seems only to be widening. This book aims to facilitate another paradigm shift in two key areas.

First, we must overcome Anglo or Eurocentric approaches and welcome linguistic diversity. Modern linguistic theories have predominantly focused on English languages, leaving other languages on the side-lines. Asian languages, despite their diversity and large number of speakers, are significantly underrepresented in English scholarship. Moreover, frameworks designed for English often do not apply to Asian languages and are therefore inadequate and problematic for explanation. We must observe, describe and analyse Asian languages from an Asian perspective. For example, many Asian languages are particle-rich and allow for structural freedom, unlike English and most Western European languages. Particles require greater attention than just their structural properties to understand Asian languages.

Second, times have changed significantly. We are currently living in the AI age, and Gen Z and Gen Alpha are 'AI natives'. The term 'digital native' was coined by Marc Prensky in 2001 to describe young people who grew up using computers, mobile phones and other tools of the digital age. However, the devices and technologies referred to in 2001 are vastly different from those we use today: thus, I coin the term 'AI native'. AI bots are now Gen Z and Gen Alpha's playmates, and virtual reality (VR) is their playground. AI is an integral part of their day-to-day experience, including learning. Social media, big data, AI and VR did not exist in 1957, but now they are ubiquitous. Despite these changes, it seems that many linguists have not been fully engaged with them. With the arrival of AI language models like ChatGPT, contemporary linguistics needs to respond to the methodological, philosophical and pedagogical challenges they present. Linguists have a responsibility to engage proactively with AI and critically explore new ways, questions and goals. Otherwise, there is no future in linguistics. Frederik Jelinek once said, 'Every time I fire a linguist, the performance of the speech recognizer goes up.' This underscores how linguistics has had a limited impact on real-world applications. This book is written with the aim of initiating a paradigm shift that our studies of languages may have a real impact on the future.

1

Challenging the Fundamentals of Linguistic Theory

Why do we need to unthink and rethink syntactic theory?

In this book, I intend to engage with some of the main issues in generative grammar and to encourage readers to unthink and rethink general linguistic properties. This book aims to show that pragmatic principles such as cost-efficiency lie at the heart of syntactic behaviours of human languages. Processing pragmatics has been what artificial intelligence (AI) has struggled with despite great leaps in recent technological advancements. For example, considering cost-efficiency, adding just one extra word to the language data input for an AI can dramatically increase the processing cost. This is in contrast to human processing, where adding more words does not significantly affect the processing cost. This pragmatic competence and instinct that I discuss occupies a central role in the syntactic competence of ordinary humans. However, advancements in AI seem to suggest that this pragmatic instinct may no longer strictly belong to only humans. I say this because nowadays, in particular the last ten years, much of our day-to-day communication has been mediated by smart devices like smartphones and tablets. This tendency will only expand and increase in the future, hence what we think is intrinsically human could mostly become interactional output that is hybridized in nature, that is, a blend of human and computer elements. The more we unconsciously feed our human linguistic data to the computer, the more likely that computers may one day, with sufficient training, be able to process the pragmatic information that is embedded in our human language. Yet, the field of syntax does not seem to be in touch with the current linguistic reality of what is happening on the ground, be it in face-to-face or online interaction.

Since the publication of Chomsky's revolutionary works such as *Syntactic Structures* in 1957 and *Aspects of the Theory of Syntax* in 1965, Chomskyan linguistics has grown and spread worldwide, becoming the dominant theory in linguistics in the latter half of the twentieth century. The development of Chomsky's generative theory has yielded numerous lessons and insights, making significant contributions to the field of theoretical linguistics. In the introduction to the second edition of Chomsky's *Syntactic Structures* (2002), Lightfoot described the book as the 'snowball which began the avalanche of the modern cognitive revolution'. However, more than six decades have passed since the birth of Chomskyan linguistics, and much has changed in the way we communicate, yet syntactic theory does not reflect these changes and is still largely focused on linguistic data from so-called 'ideal speaker-listeners'. However, more than five decades have passed since the birth of Chomskyan linguistics, and much has changed in the way we communicate, yet syntactic theory does not reflect these changes and is still largely focused on linguistic data from so-called 'ideal speaker-listeners'.

> An ideal speaker-listener, in a completely homogeneous speech-community, who knows its language perfectly and is unaffected by such grammatically irrelevant conditions as memory limitations, distractions, shifts of attention and interest, and errors (random or characteristic) in applying his knowledge of the language in actual performance.
>
> Chomsky, 1965, p. 3

This quote summarizes the main concerns of Chomskyan linguistics, which focuses on the analysis of an 'ideal' language user's competence, and downplays other aspects of his or her actual linguistic performance such as disfluencies and various other speech idiosyncrasies and neurological limitations. In addition, it emphasizes the notion of an ideal native speaker living within a monolingual speech community. However, as real-life users of language, we know that actual language use can often be very different from what is purported in linguistic theory. Spontaneous language as produced by humans in their daily communication is usually messy and not confined to neat structures or rules, unlike what linguistic theory argues for.

Many of us also do not live within strictly monolingual, homogenous communities; with the rise of globalization and transnational collaboration, the majority of us gain membership in various speech communities (such as work, school, and home) whereby we have to interact with people of various linguistic and cultural backgrounds, and often in a multitude of languages as well. The assumption that supposed native speakers living amongst each other do not vary in the way they use language is also erroneous. Even if the community speaks the same language, they do not necessarily speak in the same way – there could be morphological, phonological, syntactic, semantic differences influenced by their individual linguistic backgrounds.

In addition, technological advancements have allowed us to not only interact face-to-face, but virtually too, which has further expanded our linguistic repertoire and communities. More so than ever, communication without the constraints of time, space (and perhaps even language, if you consider the astounding capabilities of real-time translation in video chats) has become possible. This means that even if our immediate speech community is largely monolingual, the same may not be said for other communities in which we operate, be they virtual or in-person, which could be multilingual or even consist of speakers of many different varieties of a certain language. As a result, this throws doubt on the validity of just studying monolingual native speakers who use language uniformly in linguistic theory.

Furthermore, theoretical linguistics does not account for language generated online in its framework. This is a serious oversight considering the tremendous impact of human–computer interaction and the translingual, transnational possibilities of online mediums on our communication habits. Linguistic theory based on traditional Chomskyan foundations simply does not account for this diversity and transformation in human language use.

> All physical theories, their mathematical expressions apart, ought to lend themselves to so simple a description that 'even a child could understand them'.
> Einstein, cited in Elkana, 1982, p. 222

Pertaining to how linguistic theory lacks relevance in explaining natural language phenomena, another major problem with traditional linguistic theory is that it is often seen as abstruse and impractical even by students of language studies, precisely because it does not really reflect how language is actually used in real situations. If the relevancy of such theories is impalpable, then naturally learners will find them difficult to understand as they would not be able to apply these theories readily to observable linguistic phenomena. This then foregrounds the importance of simplicity. The above quote from Albert Einstein exemplifies how the most influential physicist of the twentieth century viewed simplicity as an aim for formulating scientific theories. In the same spirit as Einstein, this book intends to shed light on the need for a 'sensible' syntax – a syntactic theory that is practical and of utilitarian value. In order for this to be achieved, our theory should be simple and should not be over complicated.

In the process of exploring the idea of a 'sensible' syntax, the issues that I will attempt to investigate and question in this book are as follows:

(i) Is linguistics in danger of losing touch with reality?
(ii) Overemphasis on the final product.
(iii) The possible/impossible dichotomy.
(iv) The issue of Eurocentrism.
(v) The sidelining of verb-final languages.
(vi) The problem of independently motivated principles.
(vii) The issue of downplaying pragmatic/ecological factors.
(viii) Learning, not just acquisition, as a core aspect of language ability.

There are no easy solutions to these questions; in fact, rather than attempting to provide complex theoretical solutions, in this book I simply explore these questions. Through consideration of these issues, it should become clear to readers that a shift in perspective has become necessary in the study of syntax. This book intends to scrutinize our fundamental assumptions in order to find sensible answers to these issues, and to arrive at a sensible perspective on syntax in doing so.

(i) Is linguistics in danger of losing touch with reality?

Linguistics is a niche subject; the minutiae of the rules governing language are not of interest to everyone. Yet, most students deciding to study linguistics do so not because they want to become theoretical linguists; most do so because they wish for a greater understanding of their target language. For instance, my students study Korean linguistics in order to further their understanding of Korean. For students like these, there is the danger that too great a focus on linguistics that is not relevant to actual language use could disappoint and dishearten them from continuing their interest in linguistics. Do undergraduates hoping to better understand Korean really benefit from learning the split intransitivity hypothesis? In some languages, like Italian, split intransitivity is more relevant to conventional language use, as it is morphosyntactic in nature – yet, in Korean and Japanese the phenomenon is linked only to semantics, making it hardly relevant to standard language use. Could our resources not be used more effectively to create linguistics courses that convey what is interesting about linguistics while also enhancing students' linguistic ability? Linguistic curriculums that fail to meet these two criteria run the risk of seeming 'out of touch' with actual language, creating the impression that linguistics is something that occurs only in artificial, hypothetical scenarios that learners will never encounter. It is questionable to what extent linguistics is actually reflecting how people actually use language.

Since the advent of Chomskyan linguistics, linguistic theory has largely been focused on deriving rules and showing how language data can be used to prove the validity of these rules. Pertaining to this, Lakoff and Sutton (2017) explain how linguistic theory has been inhospitable to language data that does not follow these rules:

> Intuition was scorned: if you couldn't formalize a relationship, if you couldn't write rules, make it submit to the grammatical theory that supposedly was a tool for the understanding of language, then you'd do best to forget the whole thing. And this is just why the system was, superficially, so very elegant: the nasty complicated fuzzy parts, the parts that did not fit neatly into the scheme, were assumed not to exist, or at least, not to be of interest to the linguist.
>
> Lakoff and Sutton 2017, p. 73

Such a narrow view of linguistic analysis, which is only interested in a small subset of data that fits certain rules, invalidates a great proportion of actual language use – language use that is unstructured and does not strictly confine itself to any rules. Furthermore, linguistic theory is largely interested in language as a set of sentences (Croft, 2006, p. 97), but this may not fully reflect how we actually speak or type in real life, whereby short, incomplete utterances proliferate our speech and written language. This points to the disinterest of linguistic theory in explaining the physical reality of how people use language, but on the contrary underscores the interest of linguistic theory in exploring the abstract nature of language. While this is no doubt a venture that can be fruitful and insightful in its own right, theories which generally ignore the reality of language use on the ground can only go so far in adequately explaining linguistic phenomena.

Often, my undergraduate students complain that syntax is difficult, that out of all the areas of linguistics, syntax is the hardest to grasp. Why is this so? One of the reasons I want to write this book is to address this issue and I argue that we cannot justify overly complex theory when the data does not call for it.

> Most of the fundamental ideals of science are essentially simple, and may, as a rule, be expressed in a language comprehensible to everyone. To follow up these ideas demands the knowledge of a highly refined technique of investigation. Mathematics as a tool of reasoning is necessary if we wish to draw conclusions which may be compared with experiments. So long as we are concerned only with fundamental physical ideas we may avoid the language of mathematics.
>
> Einstein & Infeld, 1938, p. 29

Similar to an earlier quote in this chapter, the above quote from Einstein re-emphasizes that since the core ideas of scientific theories are actually simple, they should not be overly convoluted and should be expressed in a way that even a layman can understand. He emphasizes that more complex means of explanation are permissible only when developing these theories to a deeper level or when used for experimental purposes. This reflects how even much of the basic tenets of linguistic theory remain inaccessible to non-linguists, and even students of linguistics for that matter.

Furthermore, because linguistic theory is primarily concerned with abstract, ideal, native speakers living in monolingual circles, it currently lacks engagement with the latest developments in human–computer interaction. These developments, which include AI, big data and social media, along with the proliferation of smart devices like smartphones and tablets, generate massive amounts of linguistic data which contains elements produced by humans and components produced by AI. For example, language translation programs can be assisted by AI language models to analyse billions of monolingual and multilingual documents (Adeel, 2016, p. 170), which were originally written by humans. Furthermore, this hybrid human–computer-produced data is fed back into the system, which continually influences the linguistic habits of both the AI and us, the human users. However, linguistic theory in a way has lost touch with reality and is lagging behind because it does not take into account these active and fast-changing phenomena which have become part and parcel of much of the linguistic behaviour of people living in the current era. Therefore, we should question the utilitarian value of such theories that do not necessarily help us to understand how language works.

Another aspect in which linguistic theory has fallen behind is its lack of engagement with inductive, data-driven methods of linguistic study. Mendívil-Giró (2019) offers two main types of linguistic theory, functionalism and formalism, the former equalling the inductive method and the latter the deductive. Chomsky's formalisms have defined linguistic methodology and theory for several decades and his conceptions of Universal Grammar (UG) and Faculty of Languages (FL) have been influential in not only the field of linguistics but also cognitive science together, having championed the study of 'mental systems of computation and representation' rather than of 'behaviour and behavioural outcomes' (Mendívil-Giró, 2019, p. 5). Chomsky's methods may be seen as deductive methods for this reason: rather than the environmental, superimposed conditions of a language, Chomsky is interested in the basic human faculty of competence that engenders language that is then acted upon by exogenous forces, thus forming the 'languages' of social systems. On the other hand, the inductive method works in reverse by taking data from languages that have been influenced by extraneous factors and from these deriving theories about the essential notion of 'language' that underpins them.

For induction, theory and evidence are inextricable, and evidence produces theory. As for deduction, theory and evidence are separate, and theoretical constructs predict evidence. Although the deductive approach states that a single language has the ability to teach us about the faculty of language at its most rudimentary level, it does not discredit an engagement with a variety of languages. This, however, is not the main purpose of syntactic formalism, which is clearly to discover universal aspects of FL. Alternatively, the inductive approach favours as large a pool as possible from which to draw linguistic data, and theories that arise from this approach are constantly being challenged as new data emerges. On this, Mendívil-Giró (2019) states that 'the impact [of these new sources of information] can be notable for linguistic traditions based on the inductive method, but will surely have a more modest effect (although not necessarily an irrelevant one) for traditions that adopt a deductive methodology' (pp. 1–2). The Chomskyan perspective affords primacy to language, which is instantiated by neurological processes rather than data from emergent languages, which are secondary. On the other hand, according to Mendívil-Giró, functionalists believe that languages are 'cultural objects or institutions that are not the instantiation of a biologically determined FL, but are objects that must be studied in themselves and for themselves' (p. 3). Though not totally opposed to abstract frameworks, functionalists favour situations in which these frameworks arise inductively from a large sample of languages, rather than deductively from a small pool of Western European languages.

The differences between inductive and deductive reasoning are now apparent, though perhaps a combination of both methods is the solution to problems faced in contemporary linguistics. It is impossible to study all languages – living and dead – as would be ideal in the inductive approach. It may be possible to formulate sweeping theories about the nature of language, as deduction sets out to do. Yet time and time again these same theories are shown to be inadequate in practice. Therefore, in the formulation of theories, it is unwise to consider the two methods separately by going for an entirely data-driven or theory-driven approach. It is as vital to strike a balance between both inductive and deductive approaches as it is important for functionalists and formalists to be engaged in constant dialogue and strive to search for answers to the mysteries of language together, rather than to be isolated in their respective subfields. Bateman (2017, p. 24) argues for the importance of collaborations between different fields in linguistics: 'Linguistics as a whole can now benefit only when contributions across a broad range of linguistics schools are drawn upon, since no one orientation to the phenomenon of human language can claim to cover all the angles.' He goes on to emphasize the usefulness and necessity of dialogue between different schools of linguistics because the number of objectives in the study of linguistics as a whole exceeds those of any individual school of thought, and that such dialogue would require 'both an openness and a readiness to hear what others are saying and why they are saying it' (p. 24). Bateman's view echoes that of Halliday (1964, p. 13), who notes that: 'I [Halliday] would defend the view that different coexisting models in linguistics may best be regarded as appropriate to different aims, rather than as competing contenders for the same goal.'

In Chomskyan linguistics, the study of any language is the study of the 'realization of the initial state S0 under particular conditions' (Chomsky, 1986, p. 37). Rizzi (1994) showed that characterizations of English, such as finite sentence condition, do not hold in Turkish and Portuguese, in which there are subject-agreeing infinitives that function like English finite sentences. Rizzi then determines that 'the correct generalization could not have been determined on the basis of data from English alone, since in this language it is obscured by the essential overlap of the two notions of finiteness and agreement' (p. 404). Thus, purely generative formalisms are insufficient when presented with falsifying data. Newmeyer states that 'generativists study the neurophysiology of stress, typologists [functionalists] its behavioral manifestations' (1983, p. 337). Perhaps these two methods have to work in harmony to produce suitable answers to the questions that both sides wish to answer. Inductive and deductive reasoning methods should not be considered discordant, but rather complementary; the shortcomings of one may be supplemented by the other. Certainly, each side can learn from the other. Comrie advocates for the inductive method, and justifies his preference by assuming that if what 'we want to find out in work on language universals is the range of variation found across languages and the limits placed on this variation, it would be a serious methodological error to build into our research programme aphoristic assumptions about the range of variation' (1989, p. 6). Diversity in empirical evidence should be embraced at the same time as theories regarding the fundamentals of the faculty of language are conceptualized. A dialectical approach may in fact be the strongest. The deductive perspective states that the variation exhibited between two languages is a matter of degree to which exogenous forces impact natural language faculty, while from the inductive perspective it comes from an inherent validity of the languages themselves.

The aim of this book is to contribute to the discussion on the side of induction, by drawing upon data from a wide range of languages to bring into question formalisms developed from deductive methods. An engagement with real-world data, including data from newer languaging platforms which have so often been neglected by generativists, such as social media and other computer-mediated communication, brings linguistic theory back to the ground. Even if we can never realistically get data from every single language in the world nor ever collect enough data (since the notion of being sufficient is subjective), this is not a valid justification for disregarding the utility of a sizable amount of data. Descriptive linguistics has long been marginalized in Anglocentric methodologies of generative grammar, particularly data from Asian languages. Generative methods have also influenced language pedagogy in such a way that language teaching has become quite abstract and separate from actual language use out in the world. Therefore, this book seeks to frame linguistics in a way that correlates to actual data, is accessible to lay learners and teachers of language, and considers modern, technological advancements in language communication important. Both inductive and deductive approaches have their own merits, and it is important for us to bridge and reconcile the differences between these two methods so that we may derive a more comprehensive and inclusive linguistic theory. Nevertheless, such a collaboration does not mean blindly readjusting either approach to fit the other without proper due consideration of its appropriateness, to which Lakoff and Sutton (2017), as an example, caution applied linguists against forcing linguistic theories onto data without proper evaluation even if it appears 'prestigious':

> Too often the theorist, brimming with prestige from within his [sic] ivory tower, presents the applied linguist with his theory as a fait accompli: 'Here's the latest stuff, you better catch up with it and use it if you don't want to get left behind.' And the hapless applied linguist, bewildered by the formalism, figures that if it has all this technical stuff in it, it must have some merit, and willy-nilly, bends reality to meet the theory, ignores facts he knows about full well when the theory can't encompass them, and distorts his intuitive sense of the structure of a language in order that the structure he uses as a base may look like the one envisioned by the theorist, with lots of neat boxes, arrows, rules – none of the messiness he knows is really there.
>
> Lakoff and Sutton, 2017, p. 72

(ii) Overemphasis on the final product

In the study of syntax, it is often the case that the final product of syntactic representations is given more attention than the actual process of building up these representations. However, in this book, I argue that understanding this process is significant, because without it we would not be able to define even the most fundamental parts of syntactic architecture. Going through this process allows us to better comprehend the different layers of a syntactic construction, specifically resembling how we as humans construe meaning as we move from an incomplete amount of information to a more complete set of information. I argue that although the human brain is not capable of dissecting every single aspect of a construction, we are able to use pragmatic information to fill in the gaps left by having a partial knowledge of the construction, as the majority of syntactic predictions are made locally.

(iii) The possible/impossible dichotomy

The distinction between possible versus impossible has long been used as a grammaticality criterion to measure linguistic competence (Jegerski, 2014, p. 21). But why should this be the only distinction that we are interested in? For instance, what about the following contrasts: easy-and-frequent versus difficult-and-rare? As far as syntactic variation is concerned, these dichotomies are far more visible than the possible/impossible dichotomy. Surely, then, these distinctions also deserve our attention, as they would enhance our understanding of the distribution of syntactic patterns and syntactic architecture across languages. In a later chapter, I examine the frequency of syntactic patterns in different languages, and argue that the choice of syntactic structure is not merely a random occurrence – language users moderate their syntactic structures to achieve the maximum efficiency, due to physiological limitations in memory and articulation.

(iv) The problem of Eurocentrism

Eurocentrism remains widespread in linguistics. Richardson (2018) highlights how, in the social sciences, the focus on 'European social life leaves the social life and thought of other communities and nations understudied, unattended to or, worse, actively suppressed' (p. 233). As Gil (2001) notes, the development of contemporary linguistics was largely spearheaded by speakers of European languages who mainly examined European languages, a trend which continues to the present day (p. 102). In addition, the ascendancy of Chomskyan generative linguistics brought to the forefront the concept of Universal Grammar, which, in theory, aims to study as many languages as possible in order to uncover universals common to all languages, but which, in practice, is biased towards English and other Indo-European languages, as the majority of linguists are most familiar with European languages (Barrett, 2014, pp. 204–205). This led to the development of linguistic theories that 'reproduce normative assumptions about language based on a Eurocentric bias' and further marginalizes speakers of less commonly researched languages (Barrett, 2014, p. 205).

Gil (2001) further argues that this Eurocentric bias has even affected how non-European languages are analysed, because generalizations formed based on observations of European languages are applied to non-European languages. He notes that many Eurocentric linguistic frameworks assume the existence of zero elements, such as zero suffixes in morphology, even if they do not appear in the surface morphology or phonology – a generalization borrowed from observations about European languages (p. 104). He cites the example of how the Hebrew past tense of the verb 'act' is assumed to have a zero suffix form *paʕal-Ø* on the basis that its other forms (such as 1SG *paʕal-ti*, 2SG.F *paʕal-t*, and 1PL *paʕal-nu*) have overt suffixes marking different categories like gender and number (p. 104). This point is reiterated by Evans and Levinson (2009), who make the erroneous yet surprisingly common assumption that 'all languages are English-like but with different sound systems and vocabularies' (p. 429).

Regarding research on Southeast Asian languages, Gil (2001) further notes that although many researchers in the field criticize others for their indifference towards linguistic diversity and their use of abstract descriptions of languages, they often tend to commit the same error by writing grammars for these languages using terminologies based on European languages (terms such as 'subject', 'relative clause' and 'adjective') without critically evaluating their suitability for the language at hand (p. 104). Some modern linguists, however, have recognized this issue, arguing against imposing traditional Latin-based frameworks and Eurocentric concepts onto languages which diverge typologically from European languages (Zwartjes, 2011, p. 4).

Gil (2001) makes the case for the folly of shoehorning non-European languages into European models by providing an example from Riau Indonesian (see Example 1), a variety of Malay/Indonesian spoken in the Riau province of Indonesia which differs from standard Malay/Indonesian (p. 116). Although the sentence *ayam makan* could be translated as 'the chicken is eating', the sentence in isolation does not provide enough information to make a confident translation in the meaning. This is because the sentence is highly underspecified, being unmarked for number and definiteness (more so than standard varieties of

Malay/Indonesian) – a common characteristic of Southeast Asian languages, which often allow for many different interpretations of the same sentence depending on the context. Indeed, Southeast Asian languages are known for their context dependency, whereby their lack of explicit linguistic marking allows for open interpretation without sufficient context (Enfield, 2003, p. 56). Gil notes that a linguist working within Eurocentric frameworks might analyse *ayam makan* as a zero-marked passive or a zero-marked relative clause, which would cause the sentence to appear overly ambiguous with its many zero markings (p. 117). However, Gil goes on to argue that to analyse the sentence in this way would perhaps be imposing Eurocentric categories on a language which may not conform to them (p. 117), as European languages tend to clearly specify grammatical categories.

Example 1

Ayam	Makan
Chicken	Eat

'The chicken is being eaten'
'The chicken is making somebody eat'
'Somebody is eating for the chicken'
'the chicken that is eating'
'where the chicken is eating'
'when the chicken is eating'
'how the chicken is eating'

Gil argues that, because of this tendency, syntactic categories in generative linguistics are highly biased towards European languages where the various categories can easily be matched, and that the 'imposition' of these categories on Southeast Asian languages, particularly Riau Indonesian, 'provides for a facile mode of grammatical description' which is 'essentially misguided' (Newmeyer, 2005, p. 11; Gil, 1994, p. 188).

In a related observation, Kluge (2019) highlights that a significant portion of the research on terms of address in Southeast Asian languages has been primarily Eurocentric. She suggests this may be because researchers tend to overlook data from non-Indo-European languages. (p. 69). Furthermore, although there are thousands of tonal languages in the world spread across diverse regions like North, South and Meso-America, New Guinea, Africa and Asia, there is a still a tendency by some linguists to view tone systems as a kind of oddity or optional linguistic feature due to the lack of tone languages per se in Europe. This is despite the fact that tone systems are included in the majority of the world's languages (estimated at around 60 to 70 per cent of the world's languages) and are useful for conveying meaning (Dixon, 2012, p. 435; Yip, 2002, p. 17).

Similar biases exist for East Asian languages, too. For example, there has been a tendency to characterize Sinitic languages as 'simple' based on Eurocentric criteria. Edward Sapir, for instance, characterized Chinese languages as 'simple' languages on the basis that they are fully analytic and do not have inflections. He took a highly Eurocentric interpretation of what constitutes complexity in grammar, assuming that grammatical complexity equals the presence of inflection similar to that of Latin and Ancient Greek, while also assuming that Chinese syntax is simple and unchanging (Falk, 1999, pp. 61–62). This kind of approach is not limited to linguists with Western or European backgrounds; even Yuen Ren Chao, a native Chinese who studied Chinese dialects, downplayed the syntactic diversity in Chinese dialects by proclaiming that, apart from some small differences in syntax and morphology, 'one can say there is practically one universal Chinese grammar' (Chao, 1968, p. 13), a view that seems to reflect Chomskyan and Eurocentric perspectives of Universal Grammar.

Therefore, as Gil (2001) notes, it is important to describe languages on their own terms, and that by viewing the world through the lens of a non-European language, these languages, 'through familiarity, [cease] to be exotic' (p. 105). Currently, the field of theoretical linguistics is generally very unwelcoming for those who think differently or work on languages other than English. In order to formulate a syntactic theory that can accurately describe languages as they are, we need to reformulate the way we think about syntax – it should be based on inclusivity and not primarily on Eurocentric structures and ideologies. Only then can we truly develop a syntax that reflects the linguistic diversity in the world.

(v) The sidelining of verb-final languages

Despite the fact that languages with verb-final patterns outnumber those with verb-initial ones, and that there is a higher frequency of certain linguistic features such as case particles in these verb-final languages, there has been a proclivity to study only verbs and not these other features. This is reflective of Eurocentric influence in linguistic traditions, whereby the role of the verb in a sentence is emphasized, as generally case markings are only found attached to the verb. It is also claimed that, at a syntactic level, the verb contains all the combinatory information. However, these two claims are not applicable to many other languages, especially Asian languages, which have complex particle-marked cases and where not only verbs, but also particles and other constituents, have significant roles at a syntactic level. Furthermore, Asian languages, many which are verb-final, differ from Western European languages in that, for the former, meaning is created incrementally as constructive case particles that appear first provide clues for the verb that appears later in the sentence, while for the latter, the verb appears early on in the sentence and serves as a template for the constituents that will occur later. Current verb-centred models are still unable to account for such syntactic variation amongst languages in the world. Unlike in verb-initial Western European languages whereby efficiency (pragmatic needs) is explained by the verb, in verb-final languages, which include a large number of Asian languages, this is explained by flexible word order and the presence of these case particles. Therefore, I argue that these features of verb-final languages deserve attention as much as the verb does in verb-initial languages.

(vi) The problem of independently motivated principles

Another problem in current linguistics is the reliance on independently motivated principles. These are rules or exceptions that are created to support a linguistic theory or explain linguistic phenomena but which lack convincing justification beyond their immediate usefulness in ensuring the data fits with observed phenomena. In one sense, the prevalence of this within linguistics is understandable, as it is more difficult to find morphosyntactic explanations for phenomena than extralinguistic ones. One can also argue that this is a problem with the generative approach, as within generative linguistics there is no option other than to continue creating more and more rules to explain phenomena, without necessarily getting any closer to understanding *why* the data conforms with said rules. The issue with this is that it presents language as an abstract entity without reflecting how language actually works when used spontaneously and in an unplanned manner, which comprises the majority of our language use. By relying on such frameworks, not only do we fail to account for actual language performance, but the utility of these frameworks also becomes questionable if we are unable to apply it to what we observe, and we end up with circular explanations. Schroeder (2017), citing Wittgenstein, argues that linguistic rules cannot account for how language actually works and can only briefly describe language use, suggesting that these rules only provide superficial explanations for linguistic phenomena:

> Linguistic rules for natural languages are not necessary for the actual use of a language; they are only summarizing descriptions of that use. As such they can still be called 'rules of grammar,' but then the latter word is taken in a different sense: referring not to the actual workings of language, but to a systematic account of those workings.
>
> Schroeder, 2017, p. 258

This issue is further exacerbated by the fact that Chomskyan linguistics downplays the importance of linguistic diversity in favour of abstract and biological explanations, which argue that there is only one underlying language at a deeper grammatical level (Wilkin, 2015, p. 63). As previously explained, the study of linguistics as a whole suffers from Eurocentrism, with many linguistic theories being based on data from European languages. By basing the theories on a small set of data as Nagao mentions below, the extent to which such theories can satisfactorily account for the range present in natural language, or provide explanations well supported by data for these diverse linguistic phenomena is doubtful. In line with this, Nagao (1989, p. 380) argues that the weakness of linguistic theory is that it can only account for a small subset of linguistic phenomena and is incapable of accounting for real language use: 'Generally speaking, linguistic theories provide us with the basic philosophy of language. Actual language data (sentences) are so complex that the theories cannot explain the reasons for many of them. Linguistic theories are usually based on a very small set of linguistic phenomena, and explains only a small part of language phenomena.'

(vii) The issue of downplaying pragmatic/ecological factors

As linguistic theory is more interested in the abstract aspect of human language, it is often observed that pragmatic/ecological issues surrounding language have been sidestepped in theoretical linguistics. The emphasis on linguistic competence in Chomskyan linguistics foregrounds the notion that because there is a common 'template' for language shared by all humans, it is not important to study what people use in their actual linguistic performance (Burkette, 2015, p. 31). In doing so, Chomskyan linguistics is essentially sidelining 'contextual, discourse, cultural, and pragmatic (ecological) dimensions of language use, as well as attitudinal factors of linguistic performance' (Wilss, 1996, p. 16). These are all vital aspects of what makes human language so vibrant, complex and adaptable to different situations, and to ignore them in analysis would be to miss out on clues which are crucial in helping us make sense of language under various contexts. While all utterances have a general meaning which may not be tied to a specific context, there are many situations in which utterances can be interpreted in a multitude of ways. In these cases, if the appropriate pragmatic and/or ecological information is not provided, it can lead to misinterpretation and misunderstanding, which can then incur severe consequences in human interaction. Therefore, it is essential that linguistic theory take into account such metalinguistic aspects of language in order to describe human language in a comprehensive manner. To formulate theories about human languages on the basis of endless rules without reflecting the contexts of use would be akin to a person continuously engaging in a monologue with him- or herself. Garten et al. (2019) succinctly explain the importance of context in human language processing:

> In all forms of linguistic communication, successful interpretation is dependent on our ability to make use of knowledge beyond the words themselves. If we consider the sentence, 'I want more', there is little we can conclude about the utterance without knowing the context of the 'I' (who is speaking) or the 'more' (what is wanted, why it is wanted). This fact is hugely important when attempting to formalize knowledge of the role of outside information on language's functionality. Generally speaking, when we study human language processing we cannot ignore the fact that language is fully embedded within its context, the conditions of its generation with respect to participants and environment.
>
> Garten et al, 2019, p. 480

Such pragmatic/ecological considerations are also especially important for the development of AI-based language processing technologies, in which their actual implementation is fraught with difficulties. Garten et al. (2019) note that there are two main obstacles that AI-backed deep learning language models face in quantifying contextual information in language: (i) how the language data should be interpreted (as the meaning changes 'from field to field, subfield to subfield, person to person') and (ii) how to measure this contextual information since it can exist in a multitude of forms (such as general knowledge, cultural background knowledge, and knowledge about speaker motivations) (p. 480). While current AI technologies are able to produce convincing pieces of language data that are indistinguishable from those produced by humans, they are still incapable of meaningfully comprehending pragmatic information in human language (such as ambiguity) and processing linguistic data in a cost-efficient manner akin to humans, which I argue is the main aspect of pragmatic factors in the syntactic architecture of human language. If AI language models were to simply rely on the existing abstract language principles from linguistic theory as training data, then we can expect a lot of problems when we get these models to process natural human language. This is because the models would be unable to apply any of these principles thoroughly to the language data because of how much the principles diverge from the messy, unstructured and relatively rule-free nature of actual human language use.

(viii) Learning, not just acquisition, as a core aspect of human language ability

Chomsky's Universal Grammar (UG) has long espoused the view that the ability to use language is instinctive to humans, while at the same time arguing that the language learning process is inconsequential to language acquisition. Instead, UG claims that language acquisition is dependent on activating an inner generative grammar, with experiential learning playing only a very small and distantly related role: 'It seems plain that language acquisition is based on the child's discovery of what from a formal point of view is a deep and abstract theory – a generative grammar of his language – many of the concepts and principles of which are only remotely related to experience by long and intricate chains of unconscious quasi-inferential steps' (Chomsky, 1965, p. 58). Why Chomsky thinks so, as Wilkin (2015) explains, is because Chomsky adopted a rationalist approach to language, which purports that linguistic knowledge is not obtained from an 'inductive learning process' due to the 'flawed and limited nature of our experience' (p. 63). Wilss (1996) additionally notes that, according to Chomsky, linguistic ability is 'not developed through learning', but rather develops 'on the basis of a genetic program which controls the transformation of linguistic deep structures into linguistic surface strings of words' (p. 16).

Some studies in the 1970s and 1980s which trained animals to learn human language attempted to disprove this rationalist view. One of these studies involved Nim Chimpsky, a chimpanzee whose name is a play on Noam Chomsky, the subject of an experiment in the 1970s to investigate whether chimpanzees could acquire language if they were taught in an environment similar to that of human children (Kappala-Ramsamy, 2011). Although this experiment aimed at debunking Chomsky's view that language ability is only intrinsic to humans, the results eventually suggested that Nim was not able to learn languages like humans. As a result, Chomsky appeared to have won the nature-vs-nurture debate as this failed experiment seemed to prove that even chimpanzees, one of the most intelligent animals, are not capable of grasping the ever-generative syntactic power that ordinary humans have, and that learning is not a significant aspect of one's language ability if an innate language faculty determines one's ability to acquire language.

However, learning is not a trivial aspect of human language. It consists of both acquired and learned components. Most multilingual individuals worldwide did not encounter their second or third languages from birth but rather discovered them later in life. The language learning experiences of adults also reveal fascinating insights into the nature of human languages. To truly understand this, we must consider not only how infants learn languages but also how adults acquire and adapt to new languages, as well as the underlying logic that enables this process.

While I will explore this in later chapters, let us consider the large numbers of English as a second language (ESL) and English as a foreign language (EFL) speakers, around 1.1 billion, in comparison with native speakers of English, around 400 million. The current status quo, which sidelines those who have 'learnt' rather than 'acquired' their facility with the language, has created a chasm in which these multilingual, non-native English speakers and their process of acquiring English – likely through learning – are placed in the background. As such, I argue that we must acknowledge the importance of the learning process in talking about language ability, especially since syntactic structures are actively learned by people who study English later on in their lives and not from birth. This line of argument also prompts us to consider the value of learnability when feeding data to AI models, and the importance of feeding the models training data from a diverse range of speakers so as to reduce biases such as misunderstanding of commands that might occur if the models are only trained to recognize a select few accents.

Purpose

This book does not intend to condemn current linguistic frameworks; rather, it intends to express the need for a concerted effort to move towards a more sensible grammar which accounts for the diversity of human languages (in the case of this book, our focus is on Asian languages). Many, if not all, of the architectural issues outlined in this chapter are ones that I have shied away from during my own studies and research. The purpose of this book is to show that asking such questions and exposing such problems in the theory are not themselves wrong – instead, we should be actively engaging with these matters. However, finding answers is not an easy task. Rather than bringing forward novel research, my primary goal is to present state-of-the-field discussions backed by evidence.

Since the release of Chomsky's *Aspects* in 1965, there has been significant progress in the field of linguistics – particularly in the realm of syntax. One reason for these developments is the advent of big data; the huge volumes of information we can glean from public social media like Twitter and tools like Google Trends, made available by companies like Google enable us to spot linguistic patterns that were previously invisible, allowing us to create stronger links between theory and data. This is particularly useful to our present study of syntax from Asian perspectives. Furthermore, a number of Chomskyan concepts – such as the strict separation between linguistic *competence* and *performance* – are no longer convincing to contemporary linguists, and the field has moved past them. In this book, I challenge some of the long-standing preconceptions and assumptions in linguistic theory. For instance, I believe that *competence* and *performance* should indeed be linked, as there is no use learning abstract theory if one cannot apply it (see Chapter 4). When coupled with the evident lack of research on Asian languages and the difficulties in studying said languages (exemplified through inconsistencies in glossing, for example), it is clear that there is a clear Anglocentric and Eurocentric bias in our current linguistic tools. Linguists are therefore working within an outdated framework which cannot adequately account for the data. Change is needed – we as linguists must raise our game!

More must also be done to boost the prestige of Asian languages and to encourage the specialized study of Asian languages without being bound by the norms of Eurocentric linguistic conventions – only then can some of the current linguistic injustices be properly addressed.

Diversity, inclusivity and real-world implications

In this book, I will explore the meta-discourse on publications concerning syntax and Asian languages since Chomsky's 1957 *Syntactic Structures* to guide my analysis. With the prevalence of large databases and advanced AI, it is both necessary and feasible to incorporate real-world data from diverse registers that goes beyond single, written sentences. By including more non-English languages and diverse topics, we can make linguistic discussions more inclusive and open to everyone, thus departing from Anglophone dominant academia.

It's time to move away from the notion that linguistic discussions only occur in ivory towers. We need to start focusing on practical applications in the real world. This book sheds light on the lack of impact that linguistics has had on practical applications and takes the challenge seriously, with the aim of laying a solid foundation through its pages. To make it even more engaging, I've included my own personal anecdotes.

2

The Injustices of Generative Assumptions

A linguistic vacuum?

Chomsky (1965, p. 3) writes that 'An ideal speaker-listener, in a completely homogeneous speech-community, who knows its language perfectly and is unaffected by such grammatically irrelevant conditions as memory limitations, distractions, shifts of attention and interest, and errors (random or characteristic) in applying his knowledge of the language in actual performance.' The concept Chomsky describes was foundational to contemporary linguistics. However, decades have passed, and times have clearly changed. While his impact cannot be disputed, it is crucial to thoroughly reassess this proposal.

Our linguistic environments and resources, as well as how we view languages, have progressed significantly since 1965 when Chomsky wrote those words. Chomsky's theory of the ideal speaker-listener has progressed too; not many linguists today express full agreement with Chomsky's original assumption. For instance, De Costa et al. (2021, p. 129) note that the Chomskyan definition of an ideal speaker-listener of English is that of 'white, middle- to upper-class individuals [...] who used a 'standard' variety [...]', and that this 'skewed understanding of the ideal English speaker-hearer can be attributed in part to mainstream SLA research that continues to rely on "pastoral language learning participants" [...] or individuals who are found in higher education and have the luxury of choosing to become bi/multilingual'. Yet it is equally true that within contemporary linguistic discourse, many of Chomsky's original claims – including those that are now considered outdated – continue to be cited without proper consideration. This has resulted in frequent disagreements and misunderstandings among those involved in the fields of language and linguistics. This book aims to clear up some of this confusion by providing sensible, timely approaches to some of the main concerns in contemporary linguistics.

So what is outdated about Chomsky's theory? To begin with, Chomsky's ideal speaker-listener must live in a homogenous speech community. Yet nobody lives in a homogenous speech community, and in fact no one has ever lived in such a linguistic vacuum. Nor are any of us free from memory limitations – we're not superhuman. Indeed, human communication is highly resource-sensitive and backed up by synchronic and diachronic variations available to us today. The key to making our language production as efficient as possible – or in other words, cost-effective – is what we must observe, describe and explain as linguists. In this book, I propose that within this system of resource management, it is pragmatics which is most important in optimizing our linguistic production for our daily communication.

Following this line of thinking, it is worth considering what the factors excluded from Chomsky's tradition of generative linguistics – such as human memory, prosodic weight and length, and speech errors – can tell us about the tapestry of human language. That said, these factors continue to be overlooked too often. Surprisingly little has changed in contemporary linguistics since 1965. Indeed, Chomsky wrote the following in the preface to the fiftieth anniversary edition of *Aspects*:

> A fair conclusion today, I think, is that the general framework outlined in *Aspects* remain appropriate, while the specific proposals have to be substantially modified and also extended to new domains of inquiry that have emerged in the years since.

Even today, words like 'native speaker' are still frequently used without question in contemporary syntax papers, and the native speaker's judgement still plays a crucial role in shaping analyses and arguments. A grammaticality judgement based on single sentences is still considered the most important criterion in our syntactic debates, and theoretical linguists are still obsessed with researching competence while undervaluing performance.

New realities: AI and VR

Why are we so concerned with single sentences in a vacuum and the grammatical judgement of non-existent ideal speakers? These assumptions were already questionable when they were made over sixty years ago – but they seem especially irrelevant in the twenty-first century, when the internet and social media makes our lives ever more multilingual, multimodal and multicultural. I believe our immigration to virtual spaces warrants a radical update of the foundations of our linguistic research.

Over the last fifteen years, the era of big data and social media has had a significant impact on our lives. Theoretical linguistics has not responded adequately to this revolutionary change in human communication. Gen Z and Gen Alpha have been born as AI natives: AI chatbots are their playmates and VR is their playground. Technology doesn't just mediate their languages; it often initiates them. They live with hyperscale AI like ChatGPT and they operate in the metaverse. That's their reality for both life and communication. Theoretical linguistics often overlooks this aspect and passes the ball to applied linguistics. If we don't examine the everyday language of the global youth, what are we really studying? It's no wonder that linguistic theories have hardly any connection or implication in the field of AI language studies. We need to acknowledge the impact of technology on language and communication and explore new ways to incorporate these changes into linguistic research.

Changes to our communication in the digital era are significant and deserve more attention in linguistics. They have brought new possibilities for research – big data allows us to extract patterns from enormous samples of linguistic data, while social media provides us a glimpse into the everyday spontaneous language use of users around the world. Both of these methodologies will be essential in uncovering the truth behind the new realities of communication today.

Superficial differences

My first syntax textbook was Ouhalla (1994), which I studied in 1997. As the author notes on the cover, this book covers the following aspects of linguistic theory: phrase structure grammar, X-bar, theta theory, case, binding, control, movement, parameter and cross-linguistic variation. However, before discussing cross-linguistic variation, the data was exclusively drawn from English. The final chapter on cross-linguistic variation included Romance and Germanic languages, Bantu, Japanese and Arabic – a chapter that was entirely skipped in my undergraduate syntax class, in fact. Only one short chapter was dedicated to languages across the world and, to exacerbate matters, the data consisted of a very small sample of examples.

When it comes to the inclusion of diverse languages, the generative mindset has a serious issue. What Chomsky calls a slight change in parameter might yield 'superficial' variety, however, I believe that this is not constructive for our understanding of Universal Grammar (UG). Differences are not superficial, rather, they are massive. Consider the following lines from Chomsky:

> The P&P approach largely emerged from intensive study of a range of languages, but it was also suggested by major developments in general biology, specifically Francois Jacob's account of how slight changes in the hierarchy and timing of regulatory mechanisms might yield great *superficial differences* – a butterfly or an elephant, and so on. The model seemed natural for language as well: slight changes in parameter settings might yield superficial variety, through interaction of invariant principles with parameter choices.
>
> Chomsky, 1980, p. 67; emphasis mine

A theory of language has to address two major issues. The first issue relates to the fact that languages, despite their so-called 'superficial differences', are identical at a deep and abstract level. In the theory outlined in this book, this property of human languages is accounted for by postulating the existence of a set of abstract principles common to all languages, by virtue of being genetically determined. These principles are collectively referred to as Universal Grammar.

As I remind readers, in this book, which focuses on syntax from Asian perspectives, we cannot simply use quick fixes nor continue to try to make square pegs fit into round holes. What we see in generative grammars is that examining and accounting for cross-linguistic variation is a serious issue that has persisted through the decades. While robust empirical research and individual speakers' intuitions matter, only including one or two languages in a whole book leads to an inaccurate and discomfiting view of variation. To think that an Anglocentric lens will work for all languages gives false hope to those studying linguistics. One may be led to believe that, by knowing the principles and parameters, one is then able to understand cross-linguistic variation – but this is not the reality; such differences across languages are simply dismissed as 'superficial' according to the generative mindset. However, this way of understanding variation is dangerous and has caused harm to the field over the decades. The lack of diversity in the languages examined is one of the reasons for the discomfort of many linguists from other disciplines; when using such a small sample of languages, with an Anglocentric bias, the conclusions drawn do not seem convincing enough.

A new goal: the importance of ordinary language

We cannot simply graft new ideas onto old schools of thought. In order to build an explanatory framework capable of capturing and accounting for our linguistic behaviours, we need a new goal to aim for. I believe this goal should be to observe, describe and explain *how* people manage their limited linguistic resources in their ordinary communication – which is increasingly multilingual, multimodal and multicultural – to produce a suitable combination of verbal and non-verbal output in ever more creative and *generative* ways in an efficient and context-sensitive manner which observes necessary pragmatic motivations.

What matters: from single sentences to big data in context

According to Bloomfield (1935, p. 21): 'Writing is not language, but merely a way of recording language by means of visible mark.' The stand-alone sentence has received too much attention in contemporary linguistics. It is a purely artificial unit that exists only in writing. Yet, despite this, contemporary syntax bases its analysis on the stand-alone sentence regardless. The object of study in contemporary syntax is so often the formal, well-formed, grammatical sentence existing within a vacuum. However, the grammaticality of a sentence can depend on contextual factors: by changing prosody or register, ungrammaticality can frequently be repaired. Examples of this are easily found in Asian languages that are socio-pragmatically more complex than English and many other Western European languages. When looking at Korean and Japanese data that has been explored in contemporary syntax, for example, the examples being discussed tend to be in formal registers, and grammaticality can easily be restored by simply changing the register to be less formal. Given this, how can we assert that a sentence lacking all context is grammatical or not?

We're living in the era of big data. These vast volumes of data will help us to find the patterns so important to syntacticians. Sure, a single sentence can occasionally provide an important insight. Yet by leveraging the huge samples of everyday language available to us, we can glean so much more. As we shall discuss further in a later chapter, data speaks volumes.

These days, autocorrect software is advanced enough to check not only your spelling but your grammar, too. It can also help you to choose the right tone at the right time, and can even suggest emojis relevant to your message. These predictions are close enough to what we actually want to type frequently enough to make them indispensable in our increasingly busy lives. This type of software leverages data on how we type and what words we like to use to extract patterns that are used to predict where our sentences are going. I think it is crucial that linguists engage with this type of data-driven approach in order for us to open the linguistic black box in humanities. Big data and machine learning will help us to uncover emerging patterns in language, such as which forms thrive and survive over time in which regions, and why. This will also help us to find the nature of the generative power existing in human languages.

When we talk about natural language, we often unthinkingly limit our analysis to spoken and written data. Syntax is even more limited, focusing mainly on grammatically 'well-formed' sentences. Yet if we are truly interested in the linguistic sequences that we produce daily, we must rethink and revise our definition of 'natural' language, including which linguistic units are relevant to our analysis. Ordinary people's everyday communication matters. For instance, texting and emojing make up a large proportion of our daily communication, and I believe these are worthy of consideration. Alongside writing, texting and emojing should also have some common ground concerning their underlying principles. At the same time, however, the linguistic differences should be observed and incorporated into our theory of grammar and its explanation. Another element to reconsider is whether or not the single sentence is the right unit to focus on in syntactic analysis. Our everyday language use is not necessarily based on the sentence; in online messaging, we frequently break up our thoughts into separate messages to indicate the end of a thought – but these do not necessarily correlate with traditional sentences. Our digital reality has outpaced traditional linguistic models, and these need to be updated to keep up.

Who matters: from native speakers to ordinary speakers

Who lives 'in a completely homogeneous speech-community' Chomsky (1965, p. 3)? Who has unlimited linguistic resources? Nobody. So why do we spend so much time discussing 'ideal' native speakers? It is striking how many of the arguments surrounding generative linguistics today still take for granted that a monolingual community is possible, despite how outdated Chomsky's framework proposed in the *Aspects* is. People nowadays are born translingual. We navigate the physical and virtual worlds while mixing languages and combining different semiotic repertoires. This is not something unusual – this is what ordinary communication looks like in 2022. Such change is, at its core, an important grassroots change. From a generative perspective, one no longer needs to look at 'perfect' grammatical strings. Can we truly say then that this kind of mix-and-match approach to linguistics is 'ungrammatical'? No – it is translingual. Social media has also removed the gatekeepers guarding 'proper' language. Written language no longer needs to go through an editor to reach a wide audience, and different varieties of English, for example, can mix freely online. If linguistic authorities cannot enforce grammar, how are we to define grammaticality? Does grammaticality only apply to formal language now?

The 'native speaker' debate

How do we define a native speaker? Is it the language you grew up with? The language your parents speak? Does it count if you don't speak the standard dialect? Let's take English as an example. My father-in-law was born in London, yet his parents were of Danish origin. He couldn't speak Danish, but when he was young his friends' parents all used to comment on how good his English was – despite English being the only language he could speak! In terms of his linguistic ability, he should of course be included in any definition of 'native speaker' – yet he was not seen as such by others. The term 'native' can be discriminatory, especially when we live in the peak of multiculturalism. Some people speak numerous languages, and in such cases it is often hard to say which is their 'native' language. Does it have to be limited to only one? Now that English has become a global lingua franca, we see great diversity among the Englishes spoken around the world. Many people in Hong Kong, Singapore and Southeast Asia speak English as a first language – but would English speakers in the UK consider them to be natives, given that their variety of English is so different from the 'Queen's English'?

In the generative tradition, a native speaker is an ideal language user whose actual use of the language does not diverge from certain norms (Doerr, 2009, p. 2). Monolingualism is often 'taken for granted', such that what is considered to be the 'true knowledge' of any language is that which is spoken by a monolingual native speaker (Cook & Newson, 2007, p. 221). Thus, for a long time, linguistic research has focused on investigating the linguistic competence of idealized monolingual native speakers, even if it did not reflect the actual linguistic repertoire of most people – users of only one language in fact constitute a minority (Otwinowska, 2015, pp. 3–4). Despite the longstanding influence of generative linguistics, scholars in recent decades have begun to question the validity of such a restricted definition of native speakers. Mesthrie (2006) argues that the idea of a native speaker and native proficiency is flawed because it does not reflect the multilingual environments most language users must navigate, whereby these users rely on a mixture of different languages across different contexts. She notes that:

> For many 'New English' speakers, monolingualism is the marked case, a special case outside of the multilingual prototype. Today's ideal speaker lives in a heterogeneous society (stratified along increasingly globalized lines) and has to negotiate interactions with different people representing all sorts of power and solidarity positions on a regular basis. What is this ideal speaker a native speaker of, but a polyphony of codes/languages working cumulatively (and sometimes complementarily), rather than a single, first-learned code?
>
> Mesthrie, 2006, p. 482

Duarte and Gogolin (2013) also remark on this point, noting that even research on multilingual speakers has a tendency to use categories like 'native speaker' and 'heritage language' even though, for these multilingual speakers, 'their "mother tongue" may consist of a plurilingual repertoire that can be described as a composition of a number in themselves – from a linguistic point of view, distinct languages' (p. 7). The authors further note that these categories are unable to describe 'complexities within groups of speakers' (Duarte & Gogolin, 2013, p. 7). Therefore, concepts like the native speaker are deemed as being too overgeneralized and insufficient for capturing linguistic variation between individuals and groups.

The limited definition of a native speaker as proposed by generative linguists also has negative consequences, as what is not considered 'native' may be considered to be inferior in some way. Firth and Wagner (1997) highlight the issue of how non-native speakers are characterized as inherently deficient and problematic in comparison with native speakers, specifically: i) how native speakers form the 'benchmark from which judgements of appropriateness, markedness, and so forth, can be made', ii) how distinctions/variation within native and non-native speaker groups is overlooked in favour of categorizing them as homogenous and native speakers as a person born with a mother tongue, iii) how 'identity categorizations NS (native speakers) and NNS (non-native speakers) are applied exogenously and without regard for their emic relevance', and iv) how, in Second Language Acquisition views, native speakers are viewed as superior to non-native speakers, which ignores 'the multilingual reality of communities [...] and the reality of more transient, interacting groups, throughout the world' (pp. 291–292). Referring more specifically to language teaching, Holliday (2018) notes the harmfulness of the notion of native speakerism, in that it is 'a neoracist ideology that has a wide-ranging impact on how teachers are perceived by each other and by their students. By separating teachers according to the labels of "native speakers" and "non-native speakers," it falsely positions them as culturally superior and inferior with separate roles and attributes' (p. 1). The idea of a native speaker can therefore be considered to be ideological in nature.

How, then, should the terms 'native speaker' and 'native language' be defined, if at all? Some scholars have suggested that these terms should be rethought or even discarded entirely. Cheng et al. (2021) highlight the problematic nature of the notion of native speakers, illustrating how it is used to exclude certain populations, while pointing out the contradictory nature of many of the criteria used to classify someone as a native speaker, which include factors such as language proficiency, language history (e.g. age and context of language acquisition) and language identity. Cheng et al. (2021) recommended discarding the term entirely and classifying language users instead in terms of their language experience, considering 'all aspects of linguistic identity, proficiency, usage, input, output, language contact, etc' (p. 2).

Vulchanova et al. (2022) shared similar findings, arguing for the need to re-conceptualize the notion of native speakers due to its bias towards monolingualism, issues with its current definitions and, again, its tendency to exclude certain populations. Furthermore, they noted that there is no clear agreement on how to define a native language or native speaker, as previous literature has suggested these concepts are linked to a vague and contradictory range of factors including age, language exposure, sociocultural membership, etc. Finally, Andrews (2014) noted that even 'so-called native speakers of a particular language demonstrate a broad range of differences at a variety of levels', thus making it difficult to delineate any sort of criteria or 'common baseline' that applies to every native speaker (p. 41). This argument shows the futility of relying on 'native speakers' as the judges of grammaticality.

In the discussions above, we have complicated the notions of the 'native speaker' and 'native language'. Something frequently overlooked in conceptualizations of the native speaker is multilingualism. Which language is the 'native language' of a multilingual person? Can a person have only one native language? Or can a speaker be a native of multiple languages? Think of the many unique varieties of English that have emerged in postcolonial societies or regions where English is a popular foreign language to learn. In Southeast Asia, localized varieties of English in Singapore, Malaysia and the Philippines are considered to have reached the final stage of differentiation under Schneider's Dynamic Model, which tracks the different stages of development of postcolonial Englishes in former colonies based on how deeply entrenched that variety of English is within that particular society (Kirkpatrick, 2012, p. 17; Schneider, 2007). These varieties have their own unique syntactical, lexical, morphological and phonological features which differ from the dominant Inner Circle varieties. Given that speakers identify strongly with these varieties and use them extensively on a day-to-day basis as a first language, can we really say these speakers are anything less than native speakers of a variety of English? Furthermore, multilingualism is prevalent in Southeast Asia, with a home language coexisting alongside the national language, English as a foreign/school language and localized varieties of English. In cases like these, which of these should be considered their 'native' language?

Even in the present day, native speakerism has often been erroneously, and dangerously, conflated with other factors like race, class and ethnicity. Shuck (2006) describes what she calls an ideology of nativeness, whereby the world is strictly divided into native and non-native speakers, such that speech communities are viewed as inherently monocultural and monolingual, with a particular language becoming associated with a single nation (p. 260). She argues that this ideology creates structures that bring about linguistic discrimination and racism (p. 260). There is a dangerous tendency to assume that English native speakers are white Westerners, while non-whites are often considered to be non-native speakers (Pennycook, 2016, p. 31). Such assumptions of native superiority can cause speakers to 'devalue' their own language competency, 'internalize this subordination' and be used as a weapon to discriminate against those who are not as proficient in English (Tezgiden-Cakcak, 2019, p. 77; Tsuda, 2014, p. 447). This is a common issue in some of the previously mentioned Southeast Asian countries.

Despite some recognition of the value of local varieties of English, there is governmental pressure to adhere to exonormative standards of English in some of these countries, especially in Singapore, where the localized variety, Singlish, is often downplayed in favour of exonormative varieties like British English (Silver & Bokhorst-Heng, 2020, pp. 42–43). Silver and Bokhorst-Heng (2020) note that it is ironic that, while at the state level, exonormative varieties like British English are used to build local identity, this does not reflect what happens on the ground, where Singlish is proudly touted by ordinary people as a local identity marker (p. 42). With regards to racialization, Kubota et al. (2021) found that East Asian students studying at a Canadian university were 'forced into predetermined categories of race, nationality, and language', which ultimately caused them to feel excluded from the wider university community (p. 17). Positive remarks about their English proficiency were seen as demeaning and overly patronizing because such comments assume that non-white English speakers are inherently 'deficient speakers', even for native English speakers of other ethnicities, and thus they are rarely able to be seen in the same light as white English speakers (p. 17).

Pressure to adhere to exonormative standards is particularly evident in education. An analysis of the English language tests requirements for university admission across fourteen universities in Singapore, China, Hong Kong, Japan and South Korea showed that the tests accepted were all of exonormative, Inner Circle origins, which include IELTS, TOEFL and Cambridge. The requirements were also often based on whether one's first/native language is English and whether one studied in countries deemed to be native English-speaking regions (which did not include Singapore, Malaysia or the Philippines). Despite English being spoken widely in Singapore and Hong Kong, English tests tailored to local, endonormative standards were not adopted for university admissions.

ESL and EFL learners

There is no exact calculation of the total number of English speakers globally, and different sources provide different numbers. One source estimates the number of speakers of English as a secondary language (which likely includes English as a second language (ESL) and English as a foreign language (EFL) speakers) to be around 1.1 billion, while that of first language English speakers to be approximately 400 million (Patterson & West, 2020, p. 62). Another source, Ethnologue (2022b), places these figures at 1.08 billion for non-native speakers and 373 million for native speakers. It is clear from these estimates that theoretically determined non-native speakers, which occupy around 73 to 74 per cent of the total number of English speakers, are the majority.

Despite the massive numbers of ESL and EFL speakers in comparison with native speakers, the legitimacy and influence of these non-native speakers have consistently been downplayed. In studies of second language acquisition, native speakers 'continue(s) to predominate as the baseline or target that learners should seek to emulate' while learners are portrayed as being stuck in a 'in a continuous, autonomous, cognitive, morphosyntactic struggle . . . in pursuit of the target (i.e., native speaker) competence' (Firth & Wagner, 2007b, p. 804). Birch (2014) highlights the issue of inclusivity in linguistic theory, whereby such theories are based on the assumption that ideal native speakers residing within monolingual circles should be the main research subjects (p. 24): 'If syntactic theories are based on an ideal speaker-listener in a homogenous speech community with linguistic competence, what about second language learners who live in heterogeneous speech communities, and whose language has speech errors?' Furthermore, Firth and Wagner (2007) criticize Chomsky's strict distinction between native and non-native speakers, and question the validity of viewing native speakers as exemplars in linguistic research. They note the following:

> NS [native speaker] data are thus viewed as the warranted baseline from which NNS data can be compared, and the benchmark from which judgements of appropriateness, markedness, and so forth, can be made ... As a logical extension, NNSs [non-native speakers] are unproblematically viewed as the NSs' subordinates ... At the very least, NS–NNS interactions are prejudged to be somehow unusual, anomalous or extraordinary ... NS and NNS are blanket terms, implying homogeneity throughout each group, and clearcut distinctions between them. So a NS is assumed unproblematically to be a person with a mother tongue, acquired from birth. How bilingualism, multilingualism, 'semi-lingualism,' and (first) language loss relate to the concept of NS are in large measure ignored, as is the question of whether one can become a NS in a S/FL ... The identity categorizations NS and NNS are applied exogenously and without regard for their emic relevance ... the prevailing monolingual orientation ... fails to take account of the multilingual reality of communities and the reality of more transient, interacting groups, throughout the world.
>
> Firth and Wagner, 2007a, pp 763–64

Their concerns echo what we see in the development of English as a world language currently. In the present day and age, it is no longer valid to just view English as a monolithic, homogenous Western language, nor its speakers as a bounded, fixed set of people (Marlina, 2017, p. 174). If we just consider people who speak English as a second or even third or fourth language, we are effectively looking at a billion or so English speakers who acquire and use English within a bilingual or even multilingual setting, and subsequently these are the very people who instigate the development of localized Englishes like Singaporean English and Nigerian English (Marlina, 2017, p. 174). With the onslaught of globalization, people are traversing borders virtually and in-person more often than ever before, such that individuals no longer operate only within small, localized and possibly monolingual communities, but rather, gain the opportunity to interact with people from a diverse range of linguistic and cultural backgrounds, be it native or non-native.

Traditionally non-native speakers are also taking matters into their own hands by actively shaping the English language to suit their own needs and no longer being solely dependent on the norms of native speakers, leading to the birth of local varieties of English. However, to term non-native speakers as a large homogenous entity would be erroneous, because of the differing environments in which one acquires/learns languages. Hamada (2017) argues that although 'ESL and EFL are sometimes seen as interchangeable terms', the learning environments in which they are placed in can be vastly different. For example, when compared with ESL environments whereby learners can learn 'by accident' since they are exposed to English speakers even beyond the classroom, learners in EFL environments have to make a conscious effort to study as there is no natural exposure to the language outside of classes (Hamada, 2017, p. xiii). There are also differences in access to English education across regions within and between countries, namely how well funded it is and how widespread it is in a geographical area. This underscores the importance of the learning process in language acquisition, since not everyone will have the opportunity to acquire English naturally. I will expound upon this point again in a later paragraph.

Even so-called native speakers can exhibit many differences in language use (such as in phonology and lexicon particularly) within the same community, because of their individual experiences in the virtual and physical space they frequent as well as their attitudes. Therefore, homogeneity largely does not exist anymore in most communities that are connected to the global network, and to assume any kind of uniformity would be to overlook the large amount of linguistic variation present at even the lowest levels. Non-native speakers contribute as much, perhaps even more judging by their numbers, as native speakers to the development of English on a global scale, and it is important that linguistic theories take into account their language data, otherwise we would risk continuing the suppression of non-native voices. If linguistic theories were only largely based on native speakers who are the minority, how would they be able to account for the majority of language users? Does this effectively affect the credibility of such theories? What would be the utilitarian value of such theories if they are ultimately not applicable to real language data?

Nevertheless, the chasm between native and non-native speakers is not the only issue that has been proliferated by Chomskyan linguistics. Chomskyan linguistics has constantly overlooked the role of learning in language acquisition, with Chomsky (1980) famously arguing in his work *Rules and Representations* that 'in certain fundamental respects we do not really learn language; rather, grammar grows in the mind' (p. 134), suggesting, at least in the Chomskyan perspective, that it is mostly inconsequential. Chomsky (1965) expounds upon this view by citing his renowned theory of Universal Grammar (UG), claiming at length that language acquisition is explained by the presence of an abstract grammar within humans, and that, in his view, the insignificant role of learning is attributed to how language acquisition is only distantly connected to experiential learning (p. 58): 'language acquisition is based on the child's discovery of what from a formal point of view is a deep and abstract theory – a generative grammar of his language – many of the concepts and principles of which are only remotely related to experience by long and intricate chains of unconscious quasi-inferential steps'. In essence, what this means is that, according to Chomsky, linguistic ability is 'not developed through learning' but, on the contrary, develops 'on the basis of a genetic program which controls the transformation of linguistic deep structures into linguistic surface strings of words' (Wilss, 1996, p. 16).

However, there have been doubts about Chomsky's views, since they were not based on real observations of how children actually develop language but were rather just 'rational' assessments of linguistic knowledge (Chapman, 2011, p. 150). The fact that his approach was deductive meant that Chomskyan linguistics suffered from a major shortcoming – that is to say, being too reliant on phenomena 'that cannot be proved to exist', suggesting that the idea of UG and an innate language faculty can 'never be conclusively proved' (Chapman, 2006, p. 52). Following this line of thought, since generative grammar cannot be definitively shown to exist, its connections to language acquisition are not necessarily robust. Therefore, this increases the possibility that, rather than abstract grammars, it could be the learning process that is important for acquiring language.

Furthermore, there may actually be a need for classroom instruction and learning in certain circumstances. For example, in multilingual educational environments, many individuals may not find that they are able to acquire multiple languages (three and above) naturally, and thus there is actually an increase in demand for formal instruction in a range of languages – a demand with an upward trend that will create 'more and more multilingual individuals and societies' (Wilton, 2009, pp. 46–47). This may be related to what was mentioned earlier on, that even amongst non-native English speakers there is a disparity between how ESL and EFL learners acquire English due to differences in learning environment. While natural acquisition is a common reason, learning can also play a significant role for a large proportion of those who do not have access to resources for such a process. Buschfeld (2013) reiterates this point by noting that children in non-native ESL countries can acquire English both in and out of the class due to an access to English even before the schooling period, which stands in stark contrast to traditional EFL countries where formal instruction is the basis of English learning for both children and adults (pp. 67–68). Such ESL and EFL learners should not be dismissed nor side-lined in the face of so-called native speakers; their learning experience can also provide valuable insight into human linguistic competence.

Being human: being pragmatic

We never say exactly the same thing twice. A multitude of factors affect the meaning of what we say, from our tone to the specific context of the situation. Humans are excellent at using language creatively, and we can find countless new ways of expressing the same meaning; we do not simply learn the patterns of language and repeat them – we use language with unlimited creativity and are constantly generating new expressions. This is what distinguishes human languages from that of a chimpanzee or a machine. Animals communicate pragmatically – being understood is far more important than creating new forms of expression when their communication is essential to warn of nearby predators or food. The output of machines can often seem enormously creative – we live in a time when computers can write poems (a 2016 TED talk by Oscar Schwartz (Schwartz, 2016) shows how a poem-generating algorithm can pass the poetry equivalent of the Turing Test). Yet the output of machines is still determined by the supplied input, even if randomness and algorithms can produce suitably unexpected results. Where, then, is the human element in our language?

Another myth in generative grammar relates to the idea of 'naturalness'. Often the examples of 'natural' language given in generative linguistics are created by the authors themselves or collected by the author from various written sources. Spontaneous data collected from linguistic corpora has rarely been used until recently. How do we determine whether such examples are 'natural' or not? Is the author's intuition sufficient? I believe a more robust, empirically sound method is needed to quantify the 'naturalness' of sentences, if indeed this notion is useful at all.

Very often, examples presented as 'natural' are presented in a refined, tidied-up form. As I shall explore in later chapters, most of the verbal blunders or so-called *dis*fluencies in generative grammar have been removed from the data and our analysis, leaving a glaring gap in our knowledge. Can we call such examples natural if we only see an artificially curated portion of the totality of language use? I argue in this book that these often ignored parts of our linguistic production that have been considered imperfect or flawed are the true reflection of our linguistic competence. Indeed, Levelt (1989) wrote that *uh* is the only word that's universal across languages. The fuzzy and unkempt elements of our language which machines can't easily reproduce are perhaps the key to understanding the most 'human' elements of our language. These disfluencies are also linked to the reality of our limited linguistic resources – a far cry from Chomsky's ideal speaker. Perhaps Siri and Alexa may be the ideal speakers spoken of in the *Aspects*. In reality, every aspect of our communication, from comprehension to articulation, is defined by the limits of our resources. We can't remember an infinite number of words, nor can we produce unlimited volumes of language. Our syntactic production is not only affected but also guided by our capacity for articulation. The *Aspects* often talks about being free from 'memory limitations'. Yet, as we shall see, memory limitations affect even the very core of our syntactic decisions. Our decisions to evaluate a certain linguistic sequence as acceptable or not, or even our decisions to repair or move around lexical items, are hugely influenced by our memory load. Indeed, this is the reason why people build linguistic structures in a step-by-step, incremental manner – we are not supercomputers.

> The unacceptable grammatical sentences often cannot be used, for reasons *having to do, not with grammar,* but rather with memory limitations, intonational and stylistic factors, 'iconic' elements of discourse, for example, a tendency to place logical subject and object early rather than late and so on.
>
> Chomsky, 1965, p. 11; emphasis mine

Studies into linguistic competence have long assumed that factors like intonation, prosody, memory limitations, stylistic factors, processing efficiency and frequency of use were merely peripheral issues. This is likely informed by the Chomskyan mindset, which assumes from the outset that native speakers are able to acquire their mother tongues perfectly. Is our communication really free from any limitations, however? We should reconsider whether these assumptions are truly useful to our analyses or not.

When we use language, we attempt to use our given linguistic resources with the least amount of effort. Pragmatic principles are at the heart of all of our linguistic calculations and decisions. The forms that survive and thrive are not determined arbitrarily – pragmatic motivations, namely efficiency, expressivity and empathy, are responsible for the syntactic variations we encounter daily. This also applies to our texting and emojing habits. I believe this is key to understanding the synchronic, diachronic and typological variation we encounter daily. Even in literary forms such as songs and poems, we see these pragmatic principles in effect; the prosodic structures of these genres are often chosen due to their ease of memorization, for instance.

Beyond English: an Asian perspective

Modern linguistics tends to put too much emphasis on languages and structures that resemble English. One of the main goals of this book is to challenge this Anglocentric bias. While our present focus is on Asian languages, it should be noted that the problem of representation goes beyond this group; a number of European languages have also been inadequately studied due to Anglocentrism. A famous example of this is when Maurice Gross argued in his 1979 article for how generative grammar has failed to explain French.

As for Asian languages, one could point out that they have been the subject of study frequently over the last five decades. Yet, there is often disharmony between those studying these languages from a more traditional linguistic perspective and those studying said languages from a generative perspective. For instance, in many Asian languages, socio-pragmatic considerations are more important than syntactic considerations when considering whether to realize first- or second-person pronouns. In other words, who are speaking to each other, and their relationship, determines argument realization. This is a relatively alien concept for English and other major Western European languages. Another example is that Chinese is often considered to lack tenses. Yet, many languages behave like Chinese in that there is no clear past tense (Dahl & Velupillai, 2013). According to *The World Atlas of Language Structures Online* (WALS), ninety-four languages behave like English and eighty-eight (many of them Southeast Asian languages) behave like Chinese (Dahl & Velupillai, 2013)! This makes one wonder whether tense, along with other elements of the English language, is over-emphasized as an essential part of language when describing world languages. Similarly, more languages possess a word order in which the verb comes at the final position rather than the initial position. Furthermore, most of these verb-final languages show great structural fluidity – yet, from the inception of generative grammar up until now, such flexible word orders have been considered the exception rather than the rule. These Anglocentric perspectives and traditions within linguistics must be rethought to recognize non-English languages as equals.

These methodological failings create the risk that generative linguistics will cease to be relevant. Phillips framed this in terms of the 'initiative' in 2009:

> I think that it would help a great deal if more linguists were to take more seriously the mentalistic commitments to which they profess. Most generative linguists would assent to the notion that their theories should be responsive to learnability considerations, yet there has been surprisingly little exploration of how to relate current understanding of cross-language variation to models of language learning ... In sum, I agree with many of the critics cited above that some fundamental questions must be addressed (or readdressed) if generative linguistics is to again seize the initiative in the study of language. The perception on the outside that mainstream linguistics is becoming irrelevant is unfortunately very real indeed. However, I do not think that we should be fooled into thinking that informal judgment gathering is the root of the problem or that more formalized judgment collection will solve the problem.
>
> Phillips, 2009, p. 13

If generative linguistics is to again 'seize the initiative', as Phillips put it, it needs a change in direction. Generative linguistics has been working with the same tools for too long – it needs a new box of tools with which it can reshape itself and be born anew. To regain relevance in this changing world, it needs a new set of assumptions capable of explaining all languages on an equal footing. Our language itself has been reshaped by an increasingly globalized and connected world, and generative linguistics must follow with a reconceptualized theory able to satisfactorily explain this new era of human language.

To fix or impeach?

'Should we impeach armchair linguists?', asks Phillips, who has conducted a number of crucial empirical studies. Those who have studied generative grammars will know about the problems of 'armchair' linguists. However, as Phillips sagely talks us through the discussion, we cannot be firmly black and white on this matter. A more balanced view is indeed necessary. Recall Phillips' conclusion to the paper, mentioned above. In order for generative grammar to seize the initiative, it needs to engage with other important issues around our languages. That said, my disappointment manifests again due to the lack of more robust discussion around languages other than English.

Unfortunately, it is not an easy fix. Phillips himself is at the forefront of cross-linguistic experiments to help broaden our understanding of languages beyond English. Yet in order to explain his experiments in Japanese, he had to devise a process called 'un-forced revision'. For me, what it means is that the revision is un-forced – simple enough, right? Not quite. This explanation suggests that Japanese speakers revise the structure-building due to some unknown cause. This sounds like an ad hoc explanation. Such accounts are not uncommon when we try to explain Asian languages in generative grammars, whatever version we choose; we face some sort of ad hoc mechanisms to make the explanation work. In this book, I argue against such a practice and propose instead the simplicity hypothesis. Simply speaking, what I intend to show is that simple fixes are not good enough.

3

The Injustices of Grammaticality Judgements

'This sounds better'

Chomsky (1965, p. 11) writes, 'The unacceptable grammatical sentences often cannot be used, for reasons to do, not with grammar, but rather with memory limitations, intonational and stylistic factors, "iconic" elements of discourse, for example, a tendency to place logical subject and object early rather than late and so on.' This view on pragmatic matters that has been widely touted in contemporary syntactic theories. For a long time in the studies of linguistic competence, intonation or prosody, together with memory limitations, stylistic factors and processing efficiency or frequency in use, have been understood as *peripheral* issues – not important issues. Yet, are they really?

Throughout the years, I would give my 'broken' English writings to my English husband. He would then make them sound natural and grammatical. Oftentimes, I would observe this process. The reparations were delicate, and mostly involved moving things around. Usually, he would read the words aloud and repeatedly. As part of the process, he would tend to say to me either 'this sounds better' or 'this sounds awful'. It is interesting to note that he would use the verb 'sounds'. In my own language endeavours, I often ask the question 'why is this not good?' To which my husband would normally respond with something to the effect of 'it just doesn't feel right'. Is grammaticality all about sound and feeling then?

Indeed, I felt that he was moving things around to make my collection of incomplete phrases and standalone words sound better. English grammars will often bring in the same judgement, as in the case of the so-called 'heavy NP shift' – that is to say that everything is fine and grammatical. In the past, I would give the same set of notes to other English 'native' speakers. Perhaps, unsurprisingly, there were disputes. I can still remember the one time that I had some writing corrected by my husband. Yet, back then, my supervisor told me that there were a few grammatical errors, suggesting that this was the result of my Korean grammar interfering with English. I found that among English speakers there can be disputes and disagreement – again unsurprisingly. However, looking at their corrections to my work, I also found that they were not fully in agreement with the uses of the article choices (specifically, whether to use 'a/an' or 'the'). This personal experience has stuck with me over the years. From this, I learned that what people label as (un)grammatical can often simply be the result of one's preference or style. Furthermore, what makes certain phrases feel more natural is inherently related to prosodic matters.

This chapter will look at the nature of grammaticality and its implications in our time. Over the past sixty years, grammaticality has been considered as the core criterion to reveal syntactic architecture in generative grammar. On this matter, methodological challenges are often addressed, such as the need to move towards more objective and scientific methods rather than using a subjective collection of judgements. As we shall see, there are indeed pros and cons regarding data collection itself, but what I intend to show is not so much concerned with addressing the necessity of a particular method. While methodological revision is important, I want to challenge the fundamental reasons and ethics behind grammaticality judgements.

In order to do this, I will look at the nature of grammaticality as a core criterion, describe its limitations, and engage with four key questions:

1. *Can grammaticality be relevant to efficiency and frequency?* While Chomsky's answer to this is 'no', I would disagree. Efficiency and frequency should have some contribution to grammatical constructions which also follow the patterns of use that have been repeatedly practised. Currently, there is no consideration in the framework to this aspect of asymmetry – which I call 'preference asymmetry' – to incorporate frequency and efficiency asymmetry.
2. *Is grammaticality knowledge purely syntactic?* As we can see in my short anecdote, non-grammatical or extra-grammatical factors do have an effect on one's judgement.
3. *Is grammaticality knowledge only static?* In this subsection, I show how grammaticality knowledge can be dynamic.
4. *Who decides what's right and what's wrong?* For this question, I consider the role of an individual and community – is it everyone's decision to make?

I will then examine the grammaticality of Asian languages. As it currently stands, Asian languages are all considered in the same way as in English – but I argue that this is unsuitable and unjust. For example, whether or not to use an explicit subject depends on ecological elements in many Asian languages, but our present theoretical framework does not allow for an appropriate consideration of these factors. I then investigate the grammaticality of hybrid varieties: what happens if you mix languages? An important aspect of the grammaticality discussion is the concept of the 'ideal, native speaker' in a strictly monolingual setting. Yet this is not a proper reflection of reality. While awareness of these languages and varieties is growing, when we put an asterisk or question mark, shouldn't we still consider ecological factors? At the same time, even if the focus is a particular variety of language, wouldn't it also be influenced by other ecological factors set in time?

All of these discussions will reveal that our understanding of grammaticality is no longer fitting. Looking at grammaticality from a historical perspective, we see that it has been established through repeated use. The distinction between what is more natural and what is not is established over time, through the repeated use of community practices. In other words, grammaticality is similar to habit formation – it's not just some magic box that you inherit out of the blue. We are now living in a time of individualized idiolects and social media, in which conventional nominal grammar is not relevant anymore – after all, nobody would talk about grammaticality on social media. While some may discuss punctuation and spelling online, it should be pointed out that even punctuation markers have changed in their function and meaning through the catalyst of social media; the use of an ellipsis may be entirely different on-screen and in writing. In this chapter, I engage with the underlying question of 'does grammar still matter?'

Grammaticality as the core criterion

Colorless green ideas

Grammaticality has been at the very heart of syntactic architecture since the inception of generative grammar. The following quote is from Chomsky's *Syntactic Structures* (1957).

> The fundamental aim in the linguistic analysis of a language L is to separate the grammatical sequences which are the sentences of L from the ungrammatical sequences which are not sentences of L and to study the structure of the grammatical sequences. The grammar of L will thus be a device that generates all

> of the grammatical sequences of L and none of the ungrammatical ones. One way to test the adequacy of a grammar proposed for L is to determine whether or not the sequences that it generates are actually grammatical, i.e., acceptable to a native speaker, etc.
>
> Chomsky, 1957, p. 13

Chomsky then continues to offer the famous example sentences, as below:

> Second, the notion 'grammatical' cannot be identified with 'meaningful' or 'significant' in any semantic sense. Sentences (1) and (2) are equally nonsensical, but any speaker of English will recognize that only the former is grammatical.
>
> (1) Colorless green ideas sleep furiously.
> (2) Furiously sleep ideas green colorless.
>
> Yet (1), though nonsensical, is grammatical, while (2) is not. Presented with these sentences, a speaker of English will read (1) with a normal sentence intonation, but he [sic] will read (2) with a falling intonation on each word; in fact, with just the intonation pattern given to any sequence of unrelated words. He treats each word in (2) as a separate phrase. Similarly, he will be able to recall (1) much more easily than (2), to learn it much more quickly, etc. Yet he may never have heard or seen any pair of words from these sentences joined in actual discourse.
>
> Chomsky, 1957 p. 16

However, I want to point out that, even in these core examples, Chomsky talks about prosodic/intonational resources. Considering matters through a critical lens, it is thus surprising that since the publication of *Syntactic Structures*, grammaticality has been considered solely in syntactic terms.

The limitations of grammaticality judgements

The grammaticality test has been one of the most important criteria used to attest legitimate syntactic architecture. However, as Schütze (1996) discusses in detail, though the concept of a grammaticality or acceptability judgement is regarded as the foremost criterion in shaping grammars, the method for defining degrees of grammaticality is not robust enough nor does it have a solid empirical background. Phillips (2009) further questioned whether the improvement of methodology can in fact be the real solution for puzzles around grammaticality judgement tests and some other fundamental issues which generative linguists face.[1]

Grammaticality/acceptability greatly varies between speakers too, even when they have similar linguistic backgrounds. Context is also significant. In the history of generative linguistics, socio-pragmatic sensitivity was often ignored, and the examples were studied in a vacuum-like formal, written register alone. Hence, it is easy to find that the unnaturalness is caused not because of the structural oddity but because of the register or socio-pragmatic mismatch (see later chapters for a more detailed discussion on the role of register and pragmatics).

In the following, we will discuss the limitations of output-only grammaticality judgements based only on isolated written sentences. Grammaticality judgements are known to be the most important criterion for shaping structural configuration. However, as we will see, they must have solid empirical foundations to be useful in proving linguistic theories. We shall also see that grammaticality judgements based on a 'sound-less', 'growth-less' and 'context-less' single sentences are inevitably misleading. Consider again Chomsky's famous example, shown in (1) and (2), above.

As previously noted, Chomsky's example has undoubtedly influenced decades of linguistic theory, but when we think about it, what does '*' really mean? What about '?' or '??(?)'?

Carnie (2002) defines the asterisk (*) as a symbol used to mark syntactically ill-formed (unacceptable or ungrammatical) sentences. On the other hand, the hash sign (#) is used to mark sentences that are semantically strange but syntactically well-formed. In most cases, however, it is not a simple matter to distinguish semantic oddities from syntactic oddities. Moreover, clear distinctions between '*' and '#' or between '*' and '?(?)' have not been systematically agreed upon in the literature, causing inconsistency in use between different authors. As Schütze (1996) discusses in detail, although the concept of grammaticality judgement is regarded as the foremost criterion in shaping grammars, our methods for defining degrees of grammaticality are not robust enough. The Chomskyan ethos, quoted below, explains why this is the case.

> I have no doubt that it would be possible to devise operational and experimental procedures that could replace the reliance on introspection with little loss, but it seems to me that in the present state of the field, this would simply be a waste of time and energy.
>
> Chomsky, 1969, p. 81

Would this truly have been a waste of time and energy? Is it better to decide between '?', '??' and '???' based on subjective intuition, rather than relying on agreed and consistent methods? What kinds of strangeness warrant the use of the '???' judgement rather than the '??' judgement, and why?

Another issue with this approach is that some forms of strangeness cannot be detected by typical grammaticality judgement tests. In addition to the asymmetry between grammatical and ungrammatical sequences, as shown above, this book assumes that there exists another type of interesting asymmetry, which also reveals the core aspects of linguistic universals innate to native English speakers.

Can grammaticality be relevant to efficiency and frequency?

While Chomsky would argue that grammaticality is not relevant to efficiency and frequency, I would argue otherwise. Consider (3) from Stowe (1986) and (4) from Wasow (2002):

(3) Efficiency asymmetry:

No slow-down at us:
    a.   My brother wanted to know if Ruby will bring us home to Mom at Christmas.

Slow-down at us:
    b.   *My brother wanted to know who Ruby will bring us home to at Christmas.*

(4) Frequency asymmetry:

Frequently observed:
    a.   *Pat picked up a very large mint-green hard cover book.*

Hardly observed:
    b.   *Pat picked a very large mint-green hard cover book up.*

Both pairs of sentences in (3) and (4) are grammatical, yet there are significant differences between the pairs in other respects. In the case of (3), there are significant differences in how native speakers understand the sentences in real time. In the case of (4), we can see that there are significant differences in how frequently each sentence is used in actual speech.

The differences between the sentences in (3) were recorded by Stowe (1986) using an online self-paced reading task. Stowe found a relatively slower reading time at the direct object position in (3b) compared with the same position in (3a) as underlined. This slow-down effect occurs because native speakers make predictions about the upcoming sentence structure while they read. When native speakers come across the sequence *who Ruby* in (3b), they are most likely to interpret *who* as the direct object of the upcoming sentence, yet this prediction is disproved when they reach *us*, thus causing a delay or 'surprising effect'. This phenomenon is known as the Filled-Gap Effect. If speakers did not make predictions about the future structure in the process of structure building, we would not expect this kind of surprising effect in these sentences; Stowe's study therefore provides evidence for the notion that speakers do indeed make these kinds of predictions.

The asymmetry observed in (4), on the other hand, is due to so-called Heavy NP Shift. This phenomenon was first observed by Ross (1967). Though both sentences are grammatical, native speakers strongly prefer to locate heavy NPs at the end of the sentence so that the verb and its accompanying particle come together, as in (4a). For another example, the phrasal verb *pick up* with an intervening object was found around 3,971 times in the 100 million samples in the British National Corpus. In principle, any number of words could appear between *pick* and *up* in English. Yet, 99.5 per cent of the time, only one or two lexical items with one syllable occurred between *pick* and *up*. No examples contained more than four words between *pick* and *up*.

This phenomenon has been a long-standing puzzle in generative grammar, since the weight or length effect is regarded as unrelated to innate knowledge of language. This belief, however, has recently been challenged. Hawkins (1994, 2004) and Wasow (2002), among others, have argued that grammar should have adequate ways of explaining this phenomenon. They in particular show that a processing-based account is better suited to explaining puzzling grammatical phenomena such as the Filled-Gap Effect (as in (3)) or Heavy NP Shift (as in (4)) than purely theoretical accounts. My view is more radical than that of Hawkins and Wasow in that I believe that processing considerations should be at the very heart of the grammar, and should be able to explain all structural phenomena.

Indeed, I shall argue in due course that grammar and processing are inseparable, and that understanding *how* a structure is processed should form the basis of any grammatical theory or analysis of syntactic phenomena. The aforementioned frequency effect is especially difficult to explain within the framework of generative grammar. Since both sentences in (4) are technically well-formed, the asymmetry is treated as negligible even in the most up-to-date theories of generative grammar. However, this does not mean that the asymmetry seen in (4) reveals nothing about linguistic competence. Instead, I argue that this shows the necessity of creating a grammar-formalism which *can* explain the procedural and optimizing nature of the process of building syntactic structures.

Besides grammaticality, notions such as 'felicity' (first used in Austin, 1975) and 'acceptability' (first discussed in Quirk & Svartvik, 1966) are also common judging tools in theoretical linguistics. These also deserve solid empirical foundations to enable their proper use in linguistic discussions.

Is grammaticality knowledge purely syntactic?

To cut to the chase, no – grammaticality involves dynamic processes which take into consideration non-syntactic factors such as prosody. In this book, we adopt the following conventions, explained in (5), for denoting the grammaticality of a structure or the felicity of its meaning. Note that I have adjusted the point at which abnormality is judged; rather than judging abnormality at the end of a structure, I have expanded it to a continuous process lasting throughout the process of structure building.

(5) Grammaticality Judgement Criteria
    a. *: Syntactically abnormal either during the process of understanding the structure or at the level of judging the final outcome sentence. These sentences are rarely observed in the corpus (in spontaneous speech). On the other hand, ?? represents an abnormality less severe than the kind seen in sentences marked with *.
    b. #: Semantically abnormal either during the process of understanding the structure or at the level of judging the final outcome sentence. These sentences are rarely observed in the corpus (in spontaneous speech). On the other hand, ?? represents an abnormality less severe than the kind seen in sentences marked with #.

Most of the time, it is not unambiguously clear whether strangeness is caused by syntactic or semantic factors. My approach is to identify the dominant cause of strangeness, acknowledging that other factors may also be at play: when the dominant cause of strangeness is identified as structural abnormality I use *, and when the dominant cause of strangeness is identified as semantic abnormality I use #. However, in cases when the dominant cause is unclear or irrelevant, I use ??(?). To reduce the influence of my personal subjectivity when using ??(?), I have consulted dozens of native speakers to gain a consensus.

To show where strangeness or ungrammaticality occurs during the process of structure building, I will insert the previously discussed symbols as subscripts under the corresponding word. For instance, in (6b), ?? is subscribed under the word *us* because this is where strangeness first occurs.

(6) Efficiency asymmetry
No slow-down at us:
   a. *My brother wanted to know if Ruby will bring us home to Mom at Christmas.*

Slow-down at us:
   b. *?? My brother wanted to know who Ruby will bring us?? home to at Christmas.*

Grammaticality judgements very often require one to examine multiple sentences before one can make an accurate judgement. Consider (7). Whether Sarah's utterance in (7) is grammatical or not depends on the existence of a context which plays the role of an implicitly existing first conjunct in a coordinated structure. That is, Sarah's utterance in (7) is ungrammatical without the context provided by John.

(7) *John: Why didn't you eat your dinner?*
    Sarah: Because I hate mushrooms.

Consider also (8). (8) shows the importance of prosody in grammaticality judgements. While (8a) is well-formed, (8b) is deemed ungrammatical due to its phrasing. I use curly brackets { } here to label prosodic phrasing.

(8) a. *Martin looks up to Brian and {Carol to Dani}.*
    b. *???Martin looks up to {Brian and Carol} to Dani.*

Prosody matters in structural realization. It is interesting to note that when people are asked about the grammaticality of a sentence, very often they 'speak out' the sentence or try to imagine a context that could explain the natural use of the sentence. The fact that speaking such sentences out loud can help speakers make grammaticality judgements hints at the importance of tone and phrasing information when making said judgements.

Is grammaticality only static?

No, grammaticality is not static but rather dynamic. Not only structure-building, but also assessing and assigning grammaticality is done in an incremental manner within its local grammatical unit. Consider the Korean examples below. (S<H means the hearer is senior to the speaker. S>H means the speaker is senior to the hearer.)

(9) Socio-pragmatic awkwardness/unnaturalness due to speaker–hearer relation conflict

   a.   S<H particle *nim*, S>H particle *e-la*
**Sensayng-nim, pap mek-e-la*.
teacher-respect meal eat-command
Lit. 'Dear Teacher, come and have a meal.' (Honorific is under-used.)

   b.   S>H particle *-ya* and S<H particle *–yo*.
**aki-ya pap mek-u-seyyo*.
child-vocative meal eat-polite
Lit. 'Dear baby, come and have a meal.' (Honorific is over-used.)

In the above example, native speakers detect the unnaturalness before finishing the whole sentence. (9a) is unnatural because *–nim* is an honorific particle which predicts an honorific verbal particle. Yet, in (9a), a command-denoting ending particle *-e-la* (-어라) is used, which is typically used by a superior to their junior. Hence, the socio-pragmatic expectation is jeopardized. In contrast, (9b) shows the suffix *–ya* (-야), which is used by a superior to their junior with intimacy. However, this expectation for a speaker–hearer relationship is again not met when the polite *-seyyo* (-세요) ending particle appears. The unnaturalness found in (9a) and (9b) may be broadly agreed by ordinary Korean speakers. The cause of the unnaturalness is nothing to do with grammatical structures but socio-pragmatic relevance. This shows that grammaticality or acceptability judgement is procedurally made in the process of understanding a sequence – rather than once for all at the very end of a sentence.

Is grammaticality checked globally?

Grammaticality and acceptability judgements are made locally as one goes on receiving information. That said, in spontaneous speech, if the grammaticality checking domain is too long, human parsers can easily forget to detect ungrammaticality. For instance, subject–verb mismatch in spontaneous production is frequently found in verb-final languages when the distance between the two expressions becomes too long. It is because of the limitation of resources, that is, working memory in this case. In the same way, human parsers tend to resolve filler-gap dependency as soon as possible in online processing rather than some arbitrary place in order to lower the burden of the memory load. (See Hawkins 2014 for cross-linguistic evidence for this claim.)

Along the same line, Asudeh (2011) argues that grammaticality or well-formedness in production is checked locally rather than globally, chunk by chunk. Similar claims on processing/parsing have been made by Tabor et al. (2004). Consider (10). Asudeh reports that both examples are produced and 'tolerated' – though (10b) is judged ungrammatical due to the violation of an island condition.

(10) a. *You get a rack that the bike will sit on.*
 [locally well-formed, globally well-formed]

 b. ??? *You get a rack that the bike will sit on it.*
 [locally well-formed, globally ill-formed]

According to Asudeh (2011), the reason why both sentences are produced and tolerated by ordinary speakers is because they are 'locally legitimate'. The illegitimacy of (10b) is caused by global checking of grammaticality. Asudeh argues that, due to the incremental production that initiates local checking for grammaticality, the ungrammatical examples like (10b) are sanctioned by the grammar and indeed are often produced by ordinary speakers. Unlike local checking, global checking can be loose at times and people can and do from time to time turn off the checking mechanisms in using language.[2] If indeed the operating grammar is insensitive to resources, global checking, just like local checking, should cause no problem at all to human parsers.

Who decides what's right and what's wrong?

Notions of grammaticality are hugely important to linguistic theories such as generative grammar, which rely on defining certain sentences as well-formed and others as ill-formed. As such, the question of how we can determine whether a given sentence is grammatical or not is of the utmost importance to such theories. Let's examine some of the methods we can use to determine grammaticality.

Kiaer (2014, p. 7) and Kondo et al. (2005, p. 207) suggest that there are two main criteria for judging the grammaticality of linguistic forms, which relate to the syntactic and semantic content of the form, respectively. The former criterion checks whether the form is 'morphosyntactically correct' by comparing the form with a corresponding form found in a dictionary, while the latter criterion must compare the form with created speech situations due to the limitless possibilities in actual speech (Kondo et al., 2005, pp. 207–208).

Both of these criteria are flawed, however. Indeed, we argue that imposing grammaticality judgements on linguistic forms is an inherently flawed process.

First, because the semantic criterion discussed above is only based on an artificially delimited subset of speech situations, it cannot adequately represent the semantic diversity of actual speech. Second, so-called native speakers are not good judges of well-formedness: Lefebvre (2004, p. 152) points out the issue of speaker inconsistency, a phenomenon in which one given speaker may give varying judgements of the grammaticality of a linguistic form when asked to perform judgements several times. Third, Geveler and Müller (2016, p. 45) note that grammaticality judgements can be affected by factors outside of language, such as social class and lifestyle, meaning that even among so-called native speakers, there is significant variation in grammaticality judgements that cannot simply be ignored. This also undermines the traditional conception that ideal native speakers live in homogenous speech communities. As Ellis (2003, p. 441) notes, 'variability in learners' judgements is [...] a major problem because it casts doubt on the reliability of the grammaticality judgement test'.

Grammaticality for Asian languages

Chomsky (1969, p. 81) says, 'I have no doubt that it would be possible to devise operational and experimental procedures that could replace the reliance on introspection with little loss, but it seems to me that in the present state of the field, this would simply be *a waste of time and energy*.' To this, I again ask the following: would it be really a waste of time and energy?

Schütze (1996, 2006) provides an excellent foundation for the empirical bases of grammaticality and other intuitions used in generative grammars. However, problems of the grammaticality test are in fact not only the grammaticality test itself; other types of intuition tests have also been seriously criticized. These criticisms are primarily founded on the basis that the methods are not reliable or robust enough as they can be subjective, biased and not wholly scientific. It therefore sounds sensible to have a more sound empirical foundation in order to draw more reliable linguistic judgements. In other words, it makes sense to scrutinize the method for a better, more robust analysis. Some scholars have radical views on this matter, such as positing that the grammaticality test itself is of no use at all (Gethin, 1990) or that it is blatantly informal (Derwing, 1979). Many sociolinguists, like Labov, were particularly sceptical in asking what is to stop linguists from (knowingly or unknowingly) manipulating the introspection process to substantiate their own theories (Labov, 1972, p. 199)?

In fact, many have argued that obtaining 'reliable' data from a bigger pool and a method of data collection that is more scientific, rather than using subjective, potentially biased, or 'contaminated' data, could solve the issue. Yet for me, the real problem is not so much to do with the reliability of the data from a small pool or introspective methods, but the range of languages discussed and also the under-representation of other factors in deciding the suitability of the string in the target language.

Consider the following quote from Bever (1970):

> Recent trends in linguistic research have placed increasing dependence on relatively subtle intuitions. [...] Subtle intuitions are not to be trusted until we understand the nature of their interaction with factors that are irrelevant to grammaticality. If we depend too much on such intuitions without exploring their nature, linguistic research will perpetuate the defects of introspective mentalism as well as its virtues.

The conclusion I draw from Schütze's work in the end is that linguists should not dwell on the subtle differences – after all, we can't account for all linguistic variation. Schütze thus offers a compromised view on the matter. However, as I reiterate in this book, if grammaticality and other intuition tests are crucial tools in the syntactic architecture – possibly playing important roles in Universal Grammar or in the study of all human languages – other non-European languages, such as Asian languages, and their attributes must be adequately taken into account for the discussion to hold up. It is imperative to point out that the suitability of the linguistic input in most Asian languages does not operate based on a single sentence as in English. Most of the distinctions concerning suitability or naturalness (a gradient decision but possibly binary too) are made by non-syntactic, ecological factors around the linguistic input within the context. Within a purely structural or an Anglocentric perspective, these variations may be considered 'subtle'. Indeed, most of these differences, which are obvious to ordinary speakers of relevant Asian languages, become completely lost in English when translated. Perhaps, then, this is why they are often called 'subtle' or they go unnoticed. However, such attributes of those Asian languages are caused by 'socio-pragmatic sensitivity', and in reality are not subtle to speakers at all. For instance, the dynamics of interpersonal modulation is vital in Asian languages and their morpho-syntactic variations, yet all is lost when translated into English. Instead, what's left is to decide the 'bare' single sentence.

For many Asian languages which share in-depth syntactic freedom and pragmatic sensitivity, suitability or naturalness is extremely likely to depend more on the ecological factors around the production than the language-internal, purely grammatical construction. One of the strictest and least flexible properties in these languages is verb-finality for Subject Object Verb (SOV) languages. Yet, in real language use, post-verbal expressions are very common. That said, expressions can occur freely provided that they are permitted by the possible pronunciation and the memory unit – two factors within the non-syntactic realm. The only thing then that decides the suitability of examples with post-verbal expressions is the physical 'size' of the unit.

Kim (2010) has extracted 731 examples from the Korean speech corpora where expressions occur after the verbal cluster. She found that 98 per cent of the time, only one word followed the verbal cluster at the end. She further found only fifteen examples, that is to say 2 per cent of the time, in which two words followed. Kim also found that the most frequently appearing number of syllables in the post-verbal expression is two, which comprises 34.97 per cent of the whole set of examples. Hardly any of the words had more than five syllables. In Korean, to have the verb occur alone without any arguments is fine, depending on the context. Hence, examples like (11) – in which there is no subject or object – are considered natural and grammatical.

(11) *Jinjja Joahae.*
 Really like.
 'really like.'

The above pattern is the case for most Asian languages. It is important to take this into proper consideration because the suitability of an utterance is thus decided by non-syntactic factors, such as memory, in these languages. Furthermore, since having the verb occur alone without subject or object is fine, the argument-adjunct distinction is not actually that important in deciding suitability in Asian languages (see Chapter 2 for a more detailed discussion).

One possible solution to this problem was made by Phillips (2009), in which he proposed a form of 'experimental syntax' with sophisticated tools, such as fine-grained measurements and statistics. To paraphrase, Phillips proposes a toolbox update – which I am all for. Many psychologists, for instance, complain about the weak empirical foundation of grammaticality judgements due to the reliance of informally gathered grammaticality judgements (Ferreira & Bock, 2006). While we can use an elaborate method and big data collections, Phillips suggests that the old toolkit (which includes the informal collection of grammaticality judgements) has not held back linguistics in such a significant way that we may initially think. This, I also agree with. I think both methods can be useful in some sense, but what really matters for me is the choice of languages we study. Even though Phillips' (2009) work was published in a journal for Japanese and Korean linguistics, the methodological discussion is focused on English, sadly.

As it stands, the concept of grammaticality is far too centred around the English language. In generative linguistics, our major toolbox discussions remain Anglocentric and we need a fundamental methodological discussion which is able to account for Asian languages, and other languages across the world. This is because what Asian languages present could be interpreted as subtle according to our present account – even though, crucially, they are not actually subtle. In many non-European languages, one single sentence cannot tell us much; context is key. I therefore invite us to construct a new methodological evaluation for suitability and naturalness which better accounts for languages beyond English and Western Europe. Linguists should adopt a balanced approach which is, on the one hand, scientific and data-driven, but also, on the other, driven by individuals' syntactic instincts – a notion which can be traced to Chomsky's work.

Grammaticality of hybrid varieties

It can be challenging to apply grammaticality judgements to languages and dialects that incorporate elements from multiple languages and varieties. In reality, our everyday language already exhibits a high degree of border-crossing language use. This trend is likely to continue in the future. Nation-state languages may become a thing of the past, but grammaticality on one hand represents an utmost prescriptive view that is already outdated. Our day-to-day translanguaging linguistic practices would either be unfit to be judged grammatically or deemed ungrammatical altogether.

K-pop tweets: unfit for grammaticality?

Recently, I was working with a database of 7.8 billion K-pop tweets. The vast majority of them contained some form of Korean–English border-crossing elements, as well as plenty of emojis. Should we consider these tweets unfit to be judged grammatically? Tools such as grammaticality are outdated and can serve as obstacles to making linguistic studies more diverse and inclusive. Moreover, they can easily marginalize people's languages, particularly those of minority groups, and give more power to those who have unfair linguistic authority.

Singlish: a mix of multiple languages

Singlish (Singaporean English) combines words from different local languages (mainly Malay, Hokkien and Mandarin) in an eclectic mix. One unique feature of Singlish is the use of sentence-final tonal particles, which have various pragmatic functions and are purported to originate from Southern Chinese languages (Wong, 2014). It is also common in Singlish to repurpose English words semantically and/or syntactically, giving them new meanings or fitting them into the syntax of other local languages (e.g. Sinitic and Southeast Asian) which differ significantly from standard English.

As shown below, aspects of many different languages can be found in Singlish (this list is not exhaustive). As Singlish incorporates semantic and syntactic influences from multiple different languages, grammaticality judgement criteria tuned to a single variety of language are not easily applicable. The coexistence of various semantic and syntactic variants of the same English words, as well as a rich lexicon of words from non-English languages, would make it difficult for a multilingual speaker living in Singapore to confidently judge the grammaticality of sentences due to the conflicting and competing rules from the different languages in their linguistic repertoire. Grammaticality judgement criteria promote the idea that there is only one correct linguistic form; yet with languages like Singlish that incorporate elements of multiple languages, there are multiple conflicting linguistic rules at play, making it impossible to say which rules should be observed or broken. As Mesthrie (2008, p. 268) notes: 'What is such a multilingual person a native speaker of, but a polyphony of codes/languages working cumulatively (and sometimes complementarily), rather than a single first learned code?' In this sense, such judgement criteria are therefore outdated in the case of multilinguals, as their speech constitutes an amalgamation of different coexisting linguistic influences rather than a single, homogenous entity, as these criteria are premised upon.

Case study: hybrid varieties spoken in Singaporean, online context

The following examples illustrate linguistic hybridity in Singlish, supporting my argument that traditional grammatical judgement criteria are inapplicable to Singlish. All of these examples may be considered ungrammatical at best, but there isn't a clear method to evaluate their grammaticality. Furthermore, most language use, both online and offline, displays this hybrid nature. So, what is the purpose of grammaticality if not to discriminate between speakers? The data below was collected from Facebook, WhatsApp messages, and posts on a Singaporean forum site called HardwareZone.

English

> Example 1 *I use paylah. Japan Home also no more paywave, last time have.*
>
> Squaredot, 2022b

Although the sentence shown in Example 1 is composed entirely of English words, the functions of some of the words and portions of the syntax differ from standard English. *Also no more* syntactically resembles the Chinese phrase 也不再（有）, as well as the Malay phrase *juga tiada lagi*, which means '...also no longer has...'. *Last time* here does not mean 'the previous time' or 'the most recent time', as it would in standard English, but rather refers to a distant time period with respect to the present time in which the conversation takes place (Utomo, 2020). The use of the verb *have* in *last time have* also resembles Sinitic and Southeast Asian languages in that it does not need to take an object.

English + Malay

> Example 2 *Last time heard Penangs mamak food damn tok gong. Went there then realised it's sama sama to what we see at Little India. Infact the best local google review stall is as good as any stalls at Little India*
>
> testerjp, 2022

In Example 2, *Mamak* is a Malay term mostly used in Malaysia and Singapore that refers to a street stall selling Tamil Muslim food (Lexico, n.d.). *Damn* is often used as an expletive or curse word in English, but in Singlish it functions as an adverb of degree, with a similar meaning to 'very' or 'extremely'. This is also occasionally seen colloquially in some variants of American and British English. *Tok gong* is a Hokkien term and is used to compliment something as 'very good' (mrbrown, 1998). *Sama sama* is a Malay-derived phrase that literally means 'same same', which indicates that something is identical to something else. The original meaning in Malay, however, is 'you're welcome', or 'together' (Wiktionary, 2022a). *Stall* in Singlish has a slightly different meaning from its standard English counterpart, as it does not just refer to a makeshift shop selling goods like those often seen in markets, nor a small, enclosed space, but instead refers to a building or store where cooked food is sold. Syntactically, some elements are adopted from Sinitic and Southeast Asian languages, namely copula elision (*mamak food damn tok kong* instead of *mamak food **is** damn tok kong*) and pro-drop [pronoun dropping] (*Last time heard* instead of *Last time **I** heard*).

> Example 3 *Can. I tried the spicy only. Is sedap. Bought Before at 2 for 3.95 but now even cheaper so restock again.*
>
> dude123, 2022

In Example 3, *can* does not only indicate permission and ability, but also functions as an affirmative, similar in meaning to 'sure' (Khalid & Sekkappan, 2022). *Sedap* means 'tasty' in Malay (Lee, 2004f). *Before* occurring after a verb in Singlish also obtains a different meaning to standard English: rather than meaning 'earlier than the time mentioned', it takes on a perfective meaning. This resembles a Chinese construction in which 过 guò directly follows the verb to create a similar meaning. Like Examples 1 and 2, pro-drop (*Is sedap* instead of ***it** is sedap*), copula elision (*now even cheaper* instead of *now it **is** even cheaper*), object elision (*Bought before* instead of ***I** bought **it** before*) and dropping of tense (*so restock again* instead of *so **I will** restock/**am** restock**ing** again*) are also observed here. Additionally, in standard English, *can* as an auxiliary verb must take a main verb, but in Singlish it can stand on its own. The use of *only* in the sentence-final position is also reminiscent of some grammatical constructions in Sinitic and Southeast Asian languages.

English + Malay + Tamil/Hindi

> Example 4 *Then mampos my fav Nasi Ayam goreng and Nasi Goreng Kampong and even prata's price will increase.*
>
> Ish Skywaalker, 2022

In Example 4, *Mampos* is another spelling of *mampus*, which literally means 'dead' in Malay. In Singlish, however, it means that something can no longer be salvaged, or that it is a lost cause (Yeoh, 2019). *Nasi ayam goreng* and *nasi goreng kampong* are names of Malay rice dishes, literally translated as 'fried chicken rice' and 'kampong fried rice', where *kampong* refers to a Malay village. *Prata* is derived from Tamil and possibly Hindi, and refers to a popular Indian flatbread dish (Wiktionary, 2022b).

> Example 5 *Indian house Deepavalli no kueh tart, something wrong. Will have that kueh makmur, kueh rose, murukku, all the biscuits that Chinese, Malay and Eurasians make.*
>
> Kumar22, 2021

In Example 5, *Deepavali* is a Tamil word referring to the festival of lights celebrated by Hindus worldwide, which is a major festival in Singapore due to the significant Hindu population (Lee, 2004b). *Kueh* is a Malay word referring to cakes and puddings, especially those of Malay origin (Lee, 2004d). *Kueh makmur* is one such kind of *kueh* made using toasted peanuts. *Murukku* is a Tamil term meaning 'to twist' and refers to a South Indian snack made from flour (Tham, 2021). As with most of the preceding examples, here too there is copula ellipsis (*something wrong* instead of *something **is** wrong*), pro-drop (*Will have that* instead of ***it** will have that*) and dropping of prepositions (*Indian house Deepavalli* instead of ***in** Indian houses **during** Deepavalli*).

English + Malay + Hokkien

> Example 6 *Here buy shoe not easy . . . display is usually what they have . . . and after try don't buy buay song . . . I lagi buay song* ☺

Example 6 showcases a number of syntactic features from Sinitic and Southeast Asian languages, such as the dropping of articles (*display* instead of ***the** display*), copula ellipsis, the dropping of tense and plural markings (*buy shoe not easy* instead of *buy**ing** shoe**s** **is** not easy*), fronting of certain elements, which is uncommon in English (fronting of *here* as emphasis/topicalization) and pro-drop (*don't buy* instead of *I don't buy*). *Lagi*, meaning 'more' or 'even more' in Malay, functions as an intensifier of the Hokkien term *buay song*, consisting of the negation particle buay, which means 'unhappy' or 'dissatisfied' (Lee, 2004a, 2004e).

> Example 7 *He attempted to book out in PT singlet and a pair of jeans but kena stopped by MP. Then he was unhappy and buay song, lucky . . . was there to simmer him down.*

The Malay term *kena* seen in Example 7 is used to form passive constructions, but usually implies a negative consequence for the action (Lee, 2004c). *MP* refers to military police. *Kena stopped* has a negative connotation as it implies that the person mentioned was stopped by the military police for doing something wrong. Similar to Example 6, *buay song* also shows up here, and the dropping of articles is also observed (*by MP* instead of ***by** the MP*). Additionally, the adjective *lucky* is used as an adverb without any inflections.

English + Malay + Chinese + Southern Chinese languages (final particle)

> Example 8 *Wa. . .! Mmmm. . . control the makan hor,* 七分饱就好 ☺

Wa (sometimes spelled *wah*), which appears in Example 8, is an interjection used in Singlish to express surprise and amazement (OED Online, 2022c). *Makan* is a Malay word meaning 'to eat', and it can be used as a noun as well in Singlish, as it is here. *Hor* is a pragmatic particle derived from Southern Chinese languages, which is used to call the listener's attention to what is being said, or to seek agreement (Fasold, 2013, p. 385). *Control the makan hor* would mean something like '(Please take note that you should) control what you are eating'. The last phrase is taken from Chinese and means 'just feeling 70% full is enough'. Pro-drop is seen here as well, as in previous examples (*control the makan* instead of **you** *control the makan*).

English + Hokkien + Chinese (literal translation)

> Example 9 *Let's chiong to store 7early8early tmr*
>
> Squaredot, 2022a

In Example 9, *chiong* is a Hokkien term meaning 'to rush' or 'to hurry up' (hoz0r, 2010). *Tmr* is simply an abbreviation of 'tomorrow'. *7early8early* is an interesting example of a direct translation of the Chinese phrase 七早八早 (*qī zǎo bā zǎo*), which is often used colloquially in Hokkien to mean so early in the morning that most people are still asleep (Singaporean, 2018). We can also see borrowed syntactic features like dropped articles (*store* instead of **the** *store*).

> Example 10 *Hi, Anyone Know where in AMK got sell good cat mountain durian?*
>
> ganster, 2013

In Example 10, *AMK* is an abbreviation of a district in Singapore called Ang Mo Kio, which means 'red-haired man's bridge' in Hokkien (Cornelius, 2005). *Cat mountain durian* is a literal Chinese–English translation of the name of a type of durian called māo shān wáng 猫山王. According to Hiramoto and Sato (2012), although the use of *got* shares certain meanings with standard British English, it also diverges greatly from it due to influences from Sinitic languages. From their analysis, it seems that *got* functions here as a habitual marker, and when used with the verb *sell* in its plain form, indicates that the place habitually/always sells this type of durian.

English + Malay + Hokkien + Southern Chinese languages (final particle)

> Example 11 *that new stall right? lol $3699 rental, initially open normal hours cannot tahan, now open 24hrs fish ball noodles residents will go heng lee and jiak, only if they not open den they go for this new stall koka close cos owner tio covid mah*
>
> daryl76, 2021

In Example 11, *tahan* is a Malay word that means 'to endure' or 'to tolerate' something (usually something unpleasant) (Wong et al., 2022). The verbs 'to endure' and 'to tolerate' are transitive in English, but here the verb *tahan* is intransitive, as in Malay. *Jiak* is borrowed from Hokkien and means 'to eat' (Singaporean, 2017), and also becomes intransitive here, even though *to eat* would usually be transitive in a standard English sentence. *Mah* (sometimes written as *ma*) is a pragmatic particle, used here to highlight information that is known to both the speaker and listener, similar to 'As you know/As you might have heard...' (Lim, 2007, p. 451). *Tio*, a Hokkien term, closely resembles *kena* from Example 7 and is often used interchangeably with it to construct the passive form when referring to negative situations (Zui, 2017). However, when not used with a verb, it can also mean something like 'to come into contact with something negative and suffer from negative consequences', so in the context of *tio covid*, *tio* means 'to come into contact with the virus and become infected'. Like previous examples, this example also features syntactic differences compared with English, such as pro-drop (*initially open* instead of **they** *initially open*), dropping of tenses and copula elision (*koka close* instead of *koka **is** closed*), dropping of prepositions (*will go heng lee* instead of *will go **to** heng lee*), dropping of articles (*owner* instead of ***the** owner*) and fronting of certain elements which are not common in English (*fish ball noodles* is fronted so as to make it the topic of the sentence).

Grammaticality of other Englishes

Just as assessing grammaticality for hybrid varieties poses a challenge, it is also problematic to apply grammaticality standards to English varieties other than the dominant, widely recognized ones like US and UK English.

English is the most studied language in contemporary linguistics. According to Ethnologue (2022c), English is also the most commonly spoken first language, totalling just over 372 million. There are almost three times as many L2 speakers of English, totalling over 1.4 billion. Despite the massive amount of L2 speakers, however, the English spoken by L2 speakers is comparatively under-researched. Yet, this is not a new issue within linguistics. Indeed, as the quotation from Murray (1911) shows, people have been aware that so-called non-standard varieties of English have not been afforded the legitimacy and respect they deserve for at least the past century.

> The English Language is the language of Englishmen! Of which Englishmen? Of all Englishmen or of some Englishmen? ... Does it include the English of Great Britain and the English of America, the English of Australia, and of South Africa, and of those most assertive Englishmen, the Englishmen of India, who live in bungalows, hunt in jungles, wear terai hats or puggaries and pyjamas, write chits instead of letters and eat kedgeree and chutni? Yes! In its most comprehensive sense, and as an object of historical study, it includes all these; they are all forms of English.
>
> Murray, 1911, p. 18

Yet, research on British English and American English still often tends to treat those varieties as the 'standard' or 'traditional' varieties of English, regarding them as more important or more worthy of study than other varieties, which are treated as peripheral. How little has changed in the last hundred years! The study of other varieties of English, such as Indian English or New Zealand English, mainly appears in applied linguistics research rather than theoretical linguistics studies examining language's core structure. Change is overdue – researchers should embrace the diversity of the many varieties of English without favour or prejudice.

Indeed, due to globalization and the highly mobile nature of populations in the present day, it is even more difficult to distinguish varieties of English based on region, such as British English or American English. North Americans are not the only English speakers who speak American English, for example, and likewise, speakers of Indian English do not only reside in India; that is the nature of English as a lingua franca. Crystal (2003) argues that how languages evolve in settings where most people are native speakers is likely to be very different from how languages evolve in settings where most people are not native speakers. Many varieties of English, including those categorized as standard, non-standard or hybrid, cannot be judged by British or American grammar standards – yet all of them require just as much linguistic competence to speak correctly. Despite this, varieties of English other than British English and American English have not been properly acknowledged or researched in the mainstream. Below, I show some examples from Hong Kong English. These may not be grammatical according to the standards of British or American English, but they are widely used and not considered ill-formed within Hong Kong English.

Example 12 Hong Kong English

Noun phrases: no distinction between count and mass nouns (Setter et al., 2010).
Verb phrases: lack of tense/aspect marking; e.g. 'He is born in Hong Kong and then just go to Hong Kong' (Li, 2000).
Clause and sentence structure: post-modifying clause structure after 'There be NP'; e.g. 'There are a lot of people died' (Li, 2000).

Despite the linguistic competence required to speak such varieties of English, they are often considered less than 'proper English' by native speakers in places like Britain or North America. Ng (2005) showed that the Hong Kong accent and dialect were accepted in both formal and informal contexts in Hong Kong, proving that Hong Kong English is considered to be a legitimate variety that is appropriate for formal situations. In his study, interviewees identified the recognizable features of Hong Kong English as distinctive features rather than errors. Speaking Hong Kong English is perceived to be equally effective as Standard English in conveying messages to the public. In a study investigating the international intelligibility of Hong Kong English, Kirkpatrick et al. (2008) also showed that Hong Kong English has few problems with intelligibility in international settings and contexts. Above, in Example 12, I listed some examples of Hong Kong English that are commonly used in Hong Kong but which would not be considered grammatical if judged against native-speaker standards. Too often, grammaticality judgements become measures of whether a given sentence follows 'standard' British or American varieties rather than judging whether the sentence is indeed grammatically well-formed within the variety being spoken.

Social media and instant messaging have also loosened the boundaries of what is acceptable language. Internet slang often involves intentional trespassing of grammatical rules in order to convey something about one's emotional state; for instance, a 'keysmash' (that is, a random sequence of characters resulting from randomly laying one's hands on a keyboard) can be used to convey extreme excitement or surprise (McCulloch, 2019, pp. 6–7). Similarly, intentional misspellings are often used to convey a variety of tones ranging from mocking to excitement. Example 13 is taken from a real conversation between a group of close friends that took place on a popular instant messaging app, Telegram.

Example 13 [M posts a picture of a new tattoo featuring illustrations of shrimp and fish]

M   Shremp
H   prawm!!!!!
H   i love he
F   Omgggg I love the shirmppppp
S   FEEEESH

Needless to say, this conversation cannot be considered grammatically correct in any traditional sense. However, within the context of internet language, it is also difficult to say that these messages are 'ill-formed' in any meaningful sense, as each instance of misusing grammar or spelling is made intentionally by the speech participants to convey information to the other participants. I believe that internet language, therefore, also needs its own specialized approach to make grammaticality judgements.

Globalization creates possibilities for new varieties of English that can travel beyond traditional nation-state boundaries, opening up new ways to communicate whereby mutual understanding is achieved through speakers' linguistic competence rather than native-like proficiency. To take an example from Crystal (2003), people in the Middle Ages would have laughed at you if you had told them Latin would die out in the future, and those in the eighteenth century would have laughed at you if you told them another language would surpass French as the world's dominant language. If English is to be the world's global language, we must systematically integrate those varieties that are unintelligible or less widely spoken into the record of theoretical linguistics. The postcolonial era has seen further promotion of multilingualism rather than prioritizing of the languages of former colonial powers. In our view, we must strive for justice and diversity, by recognizing that English is no longer simply a remnant of colonialism in colonized countries; it has evolved to take on new identities and has been shaped by new generations of speakers. Judging these new forms of English by the standards of their colonizing varieties would be a deep injustice to the rich and interesting varieties of English that have been developed in these regions.

We cannot judge the grammaticality of language based on isolated, contextless sentences alone. Grammaticality can involve myriad factors, including the particular variety of the language; the relative status of speech participants; tone and register; previous utterances in the conversation; platform of communication (e.g. offline or on a particular social media platform); and other ecological and pragmatic factors. Language does not take place in a vacuum – so how can we judge it within one? English should not be defined by American or British varieties, and other varieties should be carefully analysed and considered as equal and legitimate varieties of the English language. We hope that, in the near future, these varieties can become as widely recognized and respected as so-called standard varieties, and that people will be able to use these words and phrases freely in their own country or in an international setting without fear of being judged.

Arrival of social grammars

Over the years, a person's linguistic behaviours (including, but not limited to, text, speech or emoji use) are becoming more and more diverse and highly individualized. As a result, it is difficult to bring in some kind of (un)grammatical assessment for everyday language use. The grammaticality criteria used in current generative frameworks requires serious reconsideration in order to have some applicability in current and future linguistic theories. One such way we may change our perspectives is by considering the arrival of social grammars. I am aware that Chomsky has a strong reaction towards the word 'behaviour' since *c.* 1959 when his article 'Review of *Verbal Behavior*, by B. F. Skinner' was first published. However, in a time of idiolects, it is important to consider how our grammar has changed.

As Eckert (2012) shows, linguists no longer exclusively look at the way people communicate according to the 'static' categories of wider society, such as gender, class and ethnicity. Instead, it is generally accepted that we tailor-make our own communication styles informed by the communities and subcultures of which we are part, so-called 'communities of practice'. Communities of practice are created, maintained and adapted by the people who create them, making them very diverse, interactive and fluid in comparison with more traditional determiners such as ethnicity, class or gender. Our position in society and membership of common interest groups shape our communication behaviours into individual idiolects. What's more, we may also make use of particular bits of language we are aware of that are associated with other groups which we may not be part of, but whose attributes and values we wish to reference, display or appropriate. Crucially, the meanings of these bits of language are not fixed, but are continually reinterpreted and recombined in different contexts by diverse interlocutors.

In this way, our use of language not only reflects our position and affiliation within wider society (and our local social networks) but allows us to creatively and contextually make meaning and communicate about ourselves, our situations or the topic at hand using all the means we have at our disposal. This is true of our online communication in general, but especially so for emoji use.

Emoji competence

Emoji and texting will show the future of human languages in many respects (Kiaer 2023). First of all, due to the rapid increase of human–computer interaction, emojing and texting will be one of the major channels of human communication. This change will liberate more orthodox attitudes and environments around linguistic discourse, such as discussions surrounding grammar and the sentence.

Although there are general trends in emoji use, we all balance our needs for speed, solidarity and style in our own unique way. Fashionable emojis arise from subcultural groups, rather than one big language community. Emojis that are of interest to one person, perhaps because they are in common use in a community of practice with which they are involved, or they associate it with a particular contextual meaning, may seem lacklustre to another.

Everyone has their own emoji idiolect, but not everyone has emoji competence. Emoji competence refers to our ability to engage in multi-modal communication using the proper register (and this can be extended to a broader understanding of linguistic competence). It is about making use of the emoji repertoire and assembling the pieces together according to the person with whom you are speaking. One must 'tune in' to the situation, and decide how to employ one's idiolect accordingly. For example, emoji absence or misuse can cause misunderstanding and the breakdown of communication:

> An example I immediately think of is how my mother tends to not use emojis often and it has led to multiple misunderstandings between us. The most common one happens on a weekly basis. I get a message from her saying 'Call me' or 'Call me later', or even 'Call me as soon as possible'. Whenever I read those messages, I instantly start panicking as the lack of emoji makes the sentence sound (or look) very hurried. I always immediately message back 'Did something happen?' or 'Is everything okay?' also not using emojis as it feels like the situation is serious. The answer I always get from her is completely different from what I expect and goes along the lines of 'Nothing happened, why? I just want to talk'. The message does not come across as casual because of a lack of emoji. If she had written 'Call me later ☺' the intention of just wanting a casual conversation is understood.
>
> Extract from an interview with a twenty-year-old student

Emoji competence is also about being able to understand the multi-modal signs that we experience online. Such tech-driven images are very logical, and yet they need to be learnt. These images help for multilingual communication, but also create a digital divide between those who are familiar with them and those who are not. Age is not always the determining factor in whether one has the emoji competence to recognize these images. It can be to do with whether one is technologically keen or not, too. Image awareness is a key facet of emoji competence, and is one of the main reasons why there is a divide between emoji natives and emoji immigrants.

The key takeaway is that our grammar has changed over the years. To continue using old notions of grammaticality which are centred on the 'ideal, native speaker', rather than considering individualized idiolects which draw from different communities of practice, would be inappropriate and outdated.

Symbolic competence

Following on from the above discussion, I propose to extend this so-called 'emoji competence' to 'symbolic competence'. I think the latter is a very important notion. At present, symbolic competence in writing – particularly the formal writing in a strictly sentential level – comprises only a small portion of our daily linguistic endeavours. The way we leave linguistic footprints in this world is changing. For example, in this day and age, our linguistic activity incorporates more texting and emoji use. What's more, this trend will continue! By matters of chance, we are living in an AI age where social media is increasingly becoming the dominant mode of communication, meaning that our communication is in the process of becoming more multimodal and multilingual. We thus live in a society where a multilingual environment is the norm. Hence, in order to understand human language, we need to understand audio and visual information, as well as non-verbal information like emojis. Put simply, we need symbolic competence.

Emojis are a fairly new phenomenon. While Chomsky's *Aspects* (1965) views linguistic competence as straightforward human business, more recent developments regarding emojis and computers, for instance, mean that we have to rethink this mindset. We cannot just say that these features of human communication are not part of human language – while indeed some are explicitly related to what we're born with, some are related to how technology has developed. Crucially, our use of symbols is part of our linguistic competence that we use daily. It is not peripheral but technology-driven. This new emerging aspect of human language was born through human–computer interaction and is becoming more and more influential. As a result, understanding this multilingual, multimodal communication is an important part of understanding human language. In doing so, it's difficult to grasp this with a purely verbal understanding in which linguistic expression and communication are all embedded with text-related words. As we continue to innovate AI and technology, symbolic competence will play a more prominent role and will perhaps even be able to bridge the pre-modern understanding of linguistics to our current time.

However, we need to go beyond the boundaries of the sentence and letter words. Different semiotic repertoires – what things actually mean in context – include letter words and non-letter words like emojis. Perhaps then, symbols, emojis, and some core, translingual words may be all that we need. For example, consider how 'M' means 'metro' in many places around the world. Consider also how some symbols, such as arrows, have widely acknowledged or even universal meanings. I further argue that over time letter words and symbols will compete, as the latter will be shown as more useful in the future. This is because we will have a greater pool of resources for symbol words as technology continues to develop, leading us to become so accustomed to audio-visual messages.

Thinking of human linguistic competence as purely human, as solely what we're given, may be a limited mindset. We need to broaden our horizons. While *Aspects* (1965) points out the innateness of human linguistic abilities, I suggest that we should also consider what we develop, such as symbolic competence, which is not something we're born with. Particularly in such a time where reading and writing will no longer be as we expect, and the paper generation will gradually decrease in influence, what's essential is symbolic competence – what verbal and non-verbal words mean in the given context. Syntactic competence – how to understand and use structures – will also be part of symbolic competence too. Therefore, symbolic competence should also be the target of our study.

Is grammaticality of any use?

As technology continues to advance, and social media continues to exert a strong presence in people's everyday communication, our former understanding of grammaticality has no use. For instance, the predictive functions of digital communication software are becoming very much the norm, and autocorrect will even change input to make a word or phrase sound better. As a result, what is considered grammatical is now increasingly harder to delineate.

In fact, Google has developed a new chatbot named LaMDA (which stands for 'language model for dialogue applications') which has emerging properties of human language. In this age of rapid advancements in AI, pattern-learning and big data, the emergence of systems like LaMDA may not be surprising. In fact, while I was writing this book, LaMDA was the surprise, but by the time I finished it, ChatGPT had arrived. AI is evolving at a rapid pace, even daily. We cannot predict with certainty what the next year holds for human communication. In times like these, clinging to linguistic theories that are completely insensitive to AI advancements goes against the tide of progress and risks making linguistics increasingly disconnected from real-world applications and developments.

Now, considering that a machine can process human languages efficiently using pattern-driven learning without relying on extensive knowledge of grammaticality judgements, I wonder what value grammaticality criteria can truly offer to linguistics. Additionally, it's worth noting that speakers these days, whether intentionally or not, often have their grammaticality checked through autocorrect and other AI tools integrated into their word processors.

The concept of grammaticality has lost touch and relevance in our time. Regardless of our efforts to refine our methodology, the fact remains that we live in an era where grammaticality is no longer as useful. Excessive focus on grammaticality can hinder the promotion of inclusivity and diversity in our languages.

In such an atmosphere, it is important for us to be able to find better ways to unravel and unbox human linguistic competence. Instead of the grammatical vs ungrammatical dichotomy, it may be better to think about what AI can generate and what it can't generate through pattern extraction and deep-learning. Crucially, we can consider the following: what are the features that make human syntactic properties, in other words human generation, unique? This distinction warrants more attention, as the traditional split between grammatical and ungrammatical is no longer useful or relevant in the context of our multilingual, multimodal speakers and the optimization of human–computer interaction. It is high time we explore better ways to evaluate human linguistic competence.

4

Asian Languages from Asian Perspectives

Asian languages in syntax: an introduction

Asian languages are understudied in comparison with their European counterparts. While they have some lingering voices in the literature, they are generally depicted as minority languages and often approached in the way that English and Western European languages have been researched. To clarify, when I describe Asian languages as a 'minority', this is not quantitatively but qualitatively speaking; it is a matter of prestige, as this chapter will later explore. Finding the principles that are applicable for all human languages – in other words, searching for the Universal Grammar – has been at the heart of contemporary linguistics since Chomsky's *Aspects* (1965).

However, it is crucial to thoroughly examine whether the research process employs appropriate measures and whether the patterns and distributional characteristics of world languages are being sufficiently represented and integrated into linguistic theories. Or perhaps, is it the case – as we hear in other areas of study in the field of humanities – that Eurocentrism, especially Anglocentrism, dominates the field thereby making our observations less valid?

This chapter delves into such issues as we explore how Asian languages are perceived in contemporary linguistic theories and how they are often marginalized. At the core of the matter, there seem to exist the problems of trying to fit a square peg in a round hole when researching the core properties of Asian languages from perspectives most strongly informed by research that draws its data from English. Important features of these languages such as syntactic freedom, socio-pragmatic complexity and the rich use of particles (constructive and expressive) are broadly overlooked. As for terminology, there appears to be an Anglocentric bias. For example, when one looks at the data cross-linguistically, terms such as 'scrambling' and 'pro-drop' are very common features of world languages. Perhaps, then, it is languages like English which should be considered to have marked characteristics such as 'rigidity' and 'anti-drop'. However, attempts have constantly been made to analyse the attributes of Asian languages from an English perspective, thereby leading to ad hoc explanations or accounts and theories which are unnecessarily complex. This then deepens the chasm between traditional and contemporary linguistics and further fractures the relationship between practitioners of language pedagogy and linguistic theorists. This chapter proposes the simplicity hypothesis (the explanation for what is simple in an ordinary speaker's daily production should also be simple) and makes a case for a shift in our perspectives – hence, Asian languages from Asian perspectives.

Defining Asia

Before we get into the main discussion, we should first consider: what exactly do we mean by 'Asia'? The word 'Asia', which is found in English, other European languages and now most languages around the world, derives from the Classical Greek Ἀσία, first attested in Herodotus (about 440 BC) to refer to the Eastern regions comprising Anatolia or the Persian Empire. According to Abarim Publications (2021), Christian monks referred to the region relating to Anatolia as Asia Minor, and to the Persian region as Asia Major. From the fourth century, the term Asia also began to be used generally to refer to the entire continent. There are multiple theories regarding the origin of this term. First, the word Asia could have derived from the Akkadian word 'asu', meaning 'to go out, to rise', which is cognate with the Hebrew אסא ('asa), which means 'to heal, to rise'. This hypothesis relates to the Sun, which rises in the East, and thus the word connotes the nations which lay in the East relative to Ancient Greece. This also mirrors the Chinese name of Japan (日本), also referring to the direction from which the Sun rises, which confirms the trend of a culture naming a land to its East based on the movement of the Sun.

Another interpretation concerns the Hittites, an Anatolian people that occupied the area from approximately 1650 BCE to 1190 BCE; they called the land around Ephesus the 'Assuwa', which was also the name of various states that tried to challenge the Hittites. The term 'Assuwa' is derived from the Akkadian term 'asu', mentioned above, with the suffix '-*uwa*' attached, which was a toponymic suffix in the Hittite language. Thus, the literal meaning of 'Assuwa' was the 'land of rising', once again referencing the movement of the Sun. The Greek work 'ανατολη', from which we get Anatolia, also means the 'place of rising'. The theory that the word 'Europe' comes from the Akkadian word 'erēbu(m)', meaning 'to enter' or 'set (of the Sun)', mirrors this conceptualization. More evidence for this interpretation is offered by T. R. Reid, who notes that the Akkadian word 'asu' also means 'East', and 'ereb' means 'West'. This is once again mirrored by the Latin terms *occidens* ('setting', whence we derive 'Occident/Occidental'), and *oriens* ('rising', whence we derive 'Orient/Oriental'). The term was generally used in the Greek and Roman worlds for the huge mass of land that stretched East indeterminately.

Asian languages, then, through logical extension, are the languages spoken in the geographical areas that comprise 'Asia'. Contemporary historical linguistics, though, prioritizes taxonomy in terms of comparative language groupings and relationships, and languages that do not share common ancestry are usually handled in a discrete manner. Despite not sharing genetically proven heritage, Asian languages share linguistic characteristics, such as syntactic fluidity and pragmatic sensitivity. This is grounds for considering them as linguistically connected and thus conducting broad studies that employ data from multiple Asian languages to establish commonalities.

For example, in the strict taxonomic view, Korean, Japanese and Chinese are heterogeneous and do not share a common ancestor. Vovin (2010) examines the similarities between Korea and Japan while also emphasizing that they are etymologically and genetically different. However, as Asian states developed over time, different cultures exerted influence over each other, an ecology of language was established – one that cultivated socio-pragmatic complexity. Certainly, the influences of religion or state ideology, such as Buddhism and Confucianism, played a part in the creation of this ecology, although the factors are so complex the question of how exactly it took shape seems intractable. It is easiest to see the impact of Confucianism, that promoted rigid social hierarchical systems, which appears to be an appropriate explanation of the diachronic development of grammaticalized honorification in Korean, Japanese and, to an extent, Chinese. This socio-pragmatic complexity manifests in complex systems of grammatical, prosodic and extra-linguistic honorification and syntactic fluidity in such a way that they appear to behave as if they were genetically related. The potential to interpret these developments in light of the Sapir-Whorf hypothesis is apparent here, whereby certain shared cultural characteristics may have had some influence on the production of language. These similarities show a different dimension of linguistic relationship that goes beyond genetics, and it is certainly one that cannot and should not be ignored. A combination of diachronic and synchronic research can be conducted to offer explanations for the common socio-pragmatic features of Asian languages, which should be tackled from a mix of social, historical and linguistic perspectives.

Asian languages: what are they really?

When we hear the phrase 'Asian languages', I am certain many of us can list off a number of examples, such as Arabic, Turkish, Urdu, Japanese and Vietnamese. However, when asked to *describe* Asian languages, the replies may not be as straightforward. One may turn to linguistic literature and look for possible answers there only to discover that, first, there is a relatively small pool of research to draw from, and second, the literature is riddled with discrepancies.

Asia is a geographically massive region with an incredible amount of linguistic and cultural diversity; it can be divided into five smaller regions (Central, Southeast, South, West and East Asia), and is home to more than 2,300 languages spoken by more than 4.5 billion people (Ethnologue, 2022a). However, despite the wealth of languages which come from this region, their rich histories and their sheer number of speakers across the globe, Asian languages have been significantly side-lined in research related to languages and linguistics. Instead, a Eurocentric – and often more specifically, a Western European and Anglocentric – approach to such studies is favoured.

However, this not only applies to the field of linguistics; the lack of attention these languages receive goes beyond formal study. I will never forget the time when I asked several school children about the languages spoken in India; so many of them answered 'Indian!' There is a clear lack of awareness, arguably even education, about Asian languages, despite their many speakers in the UK and across the globe.

What's more, an article published by *The Korea Times* in 2017 bore the headline 'Korean "exceptionally difficult language to learn": US agency' (Rha & Park, 2017). According to a report by the Foreign Service Institute (FSI), which sorted seventy languages into four categories depending on the level of difficult, Category IV languages – languages that are 'exceptionally difficult for native English speakers' – included Arabic, Chinese, Japanese and Korean (Rha & Park, 2017). Notice how these are all Asian languages.

In this chapter, we delve into an examination of the seemingly widely held notion that 'Asian languages are at the margin'. In this section, I discuss three central problems concerning how Asian languages are presented: their classification, the perception that they are minority languages and their representation in the literature.

Are Asian languages modern languages?

The classification of Asian languages has shown itself to be a far from easy task. Given how Asian languages are used internationally by billions of speakers today, perhaps you might use the word 'modern' to describe them. Makes sense, right? Well, according to many 'Modern Foreign Language' teachers, perhaps not.

In 2017, I, along with colleagues teaching Modern Foreign Languages, attended a Westminster Education Forum devoted to 'The Future of Modern Foreign Languages in Higher Education' in London. The Westminster Education Forum targets policy makers, educational practitioners and academics to share their thoughts on issues related to education in the UK. The focus of the event, however, was staunchly on French, German, Italian and Spanish – in other words, on European languages. While there were a few Chinese teachers also present, I couldn't help but wonder, 'Is that it? European languages plus Chinese?' As a university educator of Korean, I strongly felt that I was the odd one out and found this Eurocentrism both somewhat surprising and alienating (see Kiaer, 2017 for more).

This Eurocentrism can be seen in the classification of languages as 'modern', 'classical' or 'oriental', whereby we are also indexing notions of prestige, in different contexts. To have a tendency to classify only certain languages as 'modern' seems to imply that the other languages which do not get called as such are archaic, or even not suited for modern usage. To have a propensity to consider only certain languages as 'classical' appears to suggest that the other languages, even those with a long and rich history of literature, are not 'prestigious' enough to become part of canonical classic works. We may observe this in how many examples of literature become part of the canon 'only when they reflect European experience and conform to the style and subject matter of the European literary tradition' (Tyson, 2006, p. 361). Lastly, to term languages as 'oriental' seems to reinforce colonial ideologies of Orientalism, highlighting the dominance of Western cultures in contrast to the 'subordinated "Orient"' (Park & Wilkins, 2005, p. 3). These various issues with nomenclature could affect how Asian languages are studied and perceived in linguistic research.

In this section, specifically, results from Singapore, the United Kingdom and the United States are compared. A total of 160 websites from these countries were surveyed to see how languages are categorized as a modern, oriental or classical language. This survey involved the websites of 150 universities, prep schools, boarding schools, high schools and a small number of associations and companies. An overwhelming majority of websites belonged to universities. These are often homepages of university departments (such as the Department of Modern and Classical Languages) or information pages for university courses (such as BA in Modern Languages). The total number of institutions (150) does not match the total number of sites (160) as some universities were surveyed more than once if they had one or more applicable departments or courses (for example, the University of Oxford has Modern Languages, Classics, and Oriental Studies courses, respectively).

These websites were investigated for any mention of what languages might be classified as modern, oriental or classical. The total number of appearances of each language being mentioned as being modern, oriental or classical was calculated. This tabulation was done for the Singaporean, UK and US websites respectively, to see if there are any differences between the three countries.

Comparing the analyses of websites from the three countries, there appears to be some variation in what is considered a modern language, an oriental language or a classical language in each country. Comparing the top five languages mentioned as 'modern languages' across the websites, only Singaporean websites feature more than one non-European language (Singapore Sign Language and Chinese) in the top five while the UK and US websites each feature only one non-European language (Chinese) in the top five. Therefore, there appears to be a difference in what Singapore, an Asian country, considers a modern language to be versus what both the United Kingdom and the United States, both Anglosphere countries, consider it to be, of which the former seems to be more Asiacentric while the latter is more Eurocentric.

Furthermore, the labelling of classical languages also differs across the three countries. In Singaporean websites, Tamil, an Asian language, recorded a far higher number of occurrences of being labelled a 'classical language' in comparison with Latin and Greek, which are more commonly considered the dominant classical languages. This contrasts with UK and US websites, where it is widely agreed that Latin and Greek, both European languages, are classical languages. While the UK results mention Arabic, it is completely absent in the US results. Here again, we see a dichotomy with an Asia-centric Singaporean definition of classical languages on one end and a shared UK and US definition on the other end, suggesting again, a Eurocentric bias.

Lastly, for the classification of oriental languages however, a different dichotomy is observed. Singaporean websites only record one occurrence of this term, and even then it does not specify what these languages are. It only vaguely refers to them as 'Asian languages' instead of specific languages. This indicates that the term 'oriental languages' is probably not commonly used at all in Singapore to the point that there is no attempt to clearly label what languages belong to this category of oriental languages. Considering the derogatory nature of the term, this phenomenon is understandable. On the other hand, the UK and US websites specified twenty-four languages and five languages, respectively, for the label 'oriental languages'. However, it is noteworthy that only one UK website (University of Oxford) and two US websites (American Oriental Society and The City University of New York) use the term 'oriental languages' as a classificatory label. Furthermore, the fact that one UK and one US website classified European languages (Yiddish and Russian, respectively) as oriental creates further ambiguity for the definition of 'oriental' as referring to something Asian. This may indicate that this term is falling out of use, which could reduce biased preconceptions of Asian languages as some minority or oddity in contrast to European languages.

To summarize, it appears that Singapore, being an Asian country, has adopted a more Asian-influenced approach to understanding what modern languages and classical languages are, while the United Kingdom and the United States have both adopted a Euro-focused approach for this matter. This is significant, as Eurocentric conceptions of what modern and classical languages are can affect both perceptions and visibility of Asian languages in the public space. A heavy Eurocentric focus in classifying and analysing languages can lead to features unique to Asian languages being overlooked in favour of viewing them through a European, Anglo-biased lens. As Kiaer (2021, p. 4) observes, several 'often-overlooked properties of Asian languages' are 'in need of proper observation, description and explanation'.

Just because such features may not be present in European languages does not mean that they are not worth investigating. Also, by indicating certain languages as modern and/or classical, and denying other languages that labelling, creates a power imbalance where the discourse of the superiority of some languages (in this case European ones) is propagated. It also seems apparent that the term 'oriental languages' is becoming very rarely used in all three countries, suggesting that it might eventually fall out of use altogether. This hints at a shift away from colonial-era stereotypes of non-European languages as oddities. Not placing the label of 'oriental' on Asian languages also points to the fact that some features of Asian languages are not anomalies but are actually found in languages across the world (Kiaer, 2021, p. 4). However, as the above results show, there was and still is generally a heavy focus on European languages in the Anglosphere. This is in spite of the huge speaker population of Asian languages which accounts for more than a third of the world's linguistic diversity and is almost twice that of European languages.

In short, the classification of Asian languages is a difficult task. There is no clear agreement across the world on how languages from this region are to be labelled, and, instead, biases govern the terms used. These preconceptions – as evidenced by the results for the United Kingdom and the United States – highlight an injustice in which Eurocentricity plays a significant part.

Are Asian languages minority languages?

Given that Asian languages have been noticeably sidelined in modern linguistic research, one might think that they can be considered minority languages. In fact, so often one groups Asia under the umbrella term 'BAME' (Black, Asian, and minority ethnic), causing one to perceive it as a minority. This is inaccurate; in fact, many Asian languages have never been considered minority languages (Kiaer, 2021, p. 7). As previously stated, Asia is home to more than 2,300 languages spoken by more than 4.5 billion people (Ethnologue, 2022a). This accounts for more than a third of the world's languages. Furthermore, in 2022, Chinese (1.1 billion) and Hindi (602 million) were among the top four languages by number of speakers (Statista Research Department, 2023), while in 2016 Chinese, Arabic, Japanese and Malay ranked among the top ten languages on the internet by number of users (Coulmas, 2018, p. 185). Southeast Asia alone is home to more than a thousand languages which span five language families (Kirkpatrick, 2020). Compare this with the number of speakers of European languages within Europe (including L2 speakers; excluding Turkish, which we classify as Asian), numbering around 2.64 billion, which is much less than that of Asian languages (Marian, n.d.).

Baker and Jones (1998, p. 100) note that the concept of 'minority' is vague, and that in the UK there are significant numbers of Asian language speakers, especially those from South Asia speaking languages like Urdu and Gujarati. The 2011 UK Census showed that the Asian or Asian British ethnic group category experienced one of the largest increases in population of national groups since 2001, comprising (4.2 million) a third of the foreign-born population of the UK (White, 2012). The 2021 UK Census found that 'Asian, Asian British or Asian Welsh' accounted for 9.3 per cent (5.5 million) of the total population in England and Wales (Office for

National Statistics, 2022). Alongside this growth in population is a growth in the number of speakers of Asian languages. Additionally, there is a rapidly increasing number of speakers of a wide variety of Asian languages such as Korean, Tagalog and Tamil in immigrant communities in the United States (Wiley & Lee, 2009, p. 12). The US Census Bureau further reveals that Asian and Pacific Island languages constitute a major portion of foreign languages spoken in the United States (Ryan, 2013). These include a wide range of languages, such as: Chinese, Korean, Japanese, Vietnamese, Hmong, Khmer, Lao, Thai, Tagalog/Filipino, the Dravidian languages of India, and other languages of the Asia and Pacific, regions including the Polynesian and Micronesian languages. Among them, Chinese, Korean and Vietnamese are among the top ten most widely spoken languages in the United States.

The situation is similar in other English-speaking countries such as Australia and Canada. In Australia, the top four foreign languages are of Asian origin: Mandarin, Arabic, Cantonese and Vietnamese. In addition, Tagalog/Filipino, Hindi and Punjabi also appear in the top ten most spoken foreign languages in Australia, whilst Tagalog and Punjabi are the two of the fastest growing foreign languages in Canada (Statista Research Department, 2023).

However, I should again clarify that 'minority' here is not so much to do with numbers but rather about prestige. For instance, Chinese languages tend to be sold as languages that people learn in order to improve their employability or for economic reasons.

Given the real presence of Asian languages across the globe, it is an injustice that they are poorly represented in linguistic discourses, as the following section will explicate. Almost all the time these languages are stigmatized in Western canons. In other words, we can say that Asian languages are not minority languages in the sense of numbers but rather minority languages in psychological terms. It is painfully true that these were not celebrated languages but, instead, were overshadowed by the current lingua franca and other European languages. To describe Asian languages as being 'at the margin' connotes that they constitute a minority, that they are unimportant. Perhaps then it is inaccurate to frame the discussion as Asian languages 'at the margin', and instead it is more a question of marginalization.

Are Asian languages underrepresented?

Despite the significant linguistic footprint left by Asian languages on the world, there has been a noticeable bias with regards to research conducted on Asian languages. Asian languages have traditionally been understudied in comparison with European languages (Musan & Rathert, 2011, p. 3), and they are severely underrepresented in modern linguistics. Oftentimes, languages spoken in India are (inaccurately) thought to be 'Indian'. For example, contemporary syntactic theory focuses predominantly on evidence from English and only a handful of other European languages. While one might argue against this claim and reference works by theoretical linguists who have indeed studied Asian languages, it is important to note that many of their studies apply the same universal theory with minimal adaptations in the explanations of their own languages and, very often, such works are not accepted by 'home-grown, more traditional linguists' (Kiaer, 2021, p. 7).

The prevalent side-lining of Asian languages is further evidenced by looking at the languages that are investigated in journal articles. Based on an analysis of the languages that were investigated in more than 1,600 articles in the *Journal of Linguistics* (Cambridge) from the 1970s to the 2000s (2006), which studied several hundred languages (between 200 to 600 for each decade), it was found that the number of languages studied steadily increased from 209 in the 1970s to 600 in the 1990s, only to then decrease to 448 in the 2000s. The investigation also showed that of the top ten languages investigated per decade by number of appearances in the journal articles, the focus has, and still is, largely on European languages and averaging only two or three Asian languages per decade (Chinese, Arabic, Japanese, Hebrew and/or Turkish). For example, English has consistently remained in the first rank from the 1970s to the 2000s, while French and German occupy the second and third spots throughout the decades. As for the Asian languages, Japanese occupies the highest rank in the 2000s, at joint-fifth place with Spanish. Evidently, European languages dominate the rankings.

The study also examined the changes in rankings of the top ten European and non-European languages being investigated for each decade from the 1970s to the 2000s. The language was selected to be included if it appeared at least once in the top ten for at least one of the decades. The rankings are calculated by comparing the number of appearances of a language in the articles of a certain decade against the total number of articles for that decade. The higher the ranking, the greater the number of appearances of a language (that is to say, the more that a language was investigated). The findings show that a few European languages stayed within the top ten throughout all the decades, namely English, Italian, Spanish, Latin, German and French. For these six languages, the majority either maintained or improved their rankings over the decades.

As for the non-Eurocentric languages, as mentioned previously, only five of these made it to the top ten over the decades – Chinese, Arabic, Japanese, Hebrew and Turkish. Of these languages, it appears that, apart from Japanese which has increased in ranking throughout the decades, the remaining four languages do not show a clear pattern, but rather experience slight dips and increases in scholarly attention over the decades. However, comparing the rankings of these languages, these are relatively lower (except for Japanese) in comparison with the six European languages which maintained or improved their already high rankings.

Therefore, the above results seem to suggest that Asian languages have been, and are still currently being, understudied in actual linguistic research; this is in sharp contrast to the attention paid to European languages. This injustice done towards Asian languages within the linguistic sphere requires rectification.

In addition, the use of highly technical terminology encouraged in the Chomskyan Minimalist Program has made it almost impossible for outsiders to participate. With these barriers, non-Chomskyans can only speak up against the reliability of the data, which Chomskyans can easily disregard due to the belief that the data does not matter as it belongs to the realm of performance. Consider the quote from Thompson (2012):

> Modern Bengali linguists (from about the 1970 onwards) have taken a giant leap away from the traditional, historic, Sanskrit-oriented grammar and have adopted western formal grammar models to test the structures of Bengali. This has resulted in a considerable body of impressive work on particular features of Bengali, however this work is highly technical in its language and largely inaccessible to non-linguists.
>
> Thompson, 2012, p. 10

This chasm is seen in other disciplines, but in linguistics as it stands now, it seems almost irrecoverable. The aim of any linguistic theory is to explain the core, innate properties of human languages. To achieve this, unprejudiced, theory-unbound observation and description are prerequisite.

Since Chomsky's *Syntactic Structures* (1957), it has been the case that categories which exist in English and Western European languages have received much attention in contemporary linguistics. However, linguistic categories and attributes that are non-existent or less relevant in these languages have been less celebrated and explored. Particles are a representative example of this. Notably, particles have failed to attract proper attention in generative grammars, which put a heavy emphasis on word orders in syntactic architecture. The following quotes are from Enfield (2007):

> The two French language grammars are similar to grammars written in Lao in that their analysis of Lao follows distinctions in grammatical meaning

traditionally made in European languages, such as categories of conjugation, mood and inflection of the verb. But a significant difference between Lao and the average European language is that Lao lacks precisely these categories. Most points of grammatical analysis of this kind are not supported with language internal arguments along lines supplied by modern standard reference grammars. Rather, the grammarian is describing Lao in terms of the resources it has for expressing the grammatical distinctions one has in French or some other 'Standard Average European' grammar.

Enfield 2007, pp. 10-11

From a modern linguistic point of view, there are a number of features of Lao not normally found in European languages which would nowadays be described on their own terms. One example is the phenomenon of serial verb constructions, a type of complex clause structure that Lao and many other languages – but not European languages like French – feature. Such structures are mentioned here and there in existing Lao grammars, but (unlike early grammars of African languages) no attention is drawn to their identity as a distinct grammatical category.

Enfield, 2007, pp. 11-12

A closer look: Central Asian languages

Montgomery (2022) characterizes the geographical region of Central Asia as consisting of the five former Soviet republics of Kyrgyzstan, Kazakhstan, Uzbekistan, Turkmenistan and Tajikistan, although he notes that depending on different contexts, this geographical boundary may be extended to include Afghanistan, Mongolia, Azerbaijani, Xinjiang, Tatarstan and various parts of Iran and Siberia. These republics were formerly part of the Soviet Union until its eventual dissolution in 1991, after which the independent republics were established (Abdullaeva, 2020, p. 39). After more than seven decades of Soviet rule in the region, the influence of Russia there is still felt in the present day – it is the most eminent foreign power in Central Asia and still leaves its mark in numerous fields like politics, culture, media, the economy and security (Oliphant, 2013, p. 1). One of the prominent Soviet legacies is the Russian language and use of the Russian-based Cyrillic script which were enforced in the Soviet period through pro-Russian language policies (Grenoble & Whaley, 1998, pp. 46–47), which continues to the present day as Russian remains the main lingua franca in the region (Chokobaeva & Ninnis, 2021, p. 217).

The former Soviet Union was a linguistically diverse space with more than 200 different languages, which include some current-day national languages of the aforementioned Central Asian republics such as Kazakh and Uzbek (Grenoble & Whaley, 1998, p. 45). Apart from these more common languages, the majority are minority languages which include language isolates and Chukotko-Kamchatkan, Samoyedic, Nakh-Daghestanian, Manchu-Tungusic and Balto-Finnic languages (Grenoble & Whaley, 1998, pp. 45–46). In the five Central Asian republics, generally Turkic languages are spoken (e.g. Kazakh, Kyrgyz, Uzbek and Turkmen as the major ones), with the exception of Tajikistan where Tajik, an Iranian language, is dominant (Hobbs, 2012, p. 125).

Despite this rich linguistic diversity, multilingualism in Central Asia has been relatively under-researched in Anglophone circles (Kalan, 2016, p. 104). Liu (2012) describes the region as 'curiously overdetermined yet understudied' and 'a neglected hole in the map' (p. 16). Luong (2004) argues that the five Central Asian republics were much more under researched as compared with the rest of the Soviet Union due to issues like language barriers and limited access, and much less was known about them than other states upon the collapse of the Soviet Union (p. 4).

Apart from Kyrgyz, Kazakh, Uzbek, Turkmen and Tajik, which were established as the official languages of the five former Soviet Central Asian republics shortly before the collapse of the Soviet Union, there is a lack of attention given to the rest of the languages in academia (Schlyter, 2001, p. 127; Bahry, 2016, p. 25). Furthermore, Smagulova and Ahn (2016) note that despite the geopolitical and historical prominence of the region of Central Asia, much of the research on the region is still in its early stages, particularly linguistics-related research, which largely went under the radar of the linguistic community and remained relatively undocumented (p. 1). Even back in the 1970s, Wheeler (1977) had noted a general lack of attention towards the Soviet language policies targeted at the Asian minorities (referring generally to the speakers of Turkic languages) in the Soviet Union, with only several publications in the United States and France dealing with this issue (p. 208). It was only with the dissolution of the Soviet Union in 1991 that Central Asia received more scholarly attention (Thibault, 2018, p. 9). In spite of this, there remain many issues in Central Asian studies, such as a lack of introductory works to introduce people to Central Asia, a paucity of comprehensive reference works, and a dearth of an associated scholarly community (Schoeberlein, 2009, pp. 39–40). In short, then, underrepresentation of Central Asian languages is a long-standing issue in linguistics.

A general lack of research on Central Asian languages until the twenty-first century might be attributed to the relative difficulty of conducting research relating to the USSR during the Soviet era (Fierman, 2015, p. 8). Fierman (2015) notes that linguistic resources for learning even major languages of the region, like Tajik and the Turkic languages, were of relatively poor quality, and there were 'close to zero' Americans studying these languages (p. 9). This lack of connection with the outside world is explained by Batsaikhan and Dabrowski (2017), who note that during Soviet times, 'the Soviet transportation network was concentrated on Russia and other Soviet republics, while connections with the outside world were almost non-existent', and in spite of some 'infrastructure investment in the last quarter-century', this lack of connection with the outside world still persists (p. 297).

Another reason for the lack of attention on Central Asian languages was the difficulty of accessing academic literature on the region. Back in the mid-twentieth century, Loewenthal (1957) noted that literature on Central Asia was divided amongst the Far East (Chinese and Japanese), Slavic (Russian) and Turkish areas, and that much of this, particularly studies of Turkic languages, were written in Russian or translated into Russian, with many of the publications in the original languages being unavailable outside of the Soviet Union (p. 8). This posed a problem as Anglo and Eurocentric circles did not have direct first-hand access to these original documents for research and could mostly only refer to Russian translated versions, and the materials for studying Russian back then were also scarce (Loewenthal, 1957, p. 8; Dadabaev, 2017, p. 30). Even in the present day, research carried out in Central Asia is underrepresented on the global stage as most research is regulated by the state, published mainly in Russian in local journals, and relatively unknown outside of the region (Adambekov et al., 2016). Stringer (2003) notes that Western scholarly interest in Central Asia has for many years been limited due to difficulties in physically accessing Central Asia as well as a lack of trustworthy source materials, especially so from the 1930s to 1980s during the Soviet era (p. 146).

This limited access to academic works from the region is often instigated by political factors. During the Soviet era, the communist government effectively prevented fieldwork in the region (Schoeberlein, 2009, pp. 23–24). Limited access and other issues, like official information manipulation and statistical misrepresentation, which were present during the Soviet times, continue to affect research in the region, especially so for the social sciences (Wooden et al., 2009, p. 37). Toktomushev (2017) notes that there is limited access to credible literature on Central Asia directly from the region itself due to various reasons such as a lack of funding (resulting from the dissolution of the Soviet Union and other issues), the questionable nature of publicly available information, and a lack of political openness (pp. 4–5). This has affected the volume and quality of publications coming from Central Asia (Toktomushev, 2017, p. 4). Janenova (2019) further reiterates Toktomushev's points by looking specifically at Kazakhstan, where she describes three main issues of doing research in the authoritarian country, namely lack of access to government officials, lack of openness by participants in interviews and focus groups, as well as ethical and safety issues (pp. 3–6). In Central Asia, Kyrgyzstan and Kazakhstan are most receptive to foreign researchers, while it is extremely challenging for foreigners to conduct research in Turkmenistan (Rasanayagam, 2010, p. 67).

Apart from lack of access, Thibault (2018) briefly explains some additional reasons for the paucity of scholarly work on Central Asia, such as 'isolation from leading publications and research centres', language barriers and challenging financial and living conditions, which have made the region less enticing for researchers (p. 9). Methodological limitations were also another factor that impeded research, particularly sociolinguistic research, during the Soviet era – there tended to be an overreliance on textual methods like surveys, as other methods were not considered 'legitimate' in the Soviet research tradition (Smagulova & Ahn, 2016, p. 6). In addition, very few foreign researchers have the adequate linguistic training (e.g. in Russian and/or Central Asian languages) to conduct detailed research in the region (Scott, 1982, p. 231). There was little motivation for scholars to learn these 'unrelated and difficult languages' of the region and to take the effort to acquire knowledge in Central Asian studies where there was a lack of foundational works, on top of the fact that Central Asia as a region did not hold an important position in scholarship (Schoeberlein, 2009, p. 24).

The paucity of studies on Central Asian languages is evident by doing a simple search on Google Scholar for scholarly articles regarding these languages. A comparison of the number of search results on Google Scholar for just the major Central Asian languages compared with major languages in other parts of Asia showcases the disparity in attention received by Central Asian languages in general. The search was conducted on 28 June 2022 by searching for 'X language', whereby X is the name of the language (such as 'Kazakh language'). This produces relevant research articles that are related to the particular language being searched for. The time range was set to 'Any time'. Table 4.1 shows the search results for twenty-six major Asian languages ranked from the largest to the smallest, with the five major Central Asian languages (highlighted in grey),

Table 4.1 Languages and their number of search results in descending order

Language	Number of search results
Chinese	3830000
Japanese	3400000
Korean	2340000
Turkish	2050000
Arabic	1800000
Hebrew	1760000
Persian	1180000
Thai	955000
Indonesian	725000
Vietnamese	571000
Tamil	386000
Malay	313000
Hindi	277000
Tibetan	246000
Tagalog	154000
Laos	149000
Urdu	134000
Bengali	131000
Mongolian	115000
Burmese	75800
Khmer	68000
Kazakh	62000
Uzbek	59100
Kyrgyz	40700
Turkmen	38200
Tajik	33800

Kazakh, Uzbek, Kyrgyz, Turkmen and Tajik, recording the five lowest search results. There is between a sixty to more than 100-fold difference in search results between the most studied Asian language (Chinese) and these five Central Asian languages. This suggests that out of all the major Asian languages, the ones in Central Asia have received the least scholarly attention, which might be attributed to the multiple factors as mentioned earlier. However, as the following section will discuss in further detail, Eurocentrism also plays a significant role in the broader side-lining of Asian languages.

Eurocentric views: since when?

Modern linguistics was greatly influenced and inspired by the works of Asian linguists' – such as Pāṇini's – grammar. Aṣṭādhyāyī by Pāṇini (dated to *c.* fourth–fifth century BC) is the very earliest extant systematic grammar of human languages. It has inspired many pioneers of modern linguistic science; Ferdinand de Saussure, Leonard Bloomfield and Roman Jakobson were all Sanskrit scholars. Staal (1967) notes that Pāṇini's grammar provided the formal foundation for contemporary linguistics due to its influence on Saussure and Chomsky.

However, during the course of its development, the Asian influence within linguistics has been lost. Throughout the history of contemporary linguistics, in accordance with the Chomskyan tradition of generative grammars, theoretical linguists have aimed to unravel universal grammars that would be applicable to all human languages. However, this search has been conducted with data taken mainly from European languages. That said, in the process of searching for and crystallizing the linguistic categories and features of world languages, mainstream Western linguists often construct their approach through the looking glass of English-like languages, implicitly assuming that the linguistic consistencies found in these languages will be applicable to all other languages with little parametric variation.

There is a great deal of opposition to the reformation of contemporary linguistics in the sense of inclusivity, and we may link this to a homogenous spirit that has underpinned studies for several decades. However, even in non-linguistic circles, Asian languages, in spite of their diversity, can be grouped altogether with little-to-no acknowledgement of their differences. This is all in the spirit of modernism, in which Eurocentrism has an influential pull. The history of Eurocentric perspectives in linguistics is closely linked to the development of this field. Early grammars were written in 'English', French, or other Western European languages, by Westerners (such as missionaries). While this was a very necessary process, in many cases, their views and the views of already-existing grammarians, were not properly communicated and therefore unreconciled. This continued throughout the twentieth century, resulting in the chasms we notice to this very day.

A closer look at some particulars of Asian languages

In this section we take a closer look at some of the particulars of Asian languages: flexible word order and a rich use of particles. These languages are non-parallel to English and other Western European languages, notably due to their robust pragmatic repertoire. Asian languages are socio-pragmatically rich, with context playing a highly important role. Classifying and studying these languages has been shown to be difficult, with few studies (relative to those on European languages) attempting to do so, because of the nature of the framework in which we analyse them. For instance, what has been argued as obligatory in the literature does not seem to be applicable to Asian languages. When looking at the actual data from these languages using online databases, such as the World Atlas of Language Structures (WALS), trying to describe and explain what we see using our current linguistic architecture which possesses a strong English bias may cause us to set up a series of exceptions for the sake of theory. When the exceptions are overdone, there is a dangerous compromise made between actual perception and linguistic predictions.

Flexible word order

First, word orders in Asian languages are relatively flexible (Kiaer, 2021, p. 11). The simultaneous unfolding of syntactic structures in languages with flexible word orders is primarily due to the important role that particles, prosody and context play. Goddard (2005, p. 7) observes that, in general, the languages of East and Southeast Asia tend to have more flexible and 'expressive' word order than English, and almost all languages within the region permit some variation in the constituent order of a simple sentence. Word order between lexical items in the same local structure is flexible and does not yield any difference in propositional meaning. This phenomenon, shifting from a so-called canonical word order into a non-canonical word order is called 'scrambling' (specifically, local or short-distance scrambling) (Ross, 1967; Saito, 1985). In other words, it assumes that there is a basic word order from which words are then re-arranged. Languages such as Japanese, Korean and Turkish are known as 'scrambling languages', and this phenomenon is one of their main defining syntactic characteristics. The following is an example of scrambling in Turkish in which the supposed basic word order (SOV (subject–object–verb) in this case) is 'scrambled' (to OSV (object–subject–verb) in this case) (taken from Hoffman, 1995):

(1) a. *Ayse* *Kitabi* *okuyor [S O V]* [Turkish]
Ayse-NOM book-ACC read
'Ayse read a book.'

b. *Kitabi*　　　　　*Ayse*　　　　　*okuyor [O S V]* [Turkish]
　　book-ACC　　　Ayse-NOM　　read
　　'Ayse read a book.'

(I explore the use of the word 'scrambling' and its implications in further detail in Chapter 5.)

Rich use of particles

Syntactic fluidity in Asian languages particularly – exemplified through flexible word order discussed above – is possible because the structure-building relies on multiple sources such as prosodic cues and morphological particles. In this section, I examine in more detail the latter feature.

It is commonly observed in Asian languages that interpersonal dynamics and sociocultural factors play a crucial role in meaningful communication; even the realization of subjects is pragmatically motivated in many of these languages. The importance of context and register echoes the Gricean maxim of quantity, where one attempts to be as informative as possible and give as much information as is needed – no more, no less.

The explicit realization of expressions therefore depends more on pragmatic elements rather than on whether the expressions are morpho-syntactically obligatory or optional. For example, the decision of whether or not to use an explicit second-person pronoun does not depend on the verb or the propositional structure, but on the relationship dynamics between the speaker and the hearer. Oftentimes, they are systematically replaced with address terms, kinship terms or even non-verbal expressions in order to avoid socio-pragmatic awkwardness.

Using Korean as an example, it is common to simply omit the second-person pronoun, unless giving emphasis or introducing the second person as the new sentential subject. In-groupness and social position are important factors to consider as to how one refers to the second person. There are numerous address terms replacing the second-person pronouns in Korean.

Turning now to particles, it may be noted that many basic syntax courses still provide analyses which assume that case particles do not exist. Tsujimura (2005, p. 164) provides a syntactic tree that features pre-X-bar schemata and pays no attention to case particles. The only notable difference between Japanese and English in this analysis appears to be word order. This approach of ignoring particles is not uncommon.

Again, broadening our reach, WALS shows us that pragmatically driven flexibility is universally observed across languages. Particles, rather than word order, are often employed to display word function in a sentence in these languages – which include a significant number of Asian languages. However, despite their clear presence, the function and meaning of particles have not been systematically studied, and particles in general have not been properly established in linguistic theories thus far. This is evident through the difficulties in glossing particles, as well as the lack of harmony between glosses in the literature. Looking at the Leipzig Glossing Rules, there are not many features that cover Asian languages, particularly their particles. Of course, adding glosses for the particles would not be so straightforward as they can carry a lot of information and have many functions – many (if not all) of which are pragmatic (see Kiaer, 2021 for more).

It is also worth noting that, despite particles playing crucial roles in both structure building and enriching meaning in Asian languages, they have received relatively little attention in the literature. In the earlier period of generative grammars, Kuno (1973, p. 4) writes in reference to Japanese that 'particles are used not only to represent case relationships, or to represent the functions that are carried in English by prepositions and conjunctions, but also after sentence-final verbs to represent the speaker's attitude towards the content of the sentence'. According to Kuno, particles are indeed important and have two primary roles – that is, constructive and expressional/attitudinal. Kuno offers the following example sentences in Japanese (Kuno 1973, p. 5):

(2) a. *Kore wa hon desu yo.* [Japanese]
This TOP book be YO
'I am telling you that this is a book.'
b. *Kore wa hon desu ne.*
This TOP book be NE
I hope you agree that this is a book.'
c. *Kore wa hon desu ka.*
This TOP book be KA
'*I ask you* if this is a book.'
d. *John wa baka sa.*
John TOP fool SA
'*It goes without saying that* John is a fool.'

The sentences (2a–d), for instance, do not elaborate in the gloss what the particles *yo*, *ne*, *ka* and *sa* mean, opting instead to keep them in their romanized form. While particles play a varied and important role in Asian languages, they have been sorely understudied by theoretical linguists whose research has focused on English and other European languages. Seeking to analyse the rich repertoire of particles of Asian languages within a Chomskyan framework seems to be problematic, with particles often being dismissed or placed on the fringe. This attests to the strong Anglocentrism and Eurocentrism of our current architecture. To elaborate, English has been widely studied in syntactics, but particles do not play as significant a role in English when compared with Asian languages such as Japanese; the tools we use for English, that we also impose onto our studies of Asian languages, do not yield convincing conclusions. In the rare instances where an attempt has been made to investigate particles, most of the theoretical linguists, particularly those who have been trained within a Chomskyan framework, come from an Anglocentric or Eurocentric perspective. Such work posits the idea that particles are largely non-existent in syntactic representation, with only a few exceptions. As I have noted previously, in linguistics textbooks designed for learners of Chinese, Japanese and Korean, for example, particles do not seem to play any role in the configuration of a structure; the particle somehow evades any mention in the majority of cases (Kiaer, 2021, p. 5). In other words, it appears that the current tools generative linguists from a Chomskyan background have at hand are simply inadequate for the analysis of Asian languages.

Problems with the 'pick-and-choose' approach

A common issue I've noticed when reading English-language linguistics textbooks and handbooks on Asian languages is what I call a 'pick-and-choose' approach. By this, I mean that authors often pick and choose theoretical frameworks depending on what serves their argument, without much regard to consistency. In most other fields, it is common practice to use the most up-to-date theories to ensure the analysis is valid and relevant, but it seems that many Western writers studying Asian linguistics tend to take a laxer approach.

Normally, this kind of writing simply sticks to a pre-minimalist approach, but their decisions can be rather inconsistent. For instance, the noun-and-particle sequence seen in many Asian languages is sometimes labelled 'NP' and sometimes 'DP', with the choice appearing completely arbitrary. Another inconsistency is that many of these books adopt the tree diagram from generative grammar while only rarely introducing other linguistic frameworks. Tree diagrams may look pretty, but surely more complex analysis is also needed. Occasionally, the pre-minimalist X-bar theory is borrowed, but how much do we need to know about phrase structure? Tsujimura (2007) says the following in the preface to the second edition:

> The fields of phonology and syntax in the generative tradition have renewed their outlook by focusing on Optimality Theory and the Minimalist program, respectively, but these changes are not mirrored in this edition. I came to this decision with the primary goal in my mind: the book is intended to present descriptions of a wider range of linguistic phenomena in Japanese and introduce a very basic level of theoretical foundation needed in linguistic analysis.

Many individuals teaching and researching Asian languages encounter the same dilemma that Tsujimura describes. While some might view this as normal, it can also be seen as a critical issue that highlights the discrepancy between theory and data. This problem needs to be addressed.

Problems with trying to fit square pegs into round holes

The grammatical properties of Asian languages have often been subjected to analyses on the basis of Eurocentric languages such as Latin (Bauer, 2017, p. 34), instead of being studied and catalogued as unique features in their own right. Recall Enfield's (2007) critique of descriptive grammars of Lao (pp. 10–11), presented above, particularly with regard to the terminological issues surrounding features of Lao that are not present in 'Standard Average European' languages, such as serial verb constructions.

The issue with such an approach is succinctly expressed by Battiste and Henderson (2000), who note that

> the underlying coherence of the Eurocentric view of language is that since Eurocentric thought mediates the entire world through its theories, then there is little possibility for an independent comparison of Eurocentric and Indigenous theories [...] To insist on analysing Indigenous thought from a Eurocentric point of view is cultural racism and cognitive imperialism [...] every Indigenous language has a right to exist without conforming to Eurocentric languages or worldviews.
>
> Battiste and Henderson, 2000, p. 74

In other words, it's like trying to fit 'square pegs into round holes'. In this analogy, the 'square pegs' are our linguistic data from Asian languages, while the 'round holes' constitute our current theoretical framework for linguistics. No matter how much we try to whittle down, cut and edit the pegs, for as long as we are making merely superficial alterations there will continue to be an irreconcilable gap between the evidence and theory. Our present framework with a strong Eurocentric bias simply does not allow a cogent analysis of Asian languages. This points to a deeper underlying problem: our theoretical mould is just not good enough. When we look at the cross-linguistic evidence and examine it from a Chomskyan perspective, it appears that we are using a theory which works for the minority of languages rather than the majority; we are making too many exceptions for the sake of leaving theory untouched. If most of our pegs are square and only a handful are somewhat round, perhaps what requires change are not the pegs themselves, but the holes in which we try to fit them.

For the past twenty-five years that I have engaged with syntax, there has been no significant change in the theoretical framework of generative grammars. In Chomsky's highly influential *Aspects* (1965), he writes of the crucial elements that linguistic theories should seek to contain: *descriptive adequacy* and *explanatory adequacy*. However, I argue that the critical element of 'observational adequacy' has been overlooked and this can be exemplified through the data we see from Asian languages which have been marginalized in the literature. It is high time that we stop trying to fit square pegs into these round holes and reform the way we approach syntactic theory.

Syntactic freedom

As previously mentioned, word orders in most Asian languages are relatively flexible. However, this freedom is not limited to Asian languages – this is the case for many other world languages, even English. Flexible ordering is indeed not a new phenomenon; it can be found in ancient languages, for instance, Latin, Greek and Sanskrit all show flexible word orders. Yet, syntactic freedom – in other words, flexible ordering – has been quite a difficult feature to analyse. This is even more so the case for Asian languages labelled as typically verb-final languages, as they are considered to cause much more trouble in the present Anglocentric syntactic architecture.

Normally, syntactic flexibility is explained as the following: you set up what the original or base structure is and then explain the rest as the variation *from* the base structure – adding a note of reason – what the cause is for the variation. This line of thought works well if the ordering is relatively fixed. If not, this causes serious trouble. How can we find the base, default structure, and explain the cause of variation? Could we find the cause for each variation particularly from a purely competence perspective, ignoring the actual production part? Human languages exhibit flexible orderings more than fixed orderings across languages, across time and across place, in other words, diachronic, synchronic and typological variation are all in line with a basic degree of flexibility. Syntactic freedom as the norm may even be what generative mindset inspires us to think. Nevertheless, in the theory as it currently stands, numerous efforts have been made as an attempt to explain that what is flexible and free in nature, is something that is inflexible and fixed. This causes syntactic theory to be almost inapproachably complex, as well as reliant upon a list of ad hoc explanations and exceptions after exceptions.

Surprising constituent isn't surprising

One example is from Japanese linguist Takano (2002, p. 258). Japanese and Korean linguists were at the forefront of studying word orders using generative schemata. The word scrambling is mostly associated with the syntax of these languages. However, a big question here is whether scrambling is even the right word to describe the syntactic freedom expressed by most world languages. (A more detailed discussion will follow in Chapter 5.) In order to explain the 'surprising' unit of expressions that become a unit even without the presence of a verb, Takano calls the unit of two words *hon-o Mary-ni* 'a book to Mary' a 'surprising constituent'; it involves a complex logical process to ensure their unity. In short, we are to assume that the unity was made through the verb which was there but then moved out. Even in this unity, however, the order should be strictly kept, as the alternative order means another layer of movement. Yet, to me, when I take off my hat as a generative linguist and put on that of an ordinary speaker of the Korean language, I find units such as these are most prevalent in our everyday language use. Verbs are often unseen, although unity is often ensured prosodically (in other words, being pronounced together). Usually, people find the unity easily without the presence of a verb and they are happy to use the expressions without many restrictions. This isn't surprising; what *is* surprising is the way the analysis was born.

A plethora of particles

Asian languages have rich particles. The main role of particles is typically twofold: (i) constructive and (ii) expressive. For (a sequence of) particles which constantly make a prediction about the on-going and up-coming structure, I use the label constructive particles or even 'little predicates'. For instance, when you see a dative particle and an accusative particle together, you are to expect a particular set of predicates and structures. If you see a complementizer particle, you will know that whatever has been read or heard is to be a part of a bigger, main structure. On the other hand, particles also decorate the proposition with all sorts of socio-pragmatic meanings and attitudes. Asian languages, though so diverse, uniformly exhibit socio-pragmatic richness, where interpersonal dynamics and other socio-cultural factors play an essential role in every aspect of communication. The complexity of interpersonal meanings is far beyond what we can observe from English and Western European languages. Oftentimes, it is through these lightweight particles that those enriched, diverse social meanings are expressed. A single particle at the very end of a construction in Korean, for instance, can set the tone and show us what the relational dynamic is between the interlocutors. To offer an example, the English translation of the two utterances, originally in Korean, may be the same: 'Jina is going to Paris.' Yet, one has the attitudinal meaning where the speaker is casual with the hearer (possibly they are social equals or the speaker is senior), whereas the other has the meaning that the speaker is polite to the hearer (possibly the hearer is senior to the speaker). All these complex meanings are contained in a one-syllable particle.

(3) a. *Jina-ka Paris* **ka** (spoken by a friend to a friend of a senior to junior)
b. *Jina-ka Paris* **ka-yo** (spoken by a junior to senior)
'Jina is going to Paris.'

Syntactic structures progress through the uses of case particles and the structures are wrapped up whenever needed through the help of prosody. Where particles don't exist, there is a set of good routines which help ordinary speakers to build meanings out of word sequences. Some complex decisions – such as whether the current structure is to be the main structure or not – also need to be guided by the particles and necessary routines as one further navigates the sequence. Kiaer (2021) shows the rich meanings, both constructive and expressive, of particles in Asian languages. Yet there is a clear lack of their study in natural language syntax. This is where a true dilemma lies: particles are what matter in the syntactic architecture of many Asian languages, yet oftentimes particles do not receive that attention, as we have seen, either from Asian syntax textbooks or systems intended for cross-linguistic description, such as the Leipzig Glossing Rules.

Verb-final languages

According to WALS, there are more languages which show verb-final word-orders than verb-initial or medial word orders. For instance, according to Dryer (2013), there are 713 languages which have a default OV (object–verb) ordering and 705 languages which have a default VO (verb–object) ordering. In the map shown in the WALS, it is noteworthy that most of the North and Central Asian as well as Southeast Asian languages are OV languages, whereas almost all European languages except Sorbian and Basque are VO languages.[1] It is also worthwhile noting, as Hawkins (1994) shows, that significantly more research has been conducted in VO languages than OV languages in contemporary linguistics.

What I try to draw attention to here is that at least half of the world's languages share verb-finality, often coupled with flexible orderings between constituents. Put radically, although half of the languages in the world behave like Korean, Japanese or Tibetan, these attributes have received hardly any attention and have been regarded as somewhat peculiar in terms of their linguistic attributes within mainstream contemporary theoretical linguistics.

On the other hand, varieties of Chinese, and the languages from the Indochinese Peninsula (or in other words, languages from Southeast Asia) roughly share SVO ordering as a preferred word order. In these languages, pragmatic knowledge is significant in structure-building as there are no morphological indicators that could give specific guidelines for future structure-building. Expressions are realized based on a simple pragmatic principle: 'Say what is needed, when it is needed'. I classify the target Asian languages as below:

a. Those with flexible word orders with rich case particles; pragmatic realization of expressions (i.e. pro-drop); particle-rich languages:

Arabic,[2] Korean, Japanese, Tamil, Hindi, Urdu, Bengali, Tibetan, Tagalog, Turkish, Persian, Mongolian, Sanskrit (most of them except Standard Arabic show strong verb-finality).

b. Those with flexible word orders with no case particles; pragmatic realization of expression (i.e. pro-drop); particle-rich languages; mostly prefer SVO order:

Mandarin Chinese, Thai, Vietnamese, Lao.

It is worth noting that none of these languages show strictly fixed word orders. Nevertheless, under contemporary linguistic theories, it is often assumed that there is a basic fixed order and other orders are derived from the base order by some purely grammatical operation such as movement.

Glossing difficulties

Wiltschko (2014) highlights several issues with the Leipzig glossing conventions (pp. 29–31). First, as these conventions provide semantic and grammatical information about 'individual' words and parts of words, they are not suitable for glossing words with multiple functions (such as words that have different grammatical properties when appearing in different parts of the sentence). Second, the Leipzig conventions assume that language-specific grammatical/semantic categories can be grouped under meta-categories (making them similar to categories with universal scope) so that they can be compared. The problem with this assumption is that in comparing languages (such as in linguistic typology), we may encounter categories specific to languages that cannot be classified under any meta-categories. Wilcox and Morford (2007) also underscore similar problems with glossing practices in general, particularly how the terms used for glossing influence readers to become attuned to particular semantic connotations produced in the transcriptions (p. 191). Using such terms to describe another language could potentially lead to biased ways of understanding the grammatical categories of the language, which may not reflect the actual nature of how it works in that language. Pederson (2010) concurs, arguing that 'semantic comparison across even moderately well-described languages largely relies on simple glossing conventions and dictionaries listing approximate translation equivalents', which results in a lack of 'accurate cross-linguistic semantic descriptions' (p. 666).

The first shortcoming could be applicable to the issue of glossing pragmatic particles which are prevalent in Asian languages, as many of these are pragmatically sensitive and may change in semantic/grammatical function in different contexts. The second shortcoming is again applicable to the glossing of Asian languages, such as in the area of pragmatic particles, as the Leipzig conventions do not have category labels that can adequately express the functions of these particles. In fact, depending on the context, particles in Asian languages can have multiple meanings and functions. This means that a one-to-one mapping of particles, while more common in European languages, is not so much the reality for Asian languages. Furthermore, unlike many European languages, in Asian languages such as Korean and Japanese, particles can even be absent; in everyday speech, case particles can be dropped for instance. These two shortcomings highlight the tendency to apply grammatical categories – which are Eurocentric in nature – onto other languages, and to subsume language-specific categories under these universal categories on the basis of easier comparison instead of glossing them as special categories in their own right.

This line of thought is succinctly expressed by Matthewson (2010), who states:

> Should we apply terms which were invented for European languages to similar – but not identical – categories in other languages? For example, should we say 'The perfect / definite determiner / subjunctive in language X differs semantically from its English counterpart', or should we say 'Language X lacks a perfect / definite determiner / subjunctive', because it lacks an element with the exact semantics of the English categories? I adopt the former approach here, as I think it leads to productive cross-linguistic comparison, and because it suggests that the traditional terms do not represent primitive sets of properties, but rather potentially decomposable ones.
>
> Matthewson, 2010, p. 13

This tendency to use Eurocentric conventions is also echoed by Murray (2012), who, in his book that guides undergraduates in writing English language and linguistics essays, specifically informs readers about doing direct comparisons of equivalents in languages during glossing (using Persian as an example), and tells readers how glossing is often done in comparison with English (pp. 149–150).

An example of the limited nature of the Leipzig rules can be seen in the example from Twi (4), a variety of the Akan language, part of the Kwa sub-group of the Niger-Congo languages on the African continent (Kuteva et al., 2019, p. 513). In the example below, the particle *à* that appears at the end of a subordinate clause is used to signify indefiniteness of 'the time frame of the event or state', and despite the importance of this particle, the abbreviation PTCL is not present in the Leipzig glossing conventions (Bartens, 2011, p. 207). Even then, this abbreviation alone is inadequate in showcasing the function of *à* within the sentence, as it does not explain how *à* is used within the context of the sentence.

(4)
Opété	tè	fúnu	nkā´	à,	nâ	ɔ-re-bá
vulture	perceive	carcass	Smell	PTCL	COMP	3SG-PROG-come

'When the vulture smells a carcass, it comes forthwith.'

Pragmatic markers are also present in non-Asian languages, such as in Macedonian, a South Slavic language. In Macedonian, *kamo* is a pragmatic marker which showcases the 'speaker's dissociative attitude towards a current belief concerning the hearer's ability and willingness to perform a certain action'

(Sévigny, 2010, p. 52). It can be used in various linguistic structures such as within questions with definite/indefinite reference and with a copula, among others. As seen from the example below (5), again, the abbreviation PART for 'particle' has been added because it is not present in the Leipzig conventions (Sévigny, 2010, p. 53). Also, like the previous example from Twi, the abbreviation PART itself does not indicate the function of the particle, other than just stating that it is a particle. This leads to various possible interpretations which cannot be deduced purely from the glossing (Sévigny, 2010, p. 53).

(5)
Kamo	Ga	mačka-ta?
Where-PART	3SG-ACC-F	cat-DEF.ART

'Where is that cat?'

This can also be interpreted as:

a. *I expected you to have produced the cat.*
b. *I believed that the cat would now be in my sight.*
c. *I am here and the cat is nowhere to be seen.*
d. *I believe that you are not able to produce the cat.*

If we were to look at Asian languages, the same issue of the inadequacy of the Leipzig conventions can also be observed. With reference to the example from Korean below (6) (Kiaer, 2021, p. 87), the abbreviations HON for honorific particle and POL for polite particle are not present in the Leipzig conventions but are absolutely essential for understanding the social hierarchy and interpersonal relations indexed through these particles which are central to the Korean language. As such, the paucity of many such abbreviations in the Leipzig conventions not only points to a lack of inclusivity which ignores much of the linguistic diversity in the world, but that some of these abbreviations are overly generic, downplaying the rich semantic/grammatical properties of these particles and other linguistic forms in their respective languages.

(6)
Kim	sensayng-nim-i	hay-yo
Kim	teacher-HON-NOM	do-POL

'Dear teacher Kim, can you please do that?' (respectful)

Nonetheless, Nordlinger and Sadler (2008) highlight the difficulties of dealing with such categorizations in glossing, namely whether to define these categories with respect to the language specifically, or with respect to existing categories:

> [W]hen confronted with unfamiliar or previously undescribed linguistic phenomena, how do we know when to establish a new category to account for it, and when to redefine an existing one? To what extent is a category to be defined in terms of the internal oppositions of the language itself (that is, in terms of its positioning within the systems of the language under description), and to what extent should we impose preconceived notions of categories and their boundaries? These seem to us to be fundamental and difficult methodological points that we constantly face in linguistic research, most especially on under-described languages, and ones that warrant further discussion and reflection by the field as a whole.
>
> Nordlinger and Sadler, 2008, p. 329

Dealing specifically with the issue of glossing pragmatic particles, Kiaer (2021) proposes a possible solution to this conundrum, a lexical matrix which can reflect the multidimensional nature of pragmatic particles. This matrix consists of two dimensions: a constructive dimension that showcases how a clause is built up and closed off, and a socio-pragmatic dimension which indexes social hierarchy, interpersonal relations, mood and emotions, style (such as dialogue and monologue) and (speaker) perspective and attitude (Kiaer, 2021, p. 129).

'To say or not to say?' – that's what pragmatics tells you

In Asian languages, it is commonly observed that even the realization of subjects is pragmatically driven, and each context and register plays a crucial role in this. Expressions are realized based on a simple pragmatic principle: 'Say what is needed, when it is needed.' This echoes the Gricean maxim of quantity where one tries to be as informative as one possibly can, and gives as much information as is needed, and no more. That is, the explicit realization of expressions depends more on context and register than on whether the expressions are morpho-syntactically obligatory (i.e. arguments) or optional (i.e. adjuncts). Indeed, the decision as to whether an expression should be 'obligatory' or 'optional' cannot be made outside of the context and the decision is inherently pragmatic. Even most typical transitive verbs can be used without a visible argument on many occasions.

In many Asian languages, for example, the decision of whether or not to have an explicit second-person subject does not depend on the verb or the propositional structure, but on the interpersonal relationship between the speaker and the hearer. From an English mindset, the second-person pronoun 'you' can be used freely to anyone. You can use it to your senior, your junior, or to a stranger. Whatever the situation, you can use 'you'. Yet, in many Asian countries, when you are speaking to your senior, but do not have a particularly suitable address term, you would not choose an arbitrary second-person pronoun. Instead, you would indicate the subjecthood or objecthood non-verbally, such as through hand gestures.

To contrast, in French and German, two different second-person pronouns exist, yet their usage is not so sensitive to socio-pragmatic, interpersonal factors as in most Asian languages. In most Asian languages, whether to use an expression or not – to pronounce it or not – depends on socio-pragmatic factors such as the above or on contextual relevance. Hence, the decision is purely pragmatic and constantly changes depending on the situation. No matter whether the expression is a subject or an object, it all depends on pragmatic choices; a speaker has to consider whether it is necessary and appropriate to articulate. However, the pragmatic aspects of these decisions have received little attention. Instead, in the generative linguistics literature, a series of terms such as 'pro-dropness', 'deletion', 'omission' and 'ellipsis' have been somewhat casually used to describe the ways grammatical expressions are realized or not as above.

The term 'pro-drop' was first introduced by Chomsky (1981) to refer to the phenomenon of pronoun omission. Chomsky understands pro-drop as a sort of free-omission phenomenon shown by the following: 'The principle suggested is fairly general but does not apply to such languages as Japanese in which pronouns can be missing much more freely' (Chomsky, 1981, p. 284, fn 47). The term pro-drop is also used in other frameworks in generative grammar, such as in lexical functional grammar (LFG), but in a more general sense: 'Pro-drop is a widespread linguistic phenomenon in which, under certain conditions, a structural NP may be unexpressed, giving rise to a pronominal interpretation' (Bresnan, 1982, p. 384).

This phenomenon, however, is neither arbitrary nor accidental. Each time, the decision is made by very careful pragmatic calculation. Yet *how* the expressions are realized – that is to say, the pragmatic mechanism itself – has received little attention. According to WALS Chapter 101 (Dryer, 2013), among the languages attested, only 12 per cent of the world languages – that is, only eighty-two languages – showed obligatory pronouns in the subject position. However, even in those languages the obligatory nature is not so universal. In English and French, for instance, it is not rare to see the subjects not being explicitly said, typed or written. In fact, most world languages, not only Asian languages, show optionality in pronominal subject realization. Nevertheless, just like scrambling, pro-drop is often used to refer to a somewhat peculiar property of a limited set of languages. This seems inaccurate; it simply isn't an exceptional property. It is rather a property that is not so much shared by English and some Western European languages.

Coining an additional term such as 'pro-drop language' to refer to a vast range of languages such as Japanese, Korean, Turkish, Chinese and Swahili, among many others, can be misleading in making readers or researchers view pragmatic realization of expressions and particles as an arbitrary and optional omission, where is it assumed that the unsaid expressions only lost their phonetic values yet anyhow exist there invisibly. More technically speaking, according to quite an up-to-date generative standpoint, this can be viewed as *arbitrary PF (Phonetic Form) deletion* without any clear morpho-syntactic trigger. Simply put, the deleted forms are there like other expressions but, for some reason, they are not pronounced. (See Chapter 5 for further discussion on pro-drop and PF-deletion.)

This book proposes that each step of our linguistic study needs to be re-thought: from observation to explanation. Not only lexical expressions, but also particles show the same patterns of behaviours. Yet often the baseline assumption was the same, in that they are there – or should have been there – but for some reason, they are not said. Given that both particles and lexical expressions systematically operate based on their structural, semantic or pragmatic needs rather than in an arbitrary way, I think the somewhat ad hoc assumption to argue for the existence of invisible-yet-existing expressions needs to be seriously re-considered. (More discussion related to this will follow in later chapters.) Particles are realized and expressions are explicitly said when they are needed structurally, semantically or pragmatically. Unpragmatically, repeated particles, though grammatically legitimate, can make an utterance unnatural.

Simplicity hypothesis

In light of the above discussion, I propose the simplicity hypothesis: for what is simple in an ordinary speaker's daily production, the explanation also should be simple. What is 'simple' can be further defined as the variation that is easy to understand and produce; in other words, what is both cost-efficient and frequently observed, typically forms that persist through synchronic and diachronic variation. For these simple forms, the grammatical analysis should also be simple, which we would take to mean that the analytical framework is suitable. Therefore, if simple forms, that are easy to process and produce, require a relatively complex explanatory mechanism or a sequence of ad hoc explanations, the explanation method needs to be re-thought.

Exceptions and ad hoc explanations should be used for phenomena that are relatively uncommon and rare. Conversely, if the phenomenon is common but has to depend on an exceptional, ad hoc explanation, something is wrong – yet this is exactly what has been done in the study of Asian languages thus far, as I have demonstrated in my discussion of scrambling and pro-drop. As I discuss in the following chapter, both labelling and explanation together have become a notable problem in many of the existing generative frameworks.

Albert Einstein once said: 'Most of the fundamental ideas of science are essentially simple, and may, as a rule, be expressed in a language comprehensible to everyone' (Einstein & Inhelder, 1938, p. 29). He is alleged to have added: 'It should be possible to explain the laws of physics to a barmaid. If you can't explain it simply, you don't understand it well enough. Any intelligent fool can make things bigger and more complex.... It takes a touch of genius and a lot of courage to move in the opposite direction.' In the same spirit, syntax should be simple in order for it to be sensible. In fact, linguistic principles in general should seek simplicity so that they may make sense not only for specialists but for laypeople, or in the words of Einstein, a 'barmaid'.

Being frustrated by Anglocentric analysis

This chapter sought to provide context and articulate the key issue which this book will examine: the injustice done to the analysis of Asian languages in linguistics. Asian languages in particular exemplify syntactic 'creativity', a key feature of language that is at the heart of Chomskyan generative grammars, yet many linguists continue to impose an Anglocentric analysis which does not yield convincing conclusions.

Throughout my career as an educator of language and linguistics, I have witnessed first-hand the frustrations of many of my Asian language students who cannot make a direct link between linguistic theory and the language itself. Oftentimes, they view the theory as entirely separate from practice and think it unnecessary for learning and understanding the language itself. I, too, have experienced these very frustrations throughout my own studies. Theoretical linguistics, particularly within the domain of syntax, can quickly become overly abstract to the point where application seems forced and unnatural, even contradicting one's own valid linguistic intuition. This is disheartening to see.

Beyond Asian languages

So far, we have focused on Asian languages, but it should be stressed that the above discussion could be expanded to include other groups, such as African and Australian languages, all of which face similar problems. These languages are all so different from English and other Western European languages yet they, too, have been studied through an unsuitable lens. Within the circle of contemporary linguistics, indigenous perspectives been considered a second-class view and are subsequently marginalized. Many hybrid languages like creoles also receive little attention, and the attention that they do receive tends to only be relevant to those studying these varieties. Such prejudices are linked to the colonial past of these languages, in which English or another Western European language was given higher value than a native one. However, as Mufwene (2001) argues, creolistics should also contribute to the understanding of issues relevant to linguistics at large.

As well as uncelebrated languages, there exist uncelebrated varieties. For instance, within English, South Asian varieties function as prime examples. By 'uncelebrated', I mean that these varieties receive less attention in studies and, when they are studied, their local and ecological factors are not properly taken into consideration. This then yields some insensible views, in which what is ordinary and normal is interpreted as surprising, exceptional, or even 'ungrammatical'.

In order to combat Eurocentrism, we are in need of a more inclusive approach to our study of linguistics, in which perspectives from other languages, such as Asian languages, are adequately taken into account. After all, Asian languages are not minority languages, and we need to investigate how and why they are different. Mufwene (2001) points out that the lives of languages are all constrained by the ecological factors that are specific to their setting and time of emergence. Therefore, we should diversify the pool of languages that we research, so that we may draw a more accurate picture of what linguistics, the study of language(s), really is.

5

The Injustices of Syntactic Terminology and Architecture

Rethinking syntactic operations

In the Preface to the 50th Anniversary edition of *Aspects of the Theory of Syntax*, Chomsky wrote: 'A fair conclusion today, I think, is that the general framework outlined in *Aspects* remains appropriate, while the specific proposals have to be substantially modified and also extended to new domains of inquiry that have emerged in the years since' (2015, p. xvii). It is true that even after sixty years, not much has changed in Chomskyan linguistics. To this day, significant operational injustice persists in generative grammars. As it stands, syntactic operations are overly complex and difficult to understand, putting off many of those who may be interested in linguistic theory but have no formal training in the field; syntax does not seem to be something you can easily dip your toes into without prior knowledge. Throughout this book, and in this chapter, I intend to expose this problem and challenge the status quo, highlighting the need for simplicity. I will also examine how we decide what is at the core and the periphery of syntax (Sag, 2010). In making this decision, a balanced consideration of both data and intuition is crucial.

Core versus periphery

As Sag (2010) remarks:

> How are we to know which phenomena belong to the core and which to the periphery? The literature offers no principled criteria for distinguishing the two, despite the obvious danger that without such criteria, the distinction seems both arbitrary and subjective. The bifurcation hence places the field at serious risk of developing a theory of language that is either vacuous or else rife with analyses

that are either insufficiently general or otherwise empirically flawed. There is the further danger that grammatical theories developed on the basis of 'core' phenomena may be falsified only by examining data from the periphery – data that falls outside the domain of active inquiry.

Sag, 2010, p. 187

In generative grammar, this is a major issue which is related to the terminology used and lies in the heart of syntactic operations, as the literature offers no principled criteria for delineating the two. For instance, is scrambling really a peripheral phenomenon? What are the implications of placing it at the margins of our studies? Without a robust criteria, it is dangerous to make such distinctions as they may very well be inherently flawed. In this chapter, the matter of which syntactic phenomena belong to the core and which to the periphery is an important undercurrent which will help to propel our discussion.

Terminal injustice

Generative grammars have shown considerable bias, particularly with regards to terminology. For example, words such as 'behaviours' and 'learning' are very often perceived as taboo as Chomskyan linguistics places emphasis on what we're born with rather than what we develop throughout our lives. As I will expose in due course, the current theoretical frameworks are in serious need of reform to help bring justice to the study of languages across the world; this can begin with a reparation of the very terms that we use in our study. In this section, I focus on three areas of terminology that I think need re-evaluation: (i) *scrambling*; (ii) *pro-drop* and (iii) *disfluency* – the first two in particular are at the heart of Asian languages.

Scrambling: at the core or periphery?

As mentioned in the previous chapter, 'scrambling' is a phenomenon that describes the shift from a so-called canonical word-order into a non-canonical word-order (Ross, 1967; Saito, 1985). In other words, scrambling refers to orders that have 'scrambled' from a language's base word order. On a deeper level, this term helps to reaffirm the assumption within generative grammars that every language has a basic word order which is fundamental to its sentence structure. In contemporary linguistics, so-called 'scrambling languages' include some Asian languages, such as Japanese, Korean and Turkish, which thus highlights their flexibility as one of their main defining syntactic characteristics. Now, consider again the following definition found in the Oxford English Dictionary (OED) which describes the 'figurative' word *scrambling*: 'To collect or gather *up* hastily or in disorder [...] To jumble or muddle (something) [...] To make [...] unintelligible by means of a scrambler' (OED Online, 2022a). As mentioned in the Preface, this term carries negative connotations. In syntactic theory, scrambling is the key phenomenon that is used to denote structural variation. However, the label itself does a great injustice to the reality of syntax. Perhaps unsurprisingly, flexible word order is the norm cross-linguistically, yet why is it that the majority of us are made to seem like we are doing something wrong, that we are 'scramblers' deviating from the standard?

As a result, this term imposes a rather biased view; labelling a group of languages as scrambling suggests that they exhibit exceptional syntactic properties when this is not the reality. On a broader scale, looking at WALS (World Atlas of Language Structures), one finds that most languages across the world exhibit a great deal of flexibility. Furthermore, in both synchronic and diachronic variations, one is able to see that rigid ordering is not so common in human languages, much less in Asian languages (Kiaer, 2021). Even languages that have been widely considered to not fall under the category of *scrambling languages*, such as French, exhibit some freedom in word order. How is it then, that the most common, natural, 'default' form (that is, word order flexibility) has ended up with such a name as this?

To help illustrate the extent to which flexibility in word orders can be found cross-linguistically, I have included examples of a range of languages – including those which have generally been considered as having more rigid word orders in the literature. To begin with, Arnaiz (1998) notes that even for French, which may be seen as canonically SVO, in colloquial French, SVO is becoming more infrequent, and there is a tendency to shift towards a flexible word order that borrows pronominal clitics (p. 71). Song (2018) says that transitive clauses containing full noun phrases are uncommon in many languages, which use bound pronouns, pronominal clitics and/or noun incorporation (p. 228), with Siewierska (1988) further noting that word order can change between text types even within the same language (p. 12). Plotkin (2006) purports that even Romance languages generally have condition-free word order due to the presence of affixes, and that there are 120 different ways to say 'Mother gave Mike a toy on his birthday' in Russian by using just five linguistic units (p. 32). This is significant as Romance languages are some of the most widely spoken European/Eurocentric languages in the world.

Balogh (2013) provides the example of flexible word order in Hungarian, which is possible due to the rich inflection (pp. 2–3), which in the following examples indicates clearly the semantic roles.

(1) Hungarian

Bemutatta	Claire	Bent	Amynek
VM_{be}-introduced	Claire	Ben.ACC	Amy.DAT
Bemutatta	Amynek	Bent	Claire
VM_{be}-introduced*	Amy.DAT	Ben.ACC	Claire

Both sentences mean 'Claire introduced Ben to Amy.'
*VM = verbal modifier

Frajzyngier and Shay (2016) provide some examples of flexible word order in Polish. In this example (2), there are two neuter nouns for 'calf' (*cielę*) and 'child' (*dziecko*), which do not differentiate between nominative and accusative case, but the noun that appears first (left-most) will be the subject (*cielę*) and the noun that appears last (right-most) will be the object (*dziecko*) (Frajzyngier & Shay, 2016, p. 102). Therefore, the two nouns can be placed anywhere in the sentence and maintain the same meaning of 'A calf frightened a/the child' as long as the word for 'calf' comes precedes the word for 'child'.

(2) Polish

cielę	Przestraszyło	dziecko
calf.N	frightened.SG.N	child.N

cielę	Dziecko	przestraszyło
calf.N	child.N	frightened.SG.N

przestraszyło	cielę	dziecko
frightened.SG.N	calf.N	child.N

'A calf frightened a/the child.'

Furthermore, Johnston and Schembri (2007) note that many languages have flexible/free word order, including Australian Aboriginal languages and even canonically classical European languages like Latin, for which they provide an example of six Latin sentences all meaning 'Mark likes the horse', due to the suffix *–us* indexing subject and *–um* indexing object (p. 216):

(3) Latin

Marcus	equum	amat
Equum	Marcus	amat

Amat	equum	Marcus
Marcus	amat	Equum
Equum	amat	Marcus
Amat	Marcus	equum

'Mark likes the horse.'

Velupillai (2012) cites the example of flexible word order in Nhanda, an Australian language from the Pama-Nyungan group, with all six sentences having the same meaning due to case marking (p. 282):

(4) Nhanda

abarla-lu	wumba-yi	wur'a-tha
child-ERG	steal-PPERF	money-1SGOBL
S	V	O

abarla-lu	wur'a-tha	wumba-yi
S	O	V

wumba-yi	wur'a-tha	abarla-lu
V	O	S

wumba-yi	abarla-lu	wur'a-tha
V	S	O

wur'a-tha	wumba-yi	abarla-lu
O	V	S

wur'a-tha	abarla-lu	wumba-yi
O	S	V

'The child stole my money.'

That being said, depending on which word is being fronted, the focus/topic of the sentence may change, giving rise to slightly different interpretations (Velupillai, 2012, p. 282):

a. The child stole my money. [SVO]
b. The child my money stole. [SOV]
c. Stole it, the child did, my money. [VSO]
d. (There it was), stealing my money, the child. [VOS]
e. My money, the child stole. [OSV]

Mycock (2015) provides the example of flexible word order in Slovene, and though the two sentences are translated as 'I must read', the choice of either construction is related to pragmatic factors, as changing the positions of *moram* and *brati* will lead to slightly different emphases on either word (p. 56):

(5) Slovene
Moram   brati
must.PRS.1SG   read.INF
'I must **read**.'

brati   moram
read.INF   must.PRS.1SG
'I **must** read.'

Kennison (2014) provides examples of flexible word order in Finnish, whereby all six sentences mean 'the fish ate the worm' (p. 7):

(6) Finnish
Kala   söi   madon
fish-NOM   ate   worm-ACC

madon   söi   kala
worm-ACC   ate   fish-NOM

Söi   kala   madon
ate   fish-NOM   worm-ACC

Söi   madon   kala
ate   worm-ACC   fish-NOM

Kala   madon   söi
fish-NOM   worm-ACC   Ate

madon   kala   Söi
worm-ACC   fish-NOM   Ate
'The fish ate the worm.'

Fischer, Gabriel and Kireva (2014) provide the following example of flexible word order in Bulgarian, in which the three sentences have the same meaning (pp. 83–84):

(7) Bulgarian

Majkata	Dade	topkata	na	Deteto
mother.the	Gave	ball.the	to	child.the

Na	Deteto	dade	majkata	Topkata
to	child.the	gave	mother.the	ball.the

Na	Deteto	majkata	dade	Topkata
To	child.the	mother.the	gave	ball.the

'The mother gave the ball to the child.'

The examples included above constitute only the tip of the iceberg. The real problem is to explain the nature of flexibility in the assumption of 'rigid, fixed' word orders and, in order to tackle this, a re-evaluation of the term *scrambling* is required. At the heart of this investigation is the following question: how do we define what is core and what is peripheral? For so long, *scrambling* has been viewed as a peripheral phenomenon which affects only a handful of languages. However, as I have shown, this is in fact not the case. What is needed is a serious empirical investigation which takes a long, hard look at the data – not only from English and other Western European languages, but also from languages which have been understudied and marginalized.

Pro-drop and tense marking: at the core or periphery?

As outlined in the previous chapter, the term 'pro-drop' was first introduced by Chomsky (1981) to refer to the phenomenon of pronoun omission. Chomsky understands pro-drop as a sort of free-omission phenomenon shown by the following: 'The principle suggested is fairly general but does not apply to such languages as Japanese in which pronouns can be missing much more freely' (Chomsky, 1981, p. 284, fn 47). While this phenomenon has been perceived as arbitrary and/or accidental in generative grammar, I argue that this is not an adequate reflection of reality. Pro-drop is not an exceptional property, and the 'dropping' of a pronoun is based on a simple pragmatic principle that echoes the Gricean maxim: 'Say what is needed, when it is needed.' Each time, the decision is made by very careful pragmatic calculation, perhaps best exemplified through many Asian languages such as Korean in which even case particles can be explicitly or implicitly realized depending on a careful calculation of the pragmatics at hand. In fact, most world languages – not only Asian languages – show optionality in pronominal subject realization. Like scrambling, pro-drop is an inaccurate label, used to refer to a supposed peculiar property of a limited set of languages when reality reveals otherwise.

To begin with, Classical Greek and Latin share certain syntactic characteristics that were not handed down to all of the languages that derived from them, such as pronoun-drop (pro-drop) and word order variation (scrambling). While Spanish, Italian, Portuguese and Romanian are considered to be pro-drop languages with liberal subject omission, both English and French, which are widely understood as non-pro-drop languages, do show a degree of syntactic flexibility. Subject pronoun omission is becoming more common for English and French in informal communication, such as social media and texting. For example, the order of the direct object and indirect object is highly flexible in a ditransitive construction. Consider the examples below from English:

(8) a. I gave Mary a book.
b. I gave a book to Mary.

Some theoretical linguists have tried to distinguish which is the base structure and which is derived, but without a solid empirical foundation it would be dangerous to set a default form. Bock (1986) and work by Branigan et al. (2005) showed that the alternation between the two object expressions is influenced by syntactic priming and other weight factors (see Chapter 6 for further discussion). In principle, what they show is that English, too, exhibits flexibility similar to that of scrambling languages. In order to explain this flexibility, one needs to consider pragmatic factors; it is no longer the case of purely syntactic considerations. Furthermore, unlike Korean and Japanese, where subjects can be inferred from pragmatics, in Latin, Greek, Spanish, Italian, Portuguese and Romanian the null subject is retrieved through verb morphology. We see here that the verb-centrality bias and syntactic rigidity fails not only in the case of East Asian languages, but also in the case of many Latin-derived European languages.

To illustrate pro-drop in Latin and Classical Greek, I will give some examples below:

(9) Latin: Bene opus facit.
He/she works well.
(10) Greek: ἐκέλευσεν εἰσελθεῖν Ξενοφῶντα
He/she invited Xenophon to come in.

In both examples above, information regarding the referent of the verb is not given past the morphology, which tells us that it is a third person, singular referent. There is no overt pronoun in either sentence, so the reader must determine the subject through context (pragmatics). If an overt pronoun were to be used in the sentence, it would be for emphatic effect, and is often translated with the reflexive pronoun to demonstrate this emphasis (e.g. ὁ αὐτός ἐκέλευσεν εἰσελθεῖν Ξενοφῶντα, 'He himself invited Xenophon to come in.') It is difficult to see how so ubiquitous a feature of language could be misrepresented in contemporary generative grammar. In theory, the constituents of the sentences above could be rearranged in any way with the meaning remaining unchanged, although stylistic convention would still favour certain word orders. According to WALS, most of the world's languages have syntactic fluidity and pro-drop to a certain extent, while English is abnormally strict regarding overt pronouns and word order. When one learns Latin and Classical Greek and is exposed to null subjects for the first time, one is taught to determine the subject of the verb through an analysis of context (except in the case of first- and second-person verb forms where the subject is obvious). Thus, even in ancient European languages, pragmatics were at the heart of syntactic variation.

Stillings et al. (1995) note that pro-drop languages can include languages like Italian and Hebrew, with sentences that often omit overt subjects, such as how the sentence 'I speak' in Italian can be translated as *Io parlo* or simply *parlo*, with the first-person pronoun *Io* being optional (p. 401). This means that pro-drop is not something unique only to Asian and/or Middle Eastern languages, but can also be found in major European languages. Duguine (2017), in citing Dryer's 2013 survey of pro-drop in WALS, notes that pro-drop and null arguments are present in the majority (70 per cent) of the world's languages, with only a small percentage (11.5 per cent, which includes English, French, German, Icelandic etc.) expressing pronominal subjects under normal conditions (pp. 3–4). That being said, non-pro-drop languages do not strictly disallow pro-drop, as there are certain conditions in which null subjects are permitted, such as in subjects of imperatives, which leads Duguine to argue that the split between pro-drop and non-pro-drop languages is exaggerated (Duguine, 2017, p. 4). Zdorenko (2010) argues that distinguishing pro-drop and non-pro-drop on the basis of verb inflection is also erroneous because it does not explain how Asian languages like Mandarin and Cantonese can allow for null subjects yet have no subject–verb agreement (p. 120).

Huang (2000) notes that null objects may be found in many languages (not limited to Asian languages) even where there is no object agreement or object clitic, and she cites several of such examples (p. 78):

(11) European Portuguese
José	sabe	que	Maria	Ø	viu
José	knows	that	Maria		saw

'José knows that Maria saw (him)'

(12) Kinande (a Bantu language)
Arlette	a-	ka-	lengekanaya	Ati	na-	abiri-anza	Ø
			a			anza	
Arlette	SUBJ	TNS	think	That	SUBJ	TNS-love	

'Arlette thinks that I have come to love (her).'

Huang (2000) further provides some more examples from German (p. 79) and Tarifit (p. 89), a Berber language:

(13) German
Ø	Kenne	das	nicht
	Recognize	that	not

'(I) don't recognise that.'

(14) Tarifit
kurižžn	y-nna	Qa	Ø	ur	y-ssin	ad	y-ghnni
everyone	AGR(3M.SG)	That		NEG	AGR(3M.SG)	to	AGR(3M.SG)
	-said				-know		-sing

'Everyone said that (he) does not know how to sing.'

Twilhaar and van den Bogaerde (2016) provide some examples of pro-drop in Sign Language of the Netherlands and Spanish (p. 161):

(15) Sign Language of the Netherlands (NGT)
*INDEX$_1$ BROTHER   TON   INDEX$_{3a}$ KNOW   INDEX$_2$
'Do you know my brother Ton?'

TOMORROW$_{3a}$visit$_{1*}$
'Tomorrow he will visit me'

*INDEX refers to a pointing gesture usually done with the index finger with different grammatical functions, such as referring to entities (e.g. speaker and listener) present physically or being referred to (Twilhaar & van den Bogaerde, 2016, p. 95).

**The verb with numbers is a verb sign that signifies movement from a location to another, used for indicating subject–verb and/or object–verb agreement. Each number indicates a location, so 1 for example refers to the signer, and 3a is another addressee (Twilhaar & van den Bogaerde, 2016, p. xi). In the preceding sentence, INDEX$_{3a}$ and INDEX$_1$ has already introduced Ton and the speaker into the conversational context, so in the following sentence, the subject (Ton) and object (speaker) are left out, only being encoded in the verb sign $_{3a}$visit$_1$ through the change in location.

(16) Spanish
Voy
go.1SG
'I go'

Siewierska (2011) cites some examples of pro-drop in European languages (Hebrew is debatable as it is also a Middle Eastern language) by looking at Finnish and Hebrew (p. 78):

(17) Finnish
Tässä　　　　　　istuu　　　　　　mukavasti
Here　　　　　　sit.PRES.3SG　　comfortably
'Here one sits comfortably.'

(18) Hebrew
šot-im　　　hamon　　mic　　　ba　　arec
drink-PL　　lots　　　juice　　in　　country
'They drink lots of juice in Israel.'

Here is an example of pro-drop in Russian from Zdorenko (2010, p. 122):

(19) Russian
Hoch-u　　　　　　jabloko
want-1SG.PRES　　apple
'(I) want an apple.'

A plethora of other examples could have also been included, yet even from the discussion above, one can see how pro-drop is not an exceptional phenomenon. Again, the underlying issue involves investigating how we decide what is core and what is peripheral and the nature of the terms which we use in this decision.

Consider also tense. Past tense marking is observed cross-linguistically, however in some languages tense is optionally marked. Tense is at the head of a VP and projects its constituents. Thus, tense is at the core of generative grammar and signals the existence of the TP in generative syntax. However, TP perhaps cannot be used as a universal condition with which to evaluate syntactic structure in all languages, particularly those in which tense markings are not obligatory.

Languages of Southeast Asia comprise the greatest part of non-past marking languages in the world. For example, in Indonesian a simple sentence such as example (20) below can be interpreted in either the past or present tense depending on pragmatics:

(20) Indonesian
Air	itu	dingin.
Water	that	Cold

'The water is/was cold.' (Dahl & Velupillai, 2013)

These languages also do not make distinctions between the imperfective and perfective aspects. One proposed reason that they lack overt tense and aspect markings is that they are isolating languages, and tense and aspect are most often marked by inflection in the languages that do have them. According to WALS (Dahl & Velupillai, 2013), in their tested languages, there are 88 languages with no past tense present tense distinction, and 134 with the distinction.

Languages with tense are subdivided into three categories:

- Past/non-past distinction marked, no remoteness distinctions.[1]
- Past/non-past distinction marked, two to three remoteness distinctions.[2]
- Past/non-past distinction marked, four or more remoteness distinctions.[3]

The fourth group consists of languages with no grammatical marking of past/non-past distinction.[4] Many languages in group 4 are found in Asia, though mainly in Southeast Asia:

Ainu, Buli (in Indonesia), Burmese, Cantonese, Cebuano, Chepang, Hmong Njua, Indonesian, Javanese, Khmer, Khmu', Lahu, Lai, Lao, Mandarin, Maybrat, Meithei, Nicobarese (Car), Nivkh, Paiwan, Palaung, Pangasinan, Semelai, Sunandese, Tagalog, Thai, Tukang Besi, Vietnamese.

Group 4 languages are also found in multitudes in Africa and the Americas. Languages that do not have marked past/present tense distinction typically retrieve tense from pragmatics, and therefore either have null value T' in the TP that projects the verb phrase, or the framework needs to be revised. These languages are highly isolating, are normally zero-marking and have almost no inflectional morphology. Pragmatics may be an engine of syntactic production just as the verb is seen to be in generative grammar. Pragmatics may also have the ability to reveal much about the nature of structure building in languages, and is not a part of linguistics that can be seen as less important than other aspects such as syntax and semantics.

Put simply, it is unclear how we decide 'marked' or 'unmarked'. As it stands, it seems that this simply means whether or not a language behaves like English in terms of tense marking. However, a significant number of languages do not have a past or non-past distinction. This leads us to question the following: is it appropriate to think that an explicit past-tense marking is the default for all languages? Likewise, so many languages show syntactic flexibility and pragmatic sensitivity but trying to explain these as 'marked' fails to work. We therefore return to the key question: on what criteria do we base our decisions concerning what to place at the core and what to place at the periphery of syntax? Is it about whether or not a language behaves like English? Or, rather, *should* it be about whether or not a language behaves like English? Anglocentrism in syntactic studies needs to be properly addressed and dealt with in order to give a more just account of languages across the world.

Disfluency: at the core or periphery?

Over the past sixty years, we have seen a gradual shift in how disfluencies are perceived within linguistics. Initially, there was a tendency to disregard disfluencies entirely as an object of study: in *Aspects* (1965), Chomsky dismissed disfluencies as random, meaningless mistakes that should be left out of linguistic theory (Kahng, 2022, p. 189). Chomsky was more concerned with the workings of 'mental grammar' and argued that the flawed language production actually produced by humans '[does] not provide useful evidence about its nature' (in Guy, 2011, p. 252). Indeed, Chomsky dismissed entirely the notion that linguistics should be about studying the 'observed use of language' if linguistics were to be 'a serious discipline' (Chomsky, 1965, p. 4). Lyons (1972, p. 58) also described 'performance errors' as 'channel noise', implying that disfluencies are simply meaningless noise that is nonetheless not an impediment to communication.

Yet, disfluencies are notable for their sheer ubiquity. Spontaneous speech is rarely ever entirely free from some form of disfluency, and Goldman-Eisler (1968) estimated that 'as much as 50% of speaking time can be taken up by *umms* and *uhhhs* and silent pauses' (Goldman-Eisler, 1968, in Bock & Ferreira, 2014). These disfluencies are 'not the result of faulty competence' and are also seen in the speech of native speakers (Loewen & Reinders, 2011, p. 33).

Given how common disfluencies are in our speech, they have gradually attracted the attention of linguists interested to find out whether there could be some meaning behind the seeming randomness of disfluencies. Fromkin et al. (2019, p. 112) point out that 'even conversational fillers such as *er, uh* and *you know* in English are constrained by the language in which they occur', suggesting that disfluencies do indeed belong in the realm of linguistics. Allison and Chanen (2012, p. 112) also note that 'fillers and blunders [...] are a marker of our speech and these markers can be interpreted by others'. In other words, the researchers are pointing out that listeners do indeed pay attention to the disfluencies of their speech partner and work to glean meaning from them in the same way that they interpret any other element of speech. As early as 1970, Cook and Lalijee also suggested that 'speech may be more comprehensible when it contains filler material during hesitations by preserving continuity and that filled pauses may serve as a signal to draw the listener's attention to the next utterance', arguing that speech disfluencies could be implicated in turn taking and listening. A similar argument was made by David et al. (2010, p. 138): 'the ability to recognize and treat speech disfluencies [...] as meaningful social properties of speech (such as indicating correction, punctuation, reordering) is a social skill necessary for communication. The sequential position of these features can impact on how turns of talk are understood and how words are heard'. In other words, interpreting disfluencies can even be viewed as a skill that must be acquired by listeners in order to aid smooth communication. In these senses, disfluency can be seen as a useful function of language, even if it is largely generated unconsciously.

Yet, in generative grammars, these so-called extra-linguistic features, which show the limitations of memory, articulation and other factors, are often dismissed and viewed as not worth researching. In other words, they are seen as performance problems and not at all relevant to linguistic competence. Yet I argue that this is simply wrong. Since early in Chomsky's career, behaviour has been perceived as irrelevant to a study of syntax and there has subsequently been less emphasis on the learning aspect of language. The famous study on Nim Chimpsky and language acquisition strengthened this stance as it showed how chimpanzees cannot be as generative as humans. Yet, to state the obvious, we are not chimpanzees! A rather pessimistic view, in line with Chomskyan theory, is that after a set number of years, that's it – we've learned all there is to language. However, I believe we need a balanced view of nature and nurture which are, in essence, two sides of the same coin. What's more, I believe an understanding of the essence and limitations of human language can be found in disfluencies. The following sections of this chapter will discuss how features like disfluencies give important insight on the nature of human language which is significantly resource-limited, as well as shed light on the different strategies which can be used to repair constructions. Examining what we consider to be core and peripheral, but more importantly, *how* we come to this distinction, is the key concern. In doing so, we can return to the root of linguistic investigation: finding out what human language can and can't do.

Operational injustice

Wittgenstein (1953, PI 66) once said, 'Don't think, but look!' I cite again the words of Wittgenstein, which remind us of the need to take a proper look at the data and our current framework, rather than remaining content with unconvincing arguments. I wish it were possible to repair these problems through quick and easy fixes – but it isn't, sadly. In particular, the attributes we see in Asian languages and their differences from English are not properly considered in the studies. In order to give them fuller justice, serious work is required. This chapter focuses on the key areas of concern regarding operational injustices and the extent to which change is necessary. We need to pause and look, before re-thinking and explaining matters in a sensible manner; we need to raise our game.

In the next half of this chapter, I will examine in more detail the following six architectural concerns:

- Output-only syntax (no procedural syntax).
- Frequency asymmetry.
- Anglocentrism in decision-making.
- Verb-centred architecture.
- Independently motivated rules.
- Pragmatic/ecological insensitivity.

Now, the solution to these problems will not be an easy fix. However, rather than constructing complex theoretical solutions within the existing framework, I simply seek to examine these matters. Upon closer inspection and more detailed explanation, it should be clear that we need a shift in perspective. For example, while syntactic flexibility and pragmatic sensitivity are shared by languages across the board, these architectural elements have been marginalized. I thus try to draw much-needed connections between these factors and linguistic theory. Throughout this book – but particularly in this chapter – I intend to make us scrutinize the fundamental assumptions in generative grammars in order to find sensible answers to these core issues.

Output-only syntax (no procedural syntax): the importance of 'how'

Syntactic architecture is in constant construction. We can gather what's happening not only from what's been built but also from the way we build – the *how* matters as much as the final product. Yet, to this day, major syntactic frameworks cannot tolerate indeterminism in structural representation. In other words, explanation is only for the 'complete sentence' – not for the 'to-be-completed' sentences. That said, without considering the procedures, we are unable to see what happens and why it happens. This is not a minor issue, but a major concern.

We build syntactic representations in a step-by-step way and process it in a step-by-step way. Without understanding this procedural nature, we cannot even define what constitutes a constituent – the very basic building block of our syntactic architecture. Phillips (1996, 2003) showed that the basics of syntax, such as defining a constituent, cannot be established without considering the resource-sensitive, procedural aspects of syntactic structure building. The same string of words can be diagnosed as a constituent by one constituent test, but not by another constituent test. Example (21) below, taken from Phillips (2003), shows a case of constituency conflict. When coordination is taken as a test for constituency, in (5a), *Gromit a biscuit* passes the coordination test and thus is regarded as a constituent. In (21b), however, *Gromit a biscuit* cannot pass the movement test and thus is not regarded as a constituent.

(21) [Gromit a biscuit] is a constituent according to the co-ordination test
a. *Wallace gave [Gromit a biscuit] and [Shawn some cheese] for breakfast.*
[Gromit a biscuit] is NOT a constituent by movement test.
b. **[VP Gromit a biscuit] Wallace gave VP* for breakfast.*

Based on the constituency shift and constituency conflict phenomena, Phillips argued for the Incrementality Hypothesis, as described in (22).

(22) *Sentence structures are built incrementally from left-to-right.*

Phillips assumed that syntactic relation must respect constituency at the point in the derivation when the relation is established. Yet, once this relation is licensed, constituency may change subsequently (i.e. be revised); and this, he argued, was the basis for such conflict. Given that defining constituency is a crucial matter in syntax, it is striking that such a core notion is difficult to sustain without considering left-to-right growth of a structure. Not only building, but repairing, evaluation and understanding all happen little by little. The principle which describes this – incrementality – is well-proved in psycholinguistic study. However, current formalisms are unable to provide a satisfactory account because they cannot tolerate indeterminate structures, that is to say structures which are not finished. As we shall see later in this chapter, this causes a serious problem for verb-final languages and many languages which allow verbless clusters. This is because, in these cases – in the absence or delay of verbs – nothing will be considered finished for they will all be considered as not-yet-finished. Phillips' example shows the importance of a new syntax which cares for the syntactic processes and not only the output, and this is also the case for this book – processes matter. Not only in more traditional generative frameworks, but also in lexicalist frameworks such as Combinatory Categorial Grammar (CCG), the structural derivation is not fully time-sensitive. What I mean by this is that, at the point of derivation, all structures have to be known, which is not intuitive. Syntactic architecture is revealed and unfolded gradually – the more you hear the linguistic sequence, the more you understand the meaning and structure. No one can fully grasp the whole structure and meaning at the word level alone. Yet, in order for an explanation to work, one has to assume the complete output and, to do so, has to go through complex processes such as type-raising (see Kiaer, 2021).

Frequency asymmetry: domain matters

Grammaticality is often considered as the window to linguistic intuition and competence, and whether or not a string was considered 'grammatical' is normally a binary distinction: possible vs impossible. Yet, what about the following contrast: easy-and-frequent vs difficult-and-rare? With regards to syntactic variation, this contrast is more visible than the possible vs impossible one. I propose that the easy-and-frequent vs difficult-and-rare distinction also warrants adequate investigation, for it can be meaningful and important for our understanding of the distribution of patterns cross-linguistically, as well as bring insight to our understanding of syntactic architecture more broadly. In line with the quote from Ball (n.d.), I posit that syntactic patterns and their frequency – the latter of which is generally ignored in generative grammars – are indeed spontaneous but by no means arbitrary.

While this proposal may be seen as odd and to go against the spirit of our time, data-driven methods are not perfect – a balanced perspective is necessary. This is why I argue in favour of the simplicity hypothesis. The big data clearly says something, but what does it say exactly? Upon closer inspection, it is noticeable that there is a 'weight effect' (such as the need for intervening expressions that separate phrasal verbs to be short). Indeed, this was discussed from the very beginning of generative grammar (see Wasow 2002 for a detailed discussion and history). However, the glaring problem was its lack of attention. If the domain becomes too long or too heavy – if it is domain-inefficient – then the structure is not easy-and-frequent. The focus for this section is therefore domain issues, which have been considered unimportant in generative grammars. In short, domain-efficient structures are preferred, whereas domain inefficient ones are avoided. Consider the constructions below:

(23) Pat picked up a very large mint-green hard cover book.

(24) ??Pat picked a very large mint-green hard cover book up.

(25) ???????? Pat picked a very large mint-green hard cover book – that's actually my Syntax book that I forgot to bring to the school … up.

Unfortunately, no grammarian can really put the '*' mark for the example of (25). The difference between (23)–(24) and (24)–(25) is hard to explain, too. From (23) to (24) to (25), grammaticality is degraded but there is nothing in generative grammar which properly explains this. Why? Well, that's because linguistic competence is believed to be insensitive to matters of weight, for example. However, in a study of the British National Corpus on phrasal verbs with intervening expressions, my colleague and I found that when the intervening expression becomes longer, the articulation speed tends to become faster (Sherr-Ziarko & Kiaer, 2019). This shows that speakers make an effort to 'squeeze' longer object expressions in order to shrink the domain of the phrasal verbs and make it prosodically memorable. The size of the domain matters in any grammatical operation because human parsers have a limited ability to produce and understand a linguistic sequence in a given time. Yet this area, too, has been under-explored. This is due to the persistent view which can be traced back to an old generative mindset: where the individual's resources are limitless, memory and articulation limitations are irrelevant in unboxing human linguistic competence. However, as discussed, domain sensitivity is relevant to grammaticality judgements. Even in evaluation then, domain matters.

The discussions on domain are further elaborated in Hawkins (1994, 2004), where he proposed the notion of minimized domain (MiD) to capture and explain the resource-sensitive, efficient nature of structure building and dependency resolution.

(26) Minimized Domains (MiD):

The human processor prefers to minimize the connected sequences of linguistic forms and their conventionally associated syntactic and semantic properties in which relations of combination and/or dependency are processed. The degree of this preference is proportional to the number of relations whose domains can be minimized in competing sequences of structures, and to the extent of the minimisation difference in each domain.

Hawkins, 1994, 2004.

The size of the domain is significant because human parsers clearly have limitations in terms of working memory and physical articulation (Gick, Wilson & Derrick, 2012). Since its beginnings, the Chomskyan mindset assumes the ordinary speaker's flawless and limitless ability to acquire their mother tongues. However, speaking and talking are highly resource-sensitive behaviours. It is clear, then, that speed and the length of the prosodic domain matter.

A short distance between the two functionally related lexical items is desirable for the sake of least effort. Yet, this isn't the complete story as the domain needs to be prosodically sensitive. Fodor (2002) and her colleagues argued that people use default 'prosodic' information even in silent reading. I take this insight to the forefront and argue that prosody is one of the most important driving forces for structural realization. In particular, the ideal domain is not just arbitrarily minimized but prosodically sensitive. For instance, we speak through the course of breathing. Though we want to express many things in a limited period of time, there is a clear limit in the number of syllables that we can pronounce 'within a span of time' (Gick et al., 2012).[5]

Cross-linguistically, speakers aim to attune syntactic structure to a prosodic structure through appropriate prosodic phrasing, using the right number of pauses and the correct speech rate. This tuning process – that is, finding the right combination – may be universally inherent to all languages. It seems that the most efficient ways of packaging syntactic and prosodic structures tend to survive and thrive over time as patterns of speech that become default among the speech community of the language. In other words, the way in which people speak in their day-to-day life naturally reflects how structure and sound are packaged in the most efficient possible way. In this book, I propose that survived and thrived forms are the ones that are produced within the remit of auditory-working memory and articulatory one-breadth limit – mostly close to one Intonational Phrase (IP). The prosody of folk song lyrics is a good example for this claim. Most folk songs that have survived and thrived over time in a given region naturally fit within the prosodic and memory structure of the language spoken by the regional community. In short, a memorable domain would survive, whereas a forgettable domain would not.

Anglocentrism in decision-making: do we need magic goggles?

Across the world, most languages have the properties which Asian languages share – that is to say, syntactic freedom and pragmatic sensitivity. However, why is it that we have to make a base assumption that languages all (should) behave like English?

Let us now briefly consider pro-drop again. Originally, Chomsky described this phenomenon as 'arbitrary', but I argue that this description is wrong. As we have already seen in this chapter, pro-drop is found not only in Asian languages, but in many languages across the world. Whether to explicitly realize a pronoun or not is not an arbitrary decision – rather, it is highly sensitive to pragmatic necessity.

That said, in generative grammars, elliptical phenomena – such as sluicing, predicate ellipsis, nominal ellipsis, gapping, stripping and fragments[6] – are perceived as being silent but actually present. Accounts have argued that the word or clause is simply unpronounced in PF (Merchant, 2001). In generative grammar the PF-deletion approach is widely adopted. According to the current status quo in the field, the PF-deletion approach is a cover term used for approaches assuming full syntactic representation and PF-non-realization of ellipsis sites. This approach has its origins in earlier accounts of deletion in which syntactic structures were subject to non-pronunciation (Ross, 1967; Sag, 1976; Hankamer, 1979).[7] PF-deletion approaches differ in stating what PF-non-realization amounts to, and how and when ellipsis 'happens' in the course of the derivation: either only in the PF branch of the grammar or already in narrow syntax. In this respect, two types of proposals can be distinguished. On the one hand, non-derivational PF-deletion proposals of ellipsis claim that ellipsis applies only in PF and does not interfere with the narrow syntactic computation. On the other hand, derivational ellipsis proposals claim that ellipsis interferes with the narrow syntactic computation in specific ways and thus it already applies in the syntax. Derivational approaches share the view that, as soon as ellipsis takes place, the ellipsis site becomes inaccessible, with the effect that no further operations can target parts of the ellipsis site.

The question of how lexical items form representations in the surface structure is one which has occupied syntacticians for fifty years. Generative grammars have proposed that passive structures were generated by movement from active structures (Chomsky, 1965). Different branches of generative grammars have varying accounts on the exact nature of the movement, but in general they all assume three empty categories (*wh*-movement, NP- movement and ellipsis). However, Ferreira et al. (2013) argue that the evidence of movement, known as 'traces' or 'gaps', requires further investigation. For example, while the study of Bock et al. (1992) is cited, its conclusion is rejected. On the basis of evidence from syntactic priming whereby the syntactic structure was only primed through the surface representation, rather than the deep structure representation, Bock et al. (1992) argued that syntactic structures are generated directly, rather than going through a two-stage process involving deep structure representation. Ferreira et al. (2013) instead argue in favour of a third alternative: that traces do not exist. While Ferreira et al. (2013) ultimately draw only the most equivocal of conclusions that the existence of traces should be examined further, perhaps with regard to the unstudied phenomenon of ellipsis, the tone, structure and phrasing of their argument mean that the connotation, rather than the denotation, is one that refutes the existence of traces in syntactic structures and thus calls into question the assumptions underpinning generative grammar.

Another proposed account is that PF-deletion involves some kind of deficiency, but this analysis is unsatisfactory. While PF-deletion accounts of ellipsis enjoy popularity in the generative framework, the PF-deletion accounts currently on the market are far from uniform about an important, but often somewhat neglected, aspect of elliptical phenomena – namely the exact *derivational timing* of the ellipsis as an operation. In order to understand the derivational timing of ellipsis, which refers to the point at which ellipsis applies in the Y-model, the matter boils down to locating ellipsis in the architecture of the grammar.

As we can see from this discussion, while all PF-deletion proposals agree that ellipsis is 'operationalized' in PF – in the sense that ellipsis manifests itself as some kind of a deficiency of certain operations at PF, resulting in missing phonetic material (thus the term 'PF-deletion') – opinions differ on what type of PF deficiency ellipsis represents and whether this deficiency has any symptoms already present in syntax. However, I draw attention to an often-dismissed aspect of PF-deletion: pragmatics.

The most popular account of PF-deletion is that it's an effort-saving approach, but I argue that it is an inherently pragmatic decision – one that is perhaps best exemplified by Asian languages. A major theme in the analysis of ellipsis is that the silence is somehow superficial (Güneş & Lipták, 2022: in their general preface). In other words, it's unpronounced but you should imagine that it's there. Does this mean we need to put on magic goggles in order to see it? This account simply lacks explanatory power. Ellipsis is systematic – not arbitrary. The key take-away is the following: you decide what to say and what not to say based on pragmatic calculations.

Verb-centred architecture: a verbal myth

The English word 'verb' derives from the Latin 'verbum', which denotes the general idea expressed in contemporary English as 'word'. The word 'verb' has adopted a more focused meaning and now denotes a specific part of speech that projects various different argument structures depending on the type of verb, and typically carries meanings associated with actions and states of being. In the plural, 'verba' stood for language and discourse in general. In the original sense of the word, all words were 'verbs'. Perhaps Latin saw no need to create such a category that exists in Anglocentric linguistics today because it had a rich case system; the verb did not hold all the combinatory power of the utterance. Instead, it was shared with case-marked nouns, which indexed the role of the noun in the utterance. The verb has taken on the predominant role in the Western European sentence, perhaps because there are no nominal case markings that provide syntactical information independent of the verb. This is not the case in many other languages, particularly Asian languages, many of which have complex systems of particle-marked cases. The verb is simply another 'verbum' in these languages, and is not seen as being more important than any other word in the syntactic architecture. Constructive case particles are used in conjunction with a verb to denote syntactic roles, but a speaker can predict ultimate sentence structure as it unfolds due to these particles. This is similar to Latin, where case-marked nouns allow readers or speakers to develop their syntactic comprehension of the sentence in an incremental manner. This reflects the original, general meaning of 'verbum', whereby all words in a sentence act as 'verbs' in some way.

While the verb carries important information, it does not contain all the combinatory information. In the Anglocentric formalism, it is claimed that the verb projects certain argument structures that must then be satisfied by the other constituents of the sentence. This is a reductionist view of syntax that is sentence-based, rather than constituent-based. In many Asian languages, it is not solely the verb that contains all the combinatory information at the syntactic level, particles and other sentential constituents also play a major role. Instead, in Asian linguistics, meaning is created incrementally through the use of constructive case particles. Thus, speakers of Asian languages are not in the dark as to the structural composition of a sentence before the verb comes, but are able to predict what type of verb may come later given the combinatorial information contained in the constructive case particles that come before it. In many Western European languages, the verb comes early in the sentence and lays the blueprint for the types of constituents that one would expect to come later in the sentence. By contrast, in Asian languages, the constituents of the sentence, including constructive case particles, allow an interlocutor to predict what type of verb may come later in the sentence. In other words, the lexical elements contain information that is then confirmed by the verb which appears later in the sentence. As it stands, generative grammar tends to account for flexible word order and verb-finality with ad hoc performance-based explanations which fail to describe the true nature of these phenomena. Thus, a verb-centred conceptualization is unsatisfactory in terms of explaining the array of variation found in the world's languages.

This leads us to the question: 'If verb-finality causes such trouble or inefficiency, why is it that there are so many verb-final languages in the world (even more than verb-initial languages)?' Verb finality tends to be a property of languages that also have flexible word ordering. In the grand scheme of things, more languages across the world exhibit verb-finality than verb-initiality. Given this, it is inconceivable to say that linguistic features of verb-final languages are inefficient or performative. Instead, efficiency cannot be explained by the verb, although it can be so in Western European languages. Asian languages that exhibit verb-finality have developed in such a way that suits the history, culture, religion and politics of the respective areas, and the complex environments that they are found in.

Kiaer (2007, 2014, 2021) argued for the constructive particles which behave like little verbs in OV languages and project the structural skeleton. Constructive particles have been shown to behave like verbs in the sense of their combinatory power. They contain syntactic information that is projected onto the remainder of the sentence, including other constructive particles. Unlike English, where strict word order is the main factor in determining a sentence constituent's syntactic role, in many Asian languages one understands the role of a constituent through the case particles attached to it. Not only do constructive particles allow interlocutors of Asian languages to create and comprehend meaning incrementally, but other multimodal cues such as prosody play an important role too.

As for scrambling, you simply can't control word order freedom with rules. Instead, we need to acknowledge that the ordering, by default, is flexible and not everything necessarily revolves around the verb. This means that we change the order of expressions due to particular pragmatic needs (see Chapter 6 for further discussion). However, generative grammars, both in the transformational and non-transformational traditions, have taken great care in terms of setting the orders and controlling them (see Kiaer, 2021, chapter 2 for more detail).

Verb-centredness also has implications on constituency (unit-hood). In order to determine what is a constituent, one needs to assume that the verb has been moved. Without this assumption, you cannot explain anything at all. What's more, to account for the variation in order within the constituent, a rule known as 'surprising constituent' was invented, when in reality the constituent would be considered natural and normal to an ordinary speaker.

Syntacticians need to acknowledge that languages across the world exhibit a degree of word order freedom. Deciding which order is used more often in certain situations involves pragmatic considerations each time. In doing so, what affects word order and the realization of arguments the most are pragmatic matters – matters which Chomsky viewed as non-linguistic, or extra-linguistic, and unimportant materials that have no place in syntax. According to Chomsky, factors like memory and cost-efficiency (what I call pragmatic matters) are not the direct cause of any syntactic variation and are therefore not worth examining. However, as I argue throughout this book, these pragmatic factors are the real causes of syntactic variation. In sum, to explain word order flexibility, Baldridge and many others have thus put more control over the lexicon. However, fundamentally, if we start restricting the lexicon, the rules become useless. After all, can we really stipulate the behaviours that are inherently free in the lexicon?

In addition, the existence of tenseless, verb-less structures poses some challenges in generative grammar. Are these exceptional? Or are the tensed verbs un-pronounced? The main problem is how theories presuppose the need for a verb and argue that it has moved out. In fact, verb-less structures are not rare but rather common cross-linguistically. Even without a verb, people can understand and build structures.

Consider the Moroccan Arabic examples below (Aoun et al., 2009).

(27) Moroccan Arabic
a. ʕomar muʕəllim
Omar teacher
'Omar is a teacher.'

(28) d-dar kbira
the-house big
'The house is big.'

If it is indeed a verb alone which projects a structural skeleton, it remains a puzzle to explain verb-less sentences that are not rare cross-linguistically.

Yet, it seems that the existence of verb-less clauses is universal to all languages.

Consider the Mandarin Chinese examples in (29) from Shei (2014, p. 106).

(29)
    (a) *Zhe4   ge5   hua4ti2   hen3   re4*   [Mandarin Chinese]
        this   topic   very   hot
       'This topic (is) very hot.'
    (b) *Dong1tian1   le5*
       Winter   SFP
       '(It is) winter already.'
    (c) *Yi4   bai3   wan4   le5*
       One   million   SFP
       '(We have) one million already.'

Similarly, in Turkish, nominal sentences in which no explicit verbal expressions are used are common, as below. (30) is from Göksel and Kerslake (2011, p. 160). In this example, there is no copular verb 'be'.

    (30) *İstanbul büyük bir şehir.*   [Turkish]
         'Istanbul [is] a big city.'

Verb-less structures are found in Burmese, too. (31) is from Jenny and Tun (2016, p. 248).

    (31) *Di shainkɛ kəlaʔ mə-pa-bù.* [Burmese]
         this motorbike clutch NEG-included-NEG
         'This motorbike doesn't have a clutch.'

Consider the Kazakh example below. This is from Muhamedowa (2015, p. 2).

    (32) *Qazaqstanda orïstar köp.* [Kazakh]
         Kazakstan-LOC Russian-PL many
         'There are many Russians in Kazakhstan.'

Looking at the above, verb-less structures can be observed cross-linguistically, as discussed in greater depth by Sadler and Nordlinger (2006). What's more, in the poetic genre, verbs are often unsaid and only assumed. In the case of Biblical Hebrew, poetic portions of the Hebrew Bible contain many examples of nominal sentences which do not have a verb at all. Instead, repeated structures or other poetic tools are used in constructing a structure.

Independently motivated rules: What's their deal?

In generative grammars there is a very theory-internal mindset of making the rules simple and efficient. Appeals to computational efficiency in generative grammar first came to the fore in the early 1990s, with the emergence of principles whose name and content evoked a concern for locality and economy – notions that invite a more general computational interpretation. One such principle is the Minimal Link Condition (Chomsky, 1995, p. 264), which states: 'Make moves as short as possible.'

While trying to simplify rules, and in doing so, to find some elegance in the theory seems to make sense, the way in which Chomsky motivates it – 'do whatever is as short as possible' –is kind of arbitrary and not philosophically, psychologically or empirically well-founded. In other words, it's a theory-internal way of making things simple. But what does it mean to be simple? Is it all about arbitrary rules and exceptions? Generative theory is known as a theory where there are exceptions to exceptions, but I think that such a strategy is not very productive if there is no solid philosophical, psychological or empirical grounding. This is why I have proposed the simplicity hypothesis (see Chapter 4).

Contemporary generative grammars are characterized by numerous independently motivated rules that are added in an ad hoc manner, as has been the case since Ross's work in 1967. Often, I find these rules to be arbitrarily made without any compelling reasons (for further discussion, see Kiaer, 2021). It's hard to deny that these rules are proposed to fit the theory rather than the data. For instance, scrambling is used to describe languages with a free word order, but even English has a degree of syntactic flexibility. While the general schema dictates that the verb comes earlier, pragmatic factors play a crucial role in shaping syntax, and it's unfair to classify languages that exhibit this flexibility as 'fixed word order languages'. Again, we find ourselves caught in the middle of an unresolved deal in which we negotiate data for theory or theory for data.

Pragmatic/ecological insensitivity: context is key

Chomsky (1965, p. 3) states: 'Linguistic theory is concerned primarily with an ideal speaker-listener, in a completely homogeneous speech-community, who knows its language perfectly and is unaffected by such grammatically irrelevant conditions as memory limitations, distractions, shifts of attention and interest, and errors (random or characteristic) in applying his knowledge of the language in actual performance'. This is quite troublesome. Chomsky describes grammar as 'unaffected' by pragmatic matters, but I refute this claim. I think that pragmatic factors are the real causes of variation and only they can make syntactic accounts sensible. Consequently, one cannot provide a satisfactory account on the argument–adjunct distinction or the big problem of ellipsis.

Considering scrambling and pro-drop as somewhat arbitrary and exceptional processes is fundamentally the output of an Anglocentric view – after all, English doesn't explicitly show these two properties. Yet, as we see in this book, according to WALS, most languages in the world – not just Asian languages – do indeed have these two properties to a certain extent. Earlier in this chapter, we even saw that English allows for some word order flexibility when it comes to ditransitive constructions. Regarding the basis on which these two properties work, it is pragmatic in nature. As I have argued in my previous works (Kiaer, 2007, 2014, 2021), pragmatics is at the heart of syntactic variation.

Pragmatic insensitivity: the primary cause of syntactic injustice

There are many reasons why there are huge operational problems in the area of syntactic theory. However, the biggest is due to pragmatic insensitivity. Whether or not to say a word or clause, how to order a sentence, these matters boil down to pragmatics. Languages across the world are highly sensitive to diverse pragmatic needs but often the key issues that help us to calculate pragmatic necessity are considered irrelevant in the grammar. Syntactic flexibility and pragmatic sensitivity are indeed language universals, but in a strict Chomskyan framework, extra-linguistic and resource-sensitive elements are unimportant (Chomsky, 1965, p. 3), thereby leading to a gaping chasm regarding theory and practice. This is where the true problem occurs and linguistic theory loses its touch! The problem isn't to do with the phenomena themselves – we can find them in languages across the world, not just in Asian languages – but rather, the problem lies in our generative toolbox in which we carry notions of strict word orders, verb-centredness and Anglocentric bias, amongst others. These architectural issues appear to be almost insurmountable, and without a thorough reevaluation that takes pragmatic factors into account, they could continue to restrict our understanding of human language.

6

Pragmatic Matters

No magical matters, but pragmatic matters

Chomsky (1965, p. 3) observed that linguistic theory primarily concerns an ideal speaker-listener, who knows the language perfectly and is unaffected by irrelevant conditions like memory limitations, distractions, shifts of attention and interest, and errors in applying language knowledge during performance. It is ironic that Chomsky's classification of 'irrelevant matters' under the umbrella of pragmatics appears to offer the most convincing explanation for the observed variations in language use. These seemingly unimportant factors play a crucial role in shaping language use in different contexts and among diverse groups. By recognizing the significance of these elements, we can gain a deeper understanding of the complexity and richness of human language. Pragmatic considerations are central to understanding variation in language, alongside other ecological and contextual factors. There are no abstract or magical features that can explain the linguistic diversity found in everyday language, as well as diachronic, synchronic and typological variation.

Resource-sensitivity

This book shows how natural language syntax *is* resource-sensitive, contrary to Chomsky's initial claims. As an Asian pragmatist, I can say that pragmatics matter and will matter more in deepening understanding of Asian languages. It may seem unusual to discuss pragmatics in a syntax book. However, the motivation behind syntax is essentially pragmatic in nature. Pragmatics plays a key role in explaining both syntactic freedom and morpho-syntactic realization of expressions. I have proposed 'pragmatic syntax' in my previous publications (Kiaer, 2014, 2021). Humans generate limitless linguistic sequences throughout their lives, but their linguistic generation is limited by given resources and circumstances. This means that we cannot remember everything we hear, nor can we produce long sentences at the speed of ChatGPT. In everyday conversation, it's common for us to use filler words like 'uh' and 'eh', which can indicate that we're struggling with our speech and listening due to limited resources. However, within these given resources and circumstances, humans make the most optimal, pragmatic choices – choices that are never arbitrary or based on magical features. This is what distinguishes human generation from AI generation. In this chapter, I will introduce three key pragmatic motivations: efficiency, expressivity and empathy. These motivations are what each situation and person juggles to produce their syntactic output. These aspects are what distinguish the human generation from the AI generation.

Prosodic matters

Syntactic analyses focus solely on soundless input and overlook prosodic cues as insignificant. For a long time, theoretical linguists studied languages in isolation, as if humans spoke in a vacuum, which is far from the reality of how we communicate. Though generative grammarians have regarded syntactic competence as being expressed in spoken – rather than written – language, ironically almost every example used in the syntactic literature is from a written source. There is some implicit belief that there is no significant difference between written and spoken syntax. However, the two can be quite different. Chomskyan linguistics often talks about spontaneous data. Yet, importantly, the data that has been studied is very much refined and of a particular form – that is the 'sentence' – rather than the data that you can collect in a real spontaneous manner. During the generative syntax years, only 'speaker-hearer-absent' written sentences are treated as manifestations of linguistic competence.

Being pragmatic means understanding that resources are limited, so we need to use them wisely, particularly when it comes to communication. Humans have several limitations when it comes to speaking and listening, such as limited articulation and memory capacity. To work around these constraints, we break long sentences into smaller, more manageable parts. The length and size of our speech play a crucial role in how effectively we communicate, and without considering prosody it's tough to explain syntactic variation. To improve grammaticality, we often need to rearrange expressions to ensure a better prosodic balance.

Human articulation matters

Articulation refers to the movement of speech organs during the production of sounds such as via the formation of words (Parker, 2012, p. 415). Physiologically, articulation is carried out by articulators such as the mouth, tongue and larynx, while mentally, this process involves the retrieval of a lemma which determines the position of a word in a sentence's syntax and triggers phonological codes for each morpheme (Parker, 2012, p. 415). According to Seikel et al. (2021), during a typical respiration cycle, inspiration constitutes 40 per cent, while expiration takes up 60 per cent of the cycle (p. 172). Speech production occurs during expiration, and one would need a very long expiration cycle in order to produce long, syntactically complex utterances, along with short inhalation in order to keep communication smooth (Seikel et al., 2021, p. 172). In speech production specifically, inspiration drops to as low as 10 per cent of the respiration cycle, while expiration takes up as much as 90 per cent of the cycle, due to the constant need for exhalation while producing speech (Gick et al., 2012, p. 50). The process of producing sentences is constrained by our breathing cycles, and by extension, our articulation capacities.

But how is articulation related to respiration in the context of speech production? The answer is that these two components, along with phonation, have to work together to facilitate the successful production of speech. To produce speech under typical circumstances, we have to coordinate phonation (sound production via the larynx and vocal folds), respiration and articulation, and in the absence of such coordination, 'intelligible speech is impossible' (Osberger & McGarr, 1982, p. 267; Gargiulo, 2012, p. 359). Furthermore, Miller (2010) notes that an 'inability to coordinate breathing with speech and with morpho-syntactic planning can severely compromise intelligibility' (p. 253). An example of how articulation affects syntactic production is in pausing, a silent interval which functions to delineate the boundaries of a syntactic unit, provide time for the listener to digest the syntactic structure of the sentences (such as through parsing) and to give the speaker time to plan out their incoming speech or to make clarifications about previously spoken utterances (Achiri-Taboh, 2022, p. 191). Pauses are not only determined by semantic and syntactic factors like the sentence composition, but also by physiological factors like articulation and respiration (Achiri-Taboh, 2022, p. 191).

Synthetic voices

The importance of articulation in human language may be further evidenced by how human-like articulation is more preferred than synthetic articulation in machine-to-human communication, as is the case with artificial intelligence, for example. With the advent of technologies like natural language processing in the twenty-first century, we have been confronted by a slew of speech recognition applications such as Google's Alexa and Apple's Siri. They are also commonly known as virtual assistants which can be used to assist humans in a range of tasks such as searching for information. There are even AI voice actors, humans who provide their voices which can be transformed using AI and used by companies for different means (Hao, 2021). These are called 'synthetic voices', and the voices of the original Siri and Alexa were composed only of segments of voices from these AI actors together, resulting in a rather unnatural-sounding and robotic voice (Hao, 2021). How these virtual assistants function is that they analyse the user's speech and convert it into something recognizable to the AI system, from which a response is generated (Japan Advanced Institute of Science and Technology, 2022). Despite the potential of virtual assistants, there are also some limitations, such as how human biases in the design of such assistants can lead to miscommunication and misunderstanding of different accents spoken by users (Ammanath & Firth-Butterfield, 2021; Harding, 2022). There is also the issue of making virtual assistants sound natural – there is often a conflict between providing social conversation (greetings and small talk etc. for indexing social relations) and transactional conversation (factual conversations carried out to get things done), whereby virtual assistants are often unable to combine the two naturally, such that one either ends up with 'an overly chatty or cold and robotic voice agent' (Yoon & McGrenere, 2021). Although the advent of deep learning has allowed AI voices to become more natural through feeding audio data to its algorithm, it is still difficult for AI voices to replace humans due to the variability of a human voice across different contexts, when 'expressive, creative, and long-form projects are still best done by humans' and the caveat that actual humans are still needed to provide the audio data (Hao, 2021).

Human versus synthetic voices

Furthermore, there are also studies which show that the use of human voices or human-like behaviour from virtual assistants is preferred by users. Chérif and

Lemoine (2019) found that, from a marketing perspective, a virtual assistant with a human voice created a greater social presence, elicited greater trust from the consumer and stronger behavioural intentions than one with a synthetic voice, leading them to argue for 'superiority of the human voice over the synthetic voice' (p. 39). However, there are also studies which show otherwise. Abdulrahman and Richards' (2022) study on human versus synthetic voices, which investigated the attitudes of more than a hundred participants on the use of a human voice versus a synthetic voice, differed from the other studies in that it found that participants showed similar attitudes towards both voices in terms of likeability, co-presence and trustworthiness. At the same time, there are also studies that recommend a balance between the two. Garcia and Lopez (2019) investigated user expectations of what the personality of a virtual assistant should be like, and one of the components which they studied was voice, specifically its gender, speed and whether it resembled a machine or a human. They found that the virtual assistant's voice should be a mix of machine and human, so users can comprehend the conversation context and react with intelligence and empathy, simultaneously indicating to the user that it is not a human.

Similarity: human vs. AI generation

Human language and artificial intelligence (AI) are not completely distinct from one another; in fact, they share numerous similarities. Like AI, humans often do not generate entirely novel sequences of words, but instead rely on what they have stored and used previously. Many of our daily conversations are repetitive and based on what we remember from past experiences. Kecskes (2019) cites three other scholars (p. 47): Hymes (1962) found that much of speech is made up of 'recurrent patterns' and 'linguistic routines' (p. 126), while Bolinger (1979) argues that the effort that language users invest in remembering is minimally equivalent to their efforts in placing linguistic units together (p. 97). Fillmore (1976) purports that much of natural language is 'formulaic, automatic and rehearsed, rather than propositional, creative or freely generated' (p. 24). The views of these scholars appear to highlight the prevalence of memory rehearsal in human language. Widdowson's (1990) view also concurs with this, as he states that a great amount of linguistic knowledge is 'acquired by means of memory and not by cognitive analysis' (p. 42).

Memory matters

Apart from articulation, there is also evidence to suggest that memory plays an important part in human communication. Studies have found that as compared with younger adults, older adults tend to produce less syntactically complex written and spoken language. Amongst the various reasons affecting this linguistic behaviour, working memory capacity seems to be a major contributing factor (Warren et al., 2018, p. 283). This is likely due to how syntactically complex sentences might be linked to high memory load demands (de Bot & Makoni, 2005, p. 32). Furthermore, the importance of memory in speech is explained by Francis, Romo and Gelman (2002), who note that speech production and comprehension necessitate information maintenance in the working memory (p. 319). The benefits of memory in verbal abilities are explained by Daneman (1991), whose study demonstrated that working memory affects individual variation in verbal fluency for speech production and oral reading, whereby 'individuals who have a greater capacity to coordinate the processing and temporary storage requirements of speaking are more verbally fluent and less prone to making articulatory errors while speaking or reading aloud' (p. 461). This significant role of memory is also applicable to language acquisition. In their investigation of executive functions and language development in Spanish-speaking pre-term and full-term children, Pérez-Pereira et al. (2017) found that verbal memory could play a role in comprehension of grammar and complex sentences while non-verbal working memory could play a vital role in morphosyntactic production (pp. 106–107).

Taking into consideration the above, we see that time and efficiency are at the core of linguistic production. The interplay between memory and prosody is crucial to how humans communicate in speech, and individually motivated rules, which fail to take into account memory and articulation (such as production cost), are the rules that are in reality irrelevant to understanding human linguistic competence. Nonetheless, this does not discredit the existence of exceptions entirely. Exceptions do exist but they should be reasonable and not excessive in number – after all, not everything can be redeemed as exceptions (Yang, 2016). Pragmatic matters – which include but are not limited to time, resource sensitivity, efficiency, memory, prosody and articulation – are at the very heart of syntactic variation along with other ecological factors. The observations of experimentalists and data linguists all point to this conclusion: pragmatic matters are the real driving forces of variation. That said, while efficiency does indeed matter, so do expressive desires. The latter are key to the limitless, generative power of linguistic output and hence creativity.

Pragmatic motivations: the 3-E Model

Syntactic variations are neither arbitrary nor accidental; they are the result of very carefully made syntactic decisions, which are inherently pragmatic. Let's say, for example, that these decisions – such as how to order expressions and whether or not to say them – are purely pragmatic. In order to make these decisions, you will need to assess necessity and resources.

The ability to make pragmatic decisions is not limited to the realm of language and communication but can also be applied in various areas of life. For instance, pragmatic decision-making skills may be useful in everyday situations. To help understand this, an analogy may be useful: Suppose you are going shopping. Before purchasing your goods, you will need to assess what you need and what you can afford. Pragmatic choices are typically made based on what is necessary and feasible given the circumstances. This is also true when it comes to communication, whether it's through talking, texting, emojing, writing or gesturing. To effectively convey a message, one must consider what is necessary to communicate and what is within the bounds of one's abilities.

Pragmatics, however, is not solely concerned with cost-efficiency. In my previous publication, Kiaer (2021), I argued that the other attitudinal and creative dimensions of language use can be incorporated into pragmatic motivations. Understanding these motives and their dynamics is key to comprehending the patterns of human languages. These pragmatic motivations can be summarized by three E-words: efficiency, expressivity and empathy. While efficiency and expressivity primarily operate on an individual level, empathy takes place at the interactional level.

As I have demonstrated in Kiaer (2021), syntactic theories have become increasingly abstract in recent years. In fact, it could be argued that current theories have become so detached from reality and actual language use that they are no longer practical. By proposing the 3-E Model, I hope to revive the link

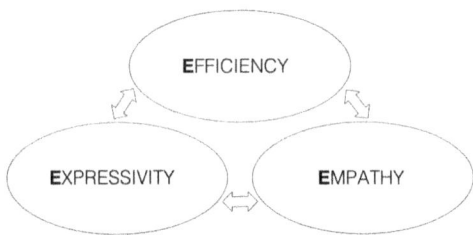

Figure 6.1 The 3-E Model.

between theory and actual language practice, for which simplicity is vital. Below, I will provide an explanation for each of the 3-Es.

Efficiency matters

Chomsky's competence-performance distinction made it crystal clear that processing considerations or, in other words, procedural aspects of human languages, have no place in mental grammar. He states, 'a generative system involves no temporal dimension' (Chomsky, 2007, p. 6). Yet, as we see in not only Asian languages, but also English and many other languages across the world, without considering the procedural aspect of linguistic representation and, indeed, time, it is impossible even to define the very basic linguistic building block (that is, the constituent) as addressed in Phillips (2003). In determining the life and destiny of every syntactic variation, time and resource efficiency matter greatly.

Simply speaking, all the variations that are selected through competition, which subsequently survive and thrive, are the ones that are produced in the most cost-saving, pragmatic manner. Hawkins (1994, 2004, 2014) shows how the very simple Zipfian least-effort principle can explain syntactic variations across time and regions. I have also argued in my previous books that linguistic choices, just as other choices we make in our life, are pragmatic in nature. Further to Hawkins, I showed that all syntactic variation is pragmatically driven (Kiaer, 2014, 2021).

Cost-efficiency can be expressed not only using minimum effort but through effective uses of given resources in a time-sensitive matter. Hawkins proposed the 'minimised domain', arguing that the smaller the grammatical domain the better. Yet, I think a small size doesn't always improve processing and production. When linguists talk about distance, they tend to count words (cf. Hawkins, 1994, 2004). However, the simple truth is that word length varies greatly and our memory and articulation cannot process all of this in the same manner. Hence, I have repeatedly shown the importance of prosody in structural choice making. Morpho-syntactic variation is not arbitrary and un-orderly. On the contrary, it is highly systematic. Although size matters, prosodic proximity plays a more essential role in morpho-syntactic variation.

Efficiency in spoken communication is limited by articulatory resource and memory capacity – though this may differ in writing or in other text-mediated communication. Though limitless generative forms are possible, not all of these variations have an equal chance of survival. Despite Chomsky's assertion that the principle of cost-efficiency has no bearing on grammar, we still see that the forms which survive and thrive are the ones that are cost-effective. This leads me to wonder, if the straightforward principle of cost-efficiency can systematically and consistently account for, and even precisely predict, the countless variations that we see in language production, why do we not consider it the primary driving force behind syntactic architecture?

Now, if cost matters, what influences the cost? We need to think about the pragmatic ecological factors that make units cost-efficient. One method is to make the unit small and compact – a shorter length is desirable. Speed is crucial. In a digital age, where communication takes place on-screen as well as off-screen, the advent of read receipts for instance has led speed to matter even more. For many, to be left unread can be annoying, even anxiety-inducing – all the more reason for communication to be efficient. Similarly, prosodic proximity also matters, as prosodically efficient forms are the ones that will survive and thrive; these forms are not necessarily short words but ones that are prosodically well put together. Consider songs and poetry; they are forms which are prosodically efficient. Their staying power is evident, and this may not only be due to their aesthetic aspect, but to their construction, which allows you to remember them more easily.

Memory weight, macro-routines, distance and locality: all these factors relate to cost-efficiency. While they may have been considered 'irrelevant' to grammar in the original generative mindset, it is these very elements that drive linguistic variation. Rather than placing them at the periphery of the discussion, they should be integrated into the centre as they can actually provide valuable insight into linguistic variations.

Perhaps the most efficient and sought-after language forms are those that have been stored as grammatical or default forms. Generative syntax has often taken a static approach, when, in reality, the time-linear process of language understanding and production cannot be ignored. Time and cost are crucial factors in all linguistic productions, whether offline or online. To dismiss the significance of time and cost in language use is to ignore a fundamental aspect of linguistic variation.

Expressivity matters

Our linguistic needs are not solely driven by efficiency. The beauty of human language lies in the fact that we do not always take the most efficient route. If we did, our linguistic variations would be limited and unremarkable. It is our emotions and attitudes that add countless layers of diversity, unpredictability and unique human expression to our language production. Linguistic variation caused by emotion and attitude is difficult to fully account for or observe in the AI generation, even when backed up by hyperscale data. While AI like ChatGPT is even able to write poetry, there is still ample room for it to catch up to emotion-filled human language. Indeed, human languages are full of spontaneous, unpredictable and sometimes inefficient expressions, many of which are driven by emotion. People do not always use the most efficient language because they want to convey their feelings and attitudes through their words, and this is where pragmatics comes into play. AI is not able to produce language brimming with spontaneity and emotion in the same way.

Pragmatics is what makes human language so versatile and fluid, enabling it to adapt to new contexts and social situations. When making linguistic decisions, there are often more factors to consider than just production costs. The ability to navigate these complexities is what sets human language apart and allows it to remain a vital and dynamic means of communication. Social interaction is different in every culture from a macro perspective, and also different to each individual human being from a micro perspective. Asian languages have very complex pragmatics based on interpersonal relations and societal hierarchies. These languages are not well understood in comparison with English and other European languages, and therefore AI translators, like Google Translate, and generative AI, like ChatGPT, have trouble translating Asian languages. Humans are able to take pragmatics into account almost instinctively and sensitively measure up what's needed in each situation. To date, AI has not been able to produce language with a natural use of pragmatics. This is not to say that it is impossible. While AI technology is advancing rapidly, there is still much work to be done before machines can fully emulate the rich complexity and nuance of human language use.

During my PhD studies, it was commonly believed that AI would never be able to understand humour. However, with the abundance of available data, AI has been able to learn how humans make humour and has made significant strides in this area. It's possible that AI could eventually acquire an understanding of pragmatics through deep learning, but as of now AI is still limited in its ability to understand and apply pragmatics in a natural and nuanced way.

While creativity is a term that is often mentioned and appreciated in describing human language within the field of generative grammar, how creativity is truly expressed in language is often considered outside the realm of linguistic speculation. This is odd because emotional aspects that drive creative variation are often left unexplored within generative grammar studies. As a result, any literary variation or other register-sensitive, emotional output is often ignored by linguists. Indeed, generative linguists have little to say about variations in poetry or songs. They narrow their scope to written and formal languages, so if the language has a literary nature, generative grammars are generally unsuitable. Creativity was always at the heart of claims made by generative linguistics, but paradoxically when the data is creative by nature, then they ultimately retreat from the discussion.

Empathy matters

That said, empathy should not be dismissed when it comes to the discussion of syntactic variation. In the 3-E Model, empathy refers to solidarity and group behaviours that influence language. This social aspect, however, has hardly been studied amongst generative linguists; it's almost like a taboo topic as it seems to veer into the territory of behaviourism. Since Chomsky's review of Skinner's verbal behaviour, behaviourism and explanations related to it are generally avoided by those following the Chomskyan framework (Wasow, 2002). Despite this, I believe it is crucial to acknowledge that the language we use is primarily a product of social interaction. Peer pressure, or more broadly, peer influence, is a powerful force that shapes our linguistic production. This interactional aspect is completely invisible when we isolate linguistic production from social interaction and present it in a vacuum. Asian languages, in particular, are rich in interpersonal decorations, where each variation is carefully chosen to project a particular relationship dynamic. Without considering the social nature of interaction, it will be challenging to pinpoint the root cause of morpho-syntactic variation in these languages.

The 3-E Model in the AI age

Each time a human speaker produces language, three motivations are carefully judged in order to create the most appropriate output. These motivations are always taken into consideration, and the challenge for speakers is to balance these factors and find the most suitable output for each situation. This requires careful thought, examination and negotiation. In my book, Kiaer (2021), I proposed a multimodal modulation approach that takes into account language-specific ecological factors, in order to better understand variations in morpho-syntactic realization. Both verbal and non-verbal patterns require proper consideration, and how they are combined and orchestrated requires further exploration.

Consideration of the 3-Es can be seen wherever humans communicate, whether it's in offline or online spaces. One of the challenges we face in modern communication is that our interactions are no longer limited to those between humans; we are constantly mediated by AI. Human–computer interaction has become an ever-present reality in our lives, and this trend is likely to continue in the years to come. I am not yet certain how the 3-E Model will apply to AI-mediated communication, as it is not a straightforward matter. For instance, whether AI will make our language more expressive and emphatic or less so remains an open question. Exploring how pragmatic motivations operate in this new reality is a crucial inquiry that awaits further investigation.

7

The Pragmatic Instinct, Natural Language and AI

This chapter describes the recent developments in artificial intelligence, focusing on how deep learning language models (specifically transformer-based models) process language, and how this differs from humans' language processing. There are two main areas of comparison: cost-efficiency and pragmatics. First, research has shown that transformer-based models like GPT and BERT have high processing capabilities, but they are less cost-efficient than the human brain's language processing. This is because of the high computational and financial costs involved in using these models. Second, these models have limitations in processing pragmatic information.

More is different

The concept of 'more is different' was introduced by physicist Philip W. Anderson in 1972. It suggests that as systems become more complex and larger in scale, new and unexpected properties emerge that cannot be explained by simply understanding the individual parts. In simpler terms, when many elements work together in a complex system, the behaviour of the system as a whole can be entirely different from that of its individual components.

It is true that having more data can make it harder to predict what the future holds. By the time this book is published in late December 2023, uncertainties await us. One thing I am certain of is that the information I provide here may no longer be up to date. In this book, I compared Google Translate and ChatGPT, but the comparison was made in early 2023, so things may have changed. More AI translations will likely be available when the book is released. This demonstrates the reality that academic research, particularly paper books, will struggle to keep up with the rapidly evolving nature of the field.

It is important to note, though, that we should never underestimate what humans can accomplish in this AI age. Human brains are not numerically inferior to Large Language Models. With an estimated 86 billion neurons, the basic units of the nervous system that transmit information throughout the body, and trillions of synapses, the human brain possesses remarkable capabilities. Each neuron can have up to 10,000 synapses, and on average, a neuron in the human brain is connected to around 10,000 other neurons, resulting in an estimated 100 trillion synapses. Most importantly, the human brain operates with exceptional efficiency. We don't require excessive energy to make educated guesses.

At the dawn of modern linguistics, generative linguists were fascinated by humans' ability to continuously generate new sentences throughout our lives. While it is true that we often reuse expressions and structures repeatedly in our daily lives, the capacity for syntactic competence was generally acknowledged as uniquely human. However, in the era of Generative AI, we now question whether endless generation is exclusive to humans, as AI can also generate different sentences to a certain extent. One aspect that I still believe remains uniquely human is the ability to create words. Generative AIs, thus far, with all their parameters, have not been able to generate a single word that we can use. It is always the task of humans to provide input to language models.

Developments in AI

Deep learning and the transformer model

The goal of AI is to be human-like and to carry out tasks that are usually done by humans. One of the key aspects of AI is machine learning, where machines acquire knowledge and experience to complete tasks without human involvement (Marr, 2018). Deep learning forms part of machine learning and focuses on the use of algorithms called artificial neural networks (ANN), which mimic the functioning of the human brain; that is to say, how neurons are interconnected and transfer information to one another in the human nervous system (Karunakaran, 2018). The applications of deep learning are vast and extend beyond language-related functions: it is used in translation, in chatbots, for facial recognition and even for disease diagnoses, amongst numerous other functions (Marr, 2018). In recent decades, the rapid development of deep learning and deep neural networks, especially in the area of natural language processing, has led to various deep learning models, of which transformers have been a highlight in the past few years. The linguistic aspect of these deep learning models is called language modelling, which refers to the application of statistical techniques to predict a sequence of words by analysing preceding textual data (Goled, 2021b).

The transformer model was first introduced in a 2017 paper by Vaswani et al. It analyses a sequence of data, such as text, as input and generates another sequence as output, such as translating a piece of text from one language to another. The model utilizes an attention mechanism that allows for the bidirectional tracking of relationships between words with long-range dependencies, which are words that are separated across a long text sequence. This approach is widely used in natural language processing (Dickson, 2022).

From BERT to GPT-3: a look at prominent transformer-based language models

The transformer model was preceded by recurrent neural networks (RNN) and long short-term memory (LSTM) networks. However, due to its feature of processing data word-by-word instead of by sequences, RNN and LSTM are inefficient in processing long sequences of data because data in preceding, far-off positions are often forgotten (Goled, 2021a). In addition to RNN and LSTM, there are convolutional neural networks (CNN), which are similar to transformers in that they can track word relationships/dependencies across various positions. Unlike transformers, CNNs are only effective when dealing with shorter sentences (Goled, 2021a). Prominent models that are based on transformers include BERT, GPT-2 and GPT-3, with each subsequent model having more parameters. Parameters are values that an ANN seeks to optimize during training (MacRae, 2021, p. 173). To quantify the scale of each model, BERT has around 340 million parameters, while GPT-2 has 1.5 billion and GPT-3 has 175 billion (Ye, 2022, p. 182; Bansal, 2021, p. 172). An upcoming model, GPT-4, is set to surpass all the previous models with 100 trillion parameters (Millman, 2022).

Highly costly: transformer-based language models

Despite the prevalence of these deep learning language models and the constant intertwining of language and AI in the current era, there are still limitations when it comes to how these models process and attempt to 'mimic' human language. The massive size of the aforementioned models also means that they not only incur high computational costs, but also significant financial costs. For example, it is estimated that the financial cost of training a GPT-3 could go as high as $10 million, while the amount of computing power needed for training is around a quadrillion neural network computations per second (Heaven, 2021). Increases in parameters in these models also result in longer training periods, such as how it would take 342 years to finish training a GPT-3 if just one Nvidia V100 GPU is used (Bansal, 2021, p. 172). Furthermore, as an example, when using a BERT model, a 100,000-word-long text would result in a mind-boggling 10 billion word pairs, which requires astronomical computing power to process (Rothman, 2021, p. 159). The high costs incurred through these AI models highlight a relatively low cost-efficiency, which stands in stark contrast to the human brain, which is highly adapted for cost-efficiency, having 'a near optimal trade-off between cost and efficiency' (Eysenck & Keane, 2020, p. 14) whereby information processing costs are minimized and growth and adaptation capacity is maximized (Stine-Morrow et al., 2022, p. 290). To highlight the efficiency of the human brain in numbers, the human brain carries out 100 trillion complex operations per second, with each operation only costing around $2 \times 10-15$ joules of energy, making it minimally 'a factor of a billion more efficient than our present technology' and 'a factor of 10 million more efficient than the best digital technology that we can imagine' (Fiorini, 2020, p. 334). This cost-efficiency of how humans process information, by extension, can be seen in how we process and use language efficiently as humans, which is related to the pragmatic usage of language.

Pragmatic translation: Google versus ChatGPT

Google Translate: 132 languages

Despite the wide range of translation applications available on the market, Google Translate is still one of the most used AI translation platforms on a global scale. Launched in 2006, Google Translate became so popular that it recorded more than 500 million daily users by 2016. It operates via neural machine translation, which essentially is an artificial neural network that predicts word sequences based on massive datasets by scanning for patterns in huge numbers (millions!) of documents which have already been translated by humans, in order to provide what it predicts is the 'best' translation (Almahasees, 2022, p. 3;

Kerr, 2014, p. 88). As of July 2022, with the recent addition of twenty-four new languages, Google Translate currently provides translation capabilities for 132 languages, including many under-resourced Asian languages like Uyghur, Pashto and Dhivehi. Out of these 132 languages, a total of fifty-five languages (fifty-six if you count Traditional and Simplified Chinese as separate languages) or 41 per cent of the languages supported by Google Translate are Asian languages. These Asian languages belong to a diverse range of language families, from Afro-Asiatic, Indo-European, Japonic, to Austronesian, Turkic, Sino-Tibetan and more. A handful of the languages supported includes the following: Arabic, Bengali, Chinese (Traditional/Simplified), Ilocano, Khmer, Lao, Maithili, Malay, Telugu, Thai and Vietnamese.[1]

Despite this achievement, there is still a long way to go for online translation efforts to truly account for the linguistic diversity in the world. It was estimated in 2016 that in machine translation, only 1 per cent of 6,000 non-endangered languages were accounted for (Moorkens, 2022, p. 135), meaning that at least more than a thousand endangered languages (as there are over 7,000 languages worldwide), and 99 per cent of 6,000 non-endangered languages, are not accorded translation resources. This highlights a great disproportion in translation resources, most of which have been accessible to only a relatively minute number of the world's languages.

Furthermore, despite the relatively significant number of languages, especially Asian languages, that continue to be included in Google Translate, the level of accuracy of translations varies across languages. Translations can often be 'misleading' – there are instances whereby the 'meaning of whole text[s]' are altered, which therefore means that translations with 'full equivalence' are infrequent (Lamichhane et al., 2021, p. 209). Thagard (2021) talks at length about the issues with Google Translate, specifically about its lack of ability to generate actual, creative translations due to its reliance on existing human translations and its inability to make sense of the grammatical features of human language on a deeper level:

> It is incapable of reasoning about why it comes up with the translations that it does, and does no abstracting about deeper grammatical features of language such as nouns, verbs, and subordinate clauses. Unlike human translators, Google Translate avoids planning, deciding, or understanding. It is devoid of feeling and has no need for acting on the world .... Human translation can sometimes be creative in coming up with original ways to convert one language into another, especially challenging for poetry, where figurative language is paramount. Google Translate relies instead on numerous translations that have already been

> done by people and therefore is incapable of producing a translation that qualifies as new and surprising as well as valuable.
>
> Thagard, 2021, p. 83

Thagard goes on to explain that Google Translate operates on a system that is different from that of human language processing, and therefore it is not equipped to process core aspects of human language such as syntax, semantics and pragmatics:

> Human translators also rely on their understanding of human intentional action to capture the meaning of action sequences. In contrast, Google Translate relies on language mechanisms that are different from the ones that support human natural language processing. ... Google Translate has no capacity for word-to-world semantics, because it knows nothing about boys and girls in the world. Google Translate does show some pragmatic sensitivity when it considers words in the context of other words, but it has no understanding of the purposes of the texts that it is translating .... Although Google Translate uses powerful computational techniques in going from text in one language to text in another, its linguistic capacities are limited by lack of deeper mechanisms for syntax, semantics, and pragmatics. It gets its results by statistical inferences in neural networks without relying on human mechanisms that include imagery, concepts, rules, analogy, emotions, intentional action, and consciousness. Google Translate works much faster and more broadly than human translators but does so by a much more superficial kind of intelligence.
>
> Thagard, 2021, p. 84

His argument is that the translational abilities of Google Translate are limited and only 'superficial'. It appears to translate much more quickly and across more languages than an actual human, but has no clear understanding of why, what and how it is translating.

ChatGPT

Differing from other popular online translation sites, ChatGPT can provide a range of pragmatically sensitive outputs. ChatGPT was released to the public on 30 November 2022. It is an AI chatbot, which is an improved version of the GPT (Generative Pretrained Transformer)-3.5 language model. GPT-3.5 is one of several versions of what is called a large language model (LLM), which relies on a massive database with 175 million parameters, making it among the biggest language processing models currently available. It is possible for users to command ChatGPT to produce a list of translations for a single sentence, and then ask it to provide reasons for why it translated the sentence in a certain way. This highlights the potential of ChatGPT for carrying out pragmatic translation, an insurmountable task for most current translation tools. I asked ChatGPT to transform a set of English sentences into informal Korean used by speakers who are friends of the same age. It was able to generate the appropriate sentences as requested, albeit with some slight inaccuracies.

In the case of English-to-Korean translations, Naver's local platform has developed an online translation service called Papago, which includes a unique feature allowing users to toggle honorifics on and off. While this is a step forward in online translation services, it is still not enough to fully capture the diverse and complex interpersonal relations in many Asian languages. Interpersonal relations are highly nuanced in Asian languages that exhibit complex interpersonal relations, and existing translation tools are very limited in their ability to reflect these subtleties, making pragmatic translation almost impossible. While people may use AI translations for the sake of speed and quantity, every output still needs to be checked by humans to ensure that it is pragmatically appropriate for real-world situations.

Tailor-made translation is possible

ChatGPT is also uniquely able to improve its translated outputs based on feedback given by users. ChatGPT engages in self-learning and self-advancement, and subsequently updates its responses after being trained on new data (Perrigo, 2022). When I was dissatisfied with a translation provided by ChatGPT, I gave it feedback and it revised the translation. Not only is it capable of translating languages, but it can also adjust the translation based on different moods and tones.

For instance, I asked ChatGPT to translate the sentence *The weather is great today* into Mandarin, and then continued to ask it to produce alternative sentences with the same meaning. Some of the alternative sentences contained added contextual information which I did not ask for. I therefore provided feedback, asking ChatGPT not to change the sentence's meaning and not to add unnecessary information.

Other translation tools generally do not allow users to give any feedback, nor do they attempt to modify the given output by suggesting improvements. Google Translate does allow users to send feedback about translations, but this is for Google's own data collection, rather than for the immediate benefit of the user. Similarly, Papago Translator also allows users to rate translations as 'good' or 'awkward', but with no immediate effect. Thus, the translation process becomes a closed loop in the sense that there is little or no communication between the translator/translation tool and the intended audience. This is especially pertinent for pragmatics because context matters when cultural concepts are being translated for audiences of a different culture. A failure in translation leads to consequences such as the other party being offended or the translation falling short of its desired function in cross-cultural contexts.

One output vs. many outputs

Unlike most other translation tools that only provide one output, ChatGPT is capable of providing multiple outputs, depending on the prompt(s) provided by the users. Even if ChatGPT only produces one translation for a particular sentence, it is possible to ask it to generate more equivalent translations. Besides ChatGPT, DeepL Translator also provides alternative translations. ChatGPT not only provides multiple translations but also constantly provides translational alternatives with different tones or registers.

Case studies

This section examines the translation capabilities of ChatGPT for nine different non-English langauges, namely, Korean, Chinese, Japanese, Vietnamese, Russian, Indonesian, Turkish, Kazakh and Mongolian. ChatGPT was fed with a series of English sentences and asked to convert them into the respective languages for an informal and formal context. It was also asked to provide justifications for the changes it made in converting the sentences from an informal to a formal style. The following sections provide summaries of my findings.

Korean

ChatGPT was able to provide pragmatically satisfactory translation if the translation was short. Other existing translation tools like Google were unable to produce pragmatically coherent translations. Even as simple as translating the second person pronouns, Google-like translations provided all different versions of translations for the given input, sometimes resulting in incoherent translations where the tone of the language did not match the intended meaning. For

ChatGPT, if we specify the relations, genre and register, one can find pretty coherent and pragmatically adequate translation.

ChatGPT is capable of switching between informal and formal styles seamlessly. When I asked ChatGPT to provide a translation for the sentence 'I need some tissue' in an informal style, as if speaking to a friend of the same age, it initially made it polite, as in 휴지 좀 주세요 (*hyuji jom juseyo*), which uses the polite speech style –요 (-yo). After informing ChatGPT that its response was overly formal and reminding it of my request to keep the sentences informal, it generated the sentence 휴지 좀 줘 (*hyuji jom jwo*), which uses the intimate style ending with –어 (-eo).

Tuning into the right social register and making the dialogue pragmatically adequate is very challenging in Korean and many Asian languages. That's why Korean is considered a super-hard language by the United States' Foreign Service Institute (FSI), along with Arabic, Japanese and Chinese. Yet, surprisingly, this practice – particularly conversational practice – seems to work well with ChatGPT. I can see that in the near future ChatGPT may provide a useful tool for language learning, particularly for languages that are understaffed and under-resourced.

However, ChatGPT is not as proficient as Google in handling long translations. Although it is capable of adjusting and refining its output, the dataset for Korean is much smaller than that of English and other Western European languages. Therefore, translations from English to Korean often include unnatural examples, incorrect particle usage or missing particles. However, I believe this issue will improve as ChatGPT users in Korea grow exponentially. With more data and a larger user base, translation practices will become more accurate and natural.

Japanese

Similarly, ChatGPT provides register-sensitive pragmatic translation in Japanese. I asked ChatGPT to translate the English sentence 'Please give me a tissue' in three different ways: as if talking to a friend, to a teacher and to a stranger. ChatGPT provided the following translations and explanations:

> When speaking to a friend in Japanese, you can use the following casual phrase to ask for a tissue: 「ティッシュくれる?」 (Tisshu kureru?), which roughly translates to 'Can you give me a tissue?' in English. This phrase is more casual and appropriate for use with friends and peers.
>
> When speaking to a teacher, it's important to use polite language in Japanese. You can use the phrase 「ティッシュをください」 (Tisshu o kudasai) to ask for a tissue politely. This phrase is a polite request that can be used in formal situations.

> When speaking to a stranger, it's common to use polite language in Japanese. You can use the phrase 「ティッシュをください」 (Tisshu o kudasai) to ask for a tissue politely. This phrase is a polite request that can be used in formal situations as well as in casual situations with people you don't know. It's important to use polite language in Japanese to show respect to others, especially to people you don't know.

The answers given by ChatGPT are correct here. The first translation is different from the others as it is posed as a question. Alternatively, it could have been translated as 「ティッシュちょうだい」 (tisshu chōdai) using plain-form language.

However, ChatGPT did experience some difficulties in finding the right pronoun in Japanese. There are thirteen different types of second-person pronouns used in the Japanese translation of *The Hobbit* (Kiaer & Cagan, 2022, p. 33). Finding the socio-pragmatically appropriate forms such as pronouns, verbs and endings in Japanese is highly complex and sensitive to the register. Although ChatGPT operates in a big dataset, it is still limited in dealing with pragmatic complexity. For example, when I asked ChatGPT to translate 'You are my best friend' into Japanese, the translation 'あなたは私の一番の友達です' (Anata wa watashi no ichiban no tomodachi desu) sounded too formal due to the use of 'anata' and 'watashi'. So, I asked ChatGPT to make it less formal and intimate. ChatGPT provided the following translation: '君は僕（or 俺）の一番の友達だ' (Kimi wa boku (or ore) no ichiban no tomodachi da), where 'kimi' (きみ) can be used instead of 'anata,' and 'boku' (ぼく) or 'ore' (おれ) can be used instead of 'watashi' to make it less formal and more intimate. As we can see, ChatGPT can adapt to further needs and changes according to each pragmatic need. Although it's not perfect, when more data is collected, the system's performance will improve.

Mandarin

Mandarin is different from Korean and Japanese because it lost much of its hierarchical language during the twentieth century, when Confucian hierarchy was abandoned, and a new Communist class system was adopted under Mao Zedong. As such, spoken language is not characterized by honorific and casual speech registers. Like English, politeness is added to an utterance by the addition of polite phrases, rather than indicated through grammatical structures. The pragmatic difficulty of the language lies in the gap between spoken and written language. Formal written language uses structures from classical Chinese, which is how Chinese was written prior to the twentieth century. Classical Chinese was only ever written, no one ever spoke in the way that they wrote. This still lingers in written Mandarin today, meaning that adopting a formal register for writing can be difficult for learners of Mandarin. To test this, I carried out the following conversation with ChatGPT:

JK Translate this sentence into Mandarin: 'I did not buy it because I wanted to save time.'

ChatGPT 我没有买它是因为我想节省时间。(Wǒ méiyǒu mǎi tā shì yīn wèi wǒ xiǎng jiéshěng shíjiān.)

JK Show me a few possible variations of the translation.

ChatGPT Certainly, here are a few possible variations of the sentence 'I did not buy it because I wanted to save time' in Mandarin:
我想节省时间，所以没有买它 (wǒ xiǎng jiéshěng shíjiān, suǒyǐ méiyǒu mǎi tā)
为了节省时间，我没有买它 (wèile jiéshěng shíjiān, wǒ méiyǒu mǎi tā)
我并没有买它，因为我想节省时间 (wǒ bìng méiyǒu mǎi tā, yīnwèi wǒ xiǎng jiéshěng shíjiān)
我为了节省时间，所以放弃了购买它 (wǒ wèile jiéshěng shíjiān, suǒyǐ fàngqìle gòumǎi tā).

These variations differ slightly in their phrasing and emphasis, but they all convey the same basic meaning: that the speaker did not buy the item because they wanted to save time. The differences in wording may be influenced by factors such as the context, the speaker's tone or style and the intended audience.

JK Now translate the same sentence using written style Mandarin (书面语)

ChatGPT 由于想要节省时间，我并没有购买它。(Yóuyú xiǎng yào jiéshěng shíjiān, wǒ bìng méiyǒu gòumǎi tā.)

JK Show me some variations in formal written Mandarin (书面语).

ChatGPT Certainly, here are some variations of the sentence 'I did not buy it because I wanted to save time' in formal written Mandarin:
本人出于时间考虑，未予购买 (běn rén chū yú shíjiān kǎolǜ, wèi yǔ gòumǎi)
为了节省时间，故未予购买 (wèi le jiéshěng shíjiān, gù wèi yǔ gòumǎi)
出于时间上的考虑，本人未能购买 (chū yú shíjiān shàng de kǎolǜ, běn rén wèi néng gòumǎi)
鉴于时间紧迫，未曾购得 (jiàn yú shíjiān jǐnpò, wèi céng gòu dé).

These variations use more formal language and differ slightly in their phrasing and vocabulary. They all convey the same basic meaning: that the speaker did not buy the item because they wanted to save time. The differences in wording may be influenced by factors such as the context, the level of formality required and the intended audience.

> **JK** These sentences add too much new information, please stick to the original sentence.
>
> **ChatGPT** I apologize for the confusion earlier. Here are some variations of the original sentence in formal written Mandarin:
>
> 本人未购买此物，因想节省时间 (běn rén wèi gòumǎi cǐ wù, yīn xiǎng jiéshěng shíjiān)
>
> 为了节省时间，本人未购买此物 (wèi le jiéshěng shíjiān, běn rén wèi gòumǎi cǐ wù)
>
> 本人因想节省时间，未购买此物 (běn rén yīn xiǎng jiéshěng shíjiān, wèi gòumǎi cǐ wù)
>
> 由于时间紧迫，本人未购买此物 (yóuyú shíjiān jǐnpò, běn rén wèi gòumǎi cǐ wù).

These variations keep the original sentence structure and convey the same basic meaning in more formal written Mandarin. The differences in wording may be influenced by factors such as the level of formality required and the intended audience. When I asked ChatGPT to rewrite the sentence in written style (书面语 *shūmiànyǔ*), it changed the conjunctions to those used in written language. For example, 因为 *yīnwēi* became 由于 *yóuyú*, or was shortened to 因 *yīn*, and 所以 *suǒyǐ* was changed to 故 *gù*, which could be ambiguous if used spoken language, but calls back to classical Chinese in a refined way in writing. In terms of verbs, ChatGPT changed the single character verb 买 *mǎi* into its two-character form 购买 *gòumǎi*, which could be used in written or spoken language, but is a must-have for written language. The first formal sentence retained 我 *wǒ* as 'I', but the formal variations of this sentence used 本人 *běn rén*, which literally means 'this person' and is more commonly used in a literary context. 它 *tā* ('it') was changed to 此物 *cǐ wù*, which means 'this object', but in a formal manner due to the use of 此 *cǐ* rather than 这个 *zhè gè* ('this, informal') and 物 *wù* ('object, literary style') rather than 东西 *dōngxī* ('thing').

Vietnamese

The Vietnamese language has a complex system of kinship and occupational terms which can function as first-, second- and third-person pronouns depending on the relationship between the speaker and their addressee. Such relationships are dynamic, and the terms that a speaker uses to refer to themselves and the addressee can vary according to changes in their relationship status. For example, two people with an age gap of a few years may refer to each other as *em* (literally 'younger sibling') and *anh* (literally 'older brother'), respectively. These terms can also be adopted by the speakers to refer to themselves. Vietnamese also has a small set of pronouns that are used in different contexts according to variations in social status and degree of intimacy. For example, *mày* is a second-person pronoun used to refer to addressees of a lower social status, while *tôi* is a formal, first-person pronoun. Still, these are often avoided in favour of kinship or occupational terms.

A major advantage of using ChatGPT to perform Vietnamese translations is that it can explain the rich range of pronouns. This is highly pertinent because displaying pragmatic competence in Vietnamese is contingent on one's awareness of the sociocultural factors underpinning one's relationship vis-à-vis the other interlocutor (e.g. gender, age, occupation, familial relation).

Google Translate generally only translates 'you' as *bạn*, which literally means 'friend' and is either used as a formal pronoun or a neutral pronoun for official documents like announcements and surveys (Ngo, 2020). Although ChatGPT generally used *bạn* for translating second-person pronouns, when I asked it for other words for *bạn*, it generated a list of alternative terms along with explanations about for whom these terms can be used and example sentences.

ChatGPT's understanding of the pragmatics of Vietnamese is sometimes flawed, often adding additional shades of meaning. For example, *My cousin is doing homework* was translated as *Cháu tớ đang làm bài tập đấy* when I asked for an informal sentence. *Tớ* is a first-person pronoun used amongst schoolmates to express intimacy, while *cháu* is used for addressing relatives who are much younger such as grandchildren or nephews and nieces (Ngo, 2011). These are relatively appropriate for the requested informal style, but the sentence-final particle *đấy*, which is used in statements to highlight factual information similar to the meaning of 'actually' or 'in fact', somewhat alters the meaning of the sentence and the context in which it might be said (Ngo, 2020, p. 202). *đấy* adds the implication that the addressee is unaware of or has a different opinion about what the speaker's cousin is doing.

Russian

Unlike most typical Asian languages, Russian does not have as complex a system of honorifics, though it does have a limited T–V (informal–formal) distinction in pronouns that is common to most European languages. This distinction is most salient in the second-person pronouns, where the type of verb ending used in a sentence depends on whether the formal or informal second-person pronoun is selected.

When ChatGPT was prompted to produce translation in an informal style suitable for usage between friends of the same age, it was able to apply the informal (Ты *ty*) second-person pronoun in a rather uniform manner across the sentences (emphasis added):

Какой **ты** добрый. *kakoj **ty** dobryj*
You are very kind.

Ты такой грубый. ***ty*** *takoj grubyj*
You're so rude.

Я дал **тебе** книгу вчера. *ja dal **tebe** knigu včera*
I gave you the book yesterday.

Джон с **тобой** дома? *džon s **toboj** doma?*
Is John at home with you?

Где **твоя** мама и папа? *gde **tvoja** mama i papa?*
Where are your mom and dad?

However, ChatGPT did not always generate appropriate responses even when prompted, and sometimes it generated responses which did not match what was requested. For example, when I asked ChatGPT to suggest address terms that could be used to replace the second-person pronouns already present in the translated sentences, it ended up changing some statements into questions, for example changing the informal translation for *Grandma is having a meal* from Бабушка кушает *babuška kušaet* into a formal interrogative Вы едите, бабушка? *vy edite, babuška?* ('Are you eating, grandmother?'). Such mistakes are commonplace on ChatGPT, but this will likely improve as more data in Russian is collected

Indonesian

As one of two standard varieties of the Malay language, Indonesian has a rich system of kinship and occupational terms that function as honorific and non-honorific titles. For Google Translate, the translation of second-person pronouns is inconsistent, with some sentences containing the informal *kamu* and others using the formal *anda*. There is also no justification or clear pattern for why this is so. Comparatively, ChatGPT is consistent in its use of *kamu* or *anda*, depending on whether it is prompted to generate translations for an informal context or a formal situation. ChatGPT can also suggest a range of other second-person pronoun substitutes such as *saudara* (second-person formal pronoun), *kalian* (second-person plural pronoun), *engkau* (second-person informal pronoun) and other kinship terms like *nenek* ('grandma'), *sahabat* ('best friend') and *teman* ('(general) friend').

Where ChatGPT lacks in its capability for Indonesian translation is that it occasionally misunderstands prompts, leading to an incorrect translation. For example, when I prompted ChatGPT to translate *You are my lovely daughter* into Indonesian, it instead generated the response *Kamu anak perempuan yang cantik*, which means 'You are a beautiful/lovely girl', completely omitting the context that this is being said by a parent to a daughter.

Turkish

Like Russian, Turkish pronouns exhibit a T–V (informal–formal) distinction, with plural forms being able to function as honorifics (Shibatani, 2009). ChatGPT is consistent when it comes to choosing informal or formal forms. When I asked ChatGPT to generate translations in informal or formal style, the results for the pronouns and their associated verbal/adjectival forms were quite consistent (see Table 7.1). Notably, usage of the formal pronoun and ending in the fourth example may come off as socially awkward as parent–child interactions are likely to be more informal in nature.

Table 7.1 Informal and formal translations into Turkish involving the second-person pronouns and associated verbal/adjectival endings

Sentence	Informal translation	Formal translation
You are very kind.	Çok kibar bir insan**sın**.	**Siz** çok nazik bir insan**sınız**.
You are so rude.	Çok kaba davranıyor**sun**.	Çok nezaketsiz davranıyor**sunuz**.
You are my best friend.	**Sen** benim en iyi arkadaşım**sın**.	**Siz** benim en iyi arkadaşım**sınız**.
You are my lovely daughter.	**Sen** benim sevimli kızım**sın**.	**Siz** benim kıymetli kızım**sınız**.
Can you meet me here?	Burada benimle buluşabilir mi**sin**?	Burada benimle buluşabilir mi**siniz**?

Note: The vowels differ due to vowel harmony.

Additionally, I asked ChatGPT to convert translations from an informal to a formal style and then subsequently prompted it to justify the changes that it made during the conversion. It was able to explain which parts were added/changed and its effect on increasing the politeness and formality of the translation.

Kazakh

Translation from English into Kazakh exposed ChatGPT's limited knowledge of the language. For example, when ChatGPT was asked to translate *You are so rude*, the given output was Сен өте кедейсің *sen öte kedeysiŋ*. However, the sentence actually means 'You (informal) are so poor', which is a mismatch with its supposed English translation 'You're so rude'. Table 7.2 shows examples of a few more mistranslations.

For Kazakh, ChatGPT is not as accurate as other translation tools. Its translations highlight that ChatGPT may not understand what is translating. Bogost (2022)

Table 7.2 Mistranslations of Kazakh in ChatGPT

Original sentence	ChatGPT's translated output	ChatGPT's English translation of translated output	Actual meaning of translated output
Come and eat.	Кел, жеңілдік іш. *kel, jeŋildik iş*	Come and eat.	Come and enjoy the discount.
Jessica is my cousin.	Жессика менің шешесім. *jessïka meniŋ şeşesim*	Jessica is my cousin.	Jessica is my mother.
My cousin is doing homework.	Менің шешем жасауды жасайды. *meniŋ şeşem jasawdı jasaydı*	My cousin is doing homework.	My mother does the making.
You are my lovely daughter.	Сен менің жүрегімдегі әйелімсің. *sen meniŋ jüregimdegi äyelimsiŋ*	You are my lovely daughter.	You (informal) are the wife in/of my heart.
Please give this to my dad.	Атамға беріңіздер деп жалғастыруыңызды сұраймын. *atamğa beriŋizder dep jalğastırwıŋızdı suraymın*	Please give this to my dad.	Please continue to give it to my grandfather.

argues that ChatGPT does not have the capacity to comprehend the intricacies of human language – it simply produces a superficial output on the basis of a certain input, without understanding what the words it produces actually mean. The lack of training data in Kazakh is likely because the language a less commonly learned and spoken language outside of Kazakhstan, and also because ChatGPT, albeit advanced, is nonetheless a relatively new technology that still needs a lot of fine tuning to better process the complexities of human language. Newer versions of ChatGPT and other AI are likely to address these flaws in the near future given that they are being trained at such a rapid pace with so much data.

Mongolian

Mongolian also has a simpler system of informal and formal second-person pronouns, and there are no differentiated verbal/adjectival endings which change according to person. Similar to Kazakh, ChatGPT made a significant number of mistakes in its translations to Mongolian (see Table 7.3). As mentioned earlier in the Kazakh section, this could be attributed to the fact that both Kazakh and Mongolian are relatively less studied and less spoken languages as compared with the other seven, which means lesser data for ChatGPT's reference.

Table 7.3 Mistranslations of Mongolian in ChatGPT

Original sentence	ChatGPT's translated output	ChatGPT's English translation of translated output	Actual meaning of translated output
Can you meet me here?	Би эндээс явж чадах уу? *bi èndèès javž čadax uu?*	Can you meet me here?	Can I go from here?
Jessica is my cousin.	Джессика надад хоёр туулай байна. *džessika nadad xoër tuulaj bajna.*	Jessica is my cousin.	Jessica, I have two rabbits.
You are very kind.	Танд их амжилттай. *tand ix amžilttaj.*	You are very kind.	You (informal) are very successful.
My cousin is doing homework.	Би хамгаалалтын ажил хийж байна. *bi xamgaalaltyn ažil xijž bajna.*	My cousin is doing homework.	I am doing security work.
You're so rude.	Та их хэтэрхий. *ta ix xètèrxij*	You're so rude.	You are too much.

Like Turkish and Kazakh, although there is also inconsistent usage of the informal and formal second-person Mongolian pronouns in other translation tools, ChatGPT's attempts at translating formal or informal Mongolian do not yield successful results either. When prompted, ChatGPT produced the same set of second-person pronouns in both cases (Ta *ta*), even though Ta *ta* is used in more formal contexts for addressing unfamiliar people or strangers. For the informal context, Чи *či* would have been more appropriate, as it used to address people who have a close relationship with the speaker (Gaunt, Baĭarmandakh, & Chuluunbaatar 2004).

Informal (ChatGPT):

Ta их сайхан. *ta ix sajxan* ('You are so good/beautiful.')
Ta миний хамгийн сайн найз. *ta minij xamgijn sajn najz* ('You are my best friend.')

Formal (ChatGPT):

Ta намайгийн хамгийн сайн найз юм. *ta namajgijn xamgijn sajn najz jum* ('You are my best friend.')
Таны ээж ба аав байгаа нь өөрийн хаана байна вэ? *tany èèž ba aav bajgaa n' öörijn xaana bajna vè?* ('Where are your (genitive) mother and father?')

ChatGPT and the future of (pragmatic) translation

Despite the various issues currently faced by ChatGPT in the area of understanding the intricacies of language use in context beyond patterns and frequencies, and its relatively poorer performance in translating lesser spoken languages like Kazakh and Mongolian, it is important to remember that ChatGPT is still in the early stages of development. Considering the scale at which it is able to digest and learn information and continuously improve itself, it may take only a short few years before the model which it is trained on enables it to produce much more seamless translations of not only dominant languages, but minority languages as well. The utility and potential of ChatGPT in pragmatic translation is undoubtable, especially so for more well-supported languages, and, with a sufficient amount of training, it could prove to be a valuable tool for learning and translating pragmatics.

Existing AI tools like Google are good for information translation, but may be problematic in pragmatic translation. For ChatGPT, its capability for pragmatic translation is better than existing AI translations but, to this day, data in languages other than English is limited. It can't handle large quantities of data as quickly as other AI translation tools. Additionally, I have experienced how ChatGPT only provides partial translations of the whole text at times. Therefore, I can say that ChatGPT's performance in non-English languages, particularly Asian languages, is not too impressive. However, for conversational translations and small amounts of text, it is still good. I am confident that it is only a matter of time before non-English data is collected and the speed improves.

The following is a summary of the strengths and weaknesses of using ChatGPT as compared with other translation tools to translate nine non-English languages, as was examined in the preceding sections. The analysis has shown that, despite its shortcomings, ChatGPT is more well attuned to translating pragmatics than the other translation tools, especially for translating between speech styles. Additionally, it potentially serves as a useful tool for learning the pragmatics of different languages, particularly for explaining the complex sociocultural factors behind address terms. This is a feature which is still missing in other translation tools, which are presently not equipped to inform users about this pragmatic information, and users who do not know the language would likely assume that the translations are correct regardless of whether this is the case. Therefore, ChatGPT can potentially aid non-speakers of a particular language in making more informed choices about the translations they use, potentially playing an important role in preventing potential misunderstanding in cross-cultural translation and communication. Given the generative abilities of ChatGPT in suggesting changes to a translated text, professional translators can also make use of ChatGPT to refine their own translations, making them more pragmatically appropriate for the intended audience and context and allowing translators to explore different translation styles beyond what they normally use.

Pragmatics is the key

There are doubts about what AI is actually doing with all this linguistic data – is it merely imitating us, or does it actually understand the data it is being fed with and use it in a multitude of ways like an actual human? Sampson (2015) is an opponent of the view that machines will eventually possess the same level of intelligence as humans, arguing that AI is a 'mindless machine' which carries out the 'automatic extraction' of the 'grammatical, semantic, and pragmatic properties' of human language (p. 8). He further purports that what computers do with natural language is simply not equivalent to what humans do with it (p. 8). While humans can understand language naturally, computers cannot process sentences in the same way, and the three core types of information – semantic, syntactic and pragmatic – need to be provided (Gopalakrishnan & Venkateswarlu, 2018, p. 130). Despite this, Vanderveken (2002) argues that, although computers can perform syntactic operations, they are incapable of carrying out 'semantic operations of relating words of language with things in the world' and, as such, are not able to truly grasp and use language, but rather can only 'simulate intelligence and understanding in verbal interactions with man', where simulation is not equivalent to the replication of human language (p. 60). Yu et al. (2019) underscore the irreplaceability of humans in comparison with machines, by arguing that many technologically advanced devices are incapable of carrying out basic human functions on a level comparable to actual human beings, and that even a young child and dog can outperform the best supercomputers on cognitive tasks like understanding languages and pattern recognition (p. 8). Although AI models can manipulate vast amounts of existing linguistic data, amounts that far exceed the capabilities of humans, to create creative linguistic entities such as new metaphors, these creations are not necessarily always greatly innovative, and, while being able to successfully imitate human linguistic production, are unable to mimic the 'refined and sophisticated language which we associate with the very best of creative writers' (Phillip, 2017, p. 229).

Amongst the various core aspects of language, pragmatics is one area that AI models have had difficulty in grasping. As mentioned previously, humans are able to process information, and subsequently language, much more efficiently than AI, which is related to the pragmatics of human language. The efficiency of humans in using language is seen in how we do not 'spend time and energy in saying explicitly what … [our] addressees already know' because if 'every sentence were a trillion words', it would fail to 'satisfy efficient human behaviour' (Azuelos-Atias, 2018, p. 106; Pym & Turk, 2000, p. 276). This is what I have also argued in my previous publications (Kiaer, 2014, 2021).

The 'ambiguity, exceptions and subjectivity' of human language, as well as the lack of a shared culture and experience with language users, make it difficult for AI to accurately and fully comprehend the meaning of words (Nelson et al., 2022, p. 84; Zhou, 2020, p. 202). For example, AI models face difficulty in processing such information like contextual clues, which hamper its ability to engage in 'unconstrained dialogue', and because the language used by an AI is not 'grounded' in experience or sensory reality nor connected with things like 'memories and cultural agreements on language', the meaningfulness of AI-produced language is doubtful (Belpaeme, 2022, p. 385).

Pragmatics is one of the most difficult aspects of human language because it varies based on person, utterance and context, and to be unable to understand pragmatics means to be unable to comprehend human language (Birner, 2021, p. 158). The inability of AI to process pragmatic information, unlike humans, can also incur dangerous consequences. As these models are based on statistical calculations of data, AI doesn't, as mentioned previously, actually comprehend the meaning of the linguistic data it receives, and as a result it may simply replicate the harmful biases that were present in its training data without the 'common sense, causal reasoning or moral judgment' that humans have when choosing our words, humanistic features which are still difficult to implement in these deep learning models (Hutson, 2021).

Rational choice theory (RCT)

Another aspect of how pragmatic usage of language by humans sets us apart from AI is how it resembles some aspects of consumer behaviour – specifically, the rational choice theory. Rational choice theory (RCT), a theory that is used in several fields such as economics and behavioural psychology, states that humans perform actions on the basis of rational decisions, that is, choices that are related to analysing the cost and benefit of something (Ballantine & Roberts, 2011, p. 52; Masoom, 2014, p. 447). Based on an economic theory of consumer behaviour, RCT argues that consumers are focused on maximizing utilitarian value, that is, on maximizing benefits and minimizing cost (Pattie & Johnston, 2011, p. 1512; Bierwald, 2014, p. 43). Individual behaviour is then determined by how people strike a balance in their actions of negotiating between the costs and benefits (Ballantine & Roberts, 2011, p. 52). This is somewhat similar to the pragmatic usage of language, whereby interlocutors attempt to minimize the cost of communication by only speaking what is necessary (therefore making their speech efficient), as well as choosing to speak in certain ways in response to contextual factors, so that one can be 'rewarded' with the desired answer. If we were to relate this to our shopping behaviours, our consumer decisions are never arbitrary – we know what we need and what we have. Of course, there's also the aspect of individual preference, regardless of the resources we have. Sometimes, we buy new clothes even if we already have enough. At times, our own preferences are superseded, and it may be more rational to 'follow the crowd' and go for something that is popular with other peers. Above all, cost is one of the most crucial factors to consider in decision-making as cost-efficiency is at the heart of consumer behaviours. When we think of ourselves as language customers, we encounter a very similar situation.

I argue in this book that cost-driven pragmatics is at the heart of every syntactic decision we find in synchronic, diachronic and typological variations. However, we do not have to make new decisions all the time in our pragmatic usage of language. Often, these cost-efficient decisions are stored as good practices and routines so we don't need to recalculate and reformulate our actions. Over time, those routines survive and thrive, and eventually form our grammatical foundations. One of the mysteries of human languages is this cost-efficiency, which is not really present in AI technologies. As mentioned previously, AI models are outstanding for their ability to process such a massive amount of information, but the problem is the significant cost that is incurred for the mere increase of one word, a cost which the human brain does not incur to such a large extent.

Blurring the linguistic lines between humans and AI

Despite the triumph of humans over AI in the efficient usage of language, it is interesting to consider the ever-growing influence of human–computer interaction (HCI) in our daily lives as mediated by AI technologies, and how it might blur the line between human language and language produced by AI. Technological advancements in the past decade have seen the proliferation of smart devices like smartphones and tablets and the drastic increase in the ownership of such devices. The number of smartphone users was approximately 708 million in 2011, which accounted for about 10 per cent of the world's population, and this has ballooned to 6.648 billion in 2021, or around 83.89 per cent of the global population (Dover, 2012; Li et al., 2022, p. 412). Increasingly, smart devices are becoming an indispensable part of our day-to-day activities, utilizing AI technologies to help us automate many different aspects of our lives (Fröhlich et al., 2020). An example of this automation, specifically in the area of language production, is predictive text and autocorrect functions, which have influenced the way in which we type. For example, when we compose an email, AI is capable of helping us finish our sentences by predicting what we might write next. The scale on which these features might be used is colossal, if we consider that more than 280 billion emails and 23 billion texts are sent per day, and that smartphone users are constantly on their devices, typically touching them 2,617 times a day (McCarthy, 2019; Naftulin, 2016; Giacomini, 2021).

With such heavy usage of smartphones and their associated AI technologies, more than ever our linguistic lives are becoming deeply intertwined with AI, to the extent that our linguistic production nowadays might even be dependent on

AI to some extent. However, this does come with some unexpected consequences. For example, China has been experiencing an unusual occurrence called 'character amnesia' whereby we suddenly forget how to spell a word when we actually attempt to write it down on paper – a survey on this showed that more than 80 per cent of respondents had had this experience, which they attributed to autocomplete (Hebbar, 2017). This suggests that we are becoming so exposed to AI-produced language that we are, in a way, becoming unconsciously 'trained' in this language, and our AI-influenced linguistic behaviour is constantly fed back into deep learning models to be used as training data. As this language data will have characteristics of both humans and AI, this blurs the line between what we can call strictly 'human' and strictly 'artificial' language since both are mutually influencing each other. Furthermore, Fracchia (2022) argues that natural languages are not necessarily 'natural' because the notion of differentiating them from purposefully created languages (such as computer programming, in the case of machines) is flawed in that human languages 'are no less artefactual than artificial languages' as they involve some form of 'human intervention' (p. 128). This leads us to question whether we should even strictly distinguish between human and AI language, since the basis for categorizing them is not necessarily a strict division between human and AI.

There are also many other ways in which AI is slowly influencing our linguistic habits: 1) texting has introduced new communication behaviours (such as how using capital letters in texting is equivalent to an emotional outburst) (Hanson, 2016, p. 347); 2) humans are increasingly projecting their interpersonal communication patterns onto computers, such as expressing emotions to, and creating friendships with, them (Xu et al., 2006, p. 227); 3) virtual and offline communications and identities are becoming so intertwined that there is 'no clear boundary between them' (Miller et al., 2016, p. 112); 4) online communication is more cost-efficient than in-person communication in that it has benefits like allowing interlocutors to adjust their self-presentation in strategic ways (Christian, 2011, p. 374; Caplan, 2006, p. 70), which questions the notion that humans are necessarily superior to machines in harnessing cost-efficiency in language usage. In the near future, we might expect digital mediums to become even more interconnected with our use of language. To emphasize this point, Harris (2008) casts doubt on the notion that face-to-face communication is necessary, by noting that the possibilities presented by online communication far exceed those of physical, in-person communication, and how online communication is overtaking face-to-face communication as the principal mode of communication (p. 430). Therefore, the omnipresence of AI in many aspects of human communication, particularly in the area of cost-efficiency, should prompt us to reconsider the role of human language vis-à-vis AI as perhaps a symbiotic relationship instead of a mutually exclusive/opposing one.

Despite the far-reaching linguistic implications of deep learning models, some scholars still cast doubt on whether AI can develop an innate ability for language. Steven Pinker (1994), in his seminal work *The Language Instinct*, argued that the innate ability to acquire and use language is unique to only human beings. His line of argument therefore suggests that when we talk about language instinct, we are unambiguously referring to humans, and that no other entity has this instinct. However, there is reason to question his view because the notion of an innate language facility is fuzzy. Hoffmann (1998) posits that intricacies about how humans learn language and the extent to which the structure for comprehending natural language is innate is 'largely unknown' (p. 231). Therefore, to simply declare that machines cannot instinctively learn (or be trained to learn) language might be a rash opinion, since what counts as 'innate' and how 'innateness' even works is never clearly defined in the first place, which affects the sturdiness of a language instinct as a benchmark to compare human and AI-produced language. Studies of natural language through machine learning have suggested that language learning could be just a probabilistic process that can occur even without explicit instruction, which is one of the main goals of machine learning – for machines to carry out tasks in the absence of explicit instruction (Railton, 2020, p. 50; Micheuz, 2020, p. 4). Furthermore, recent transformer-based models like GPT-3 are capable of producing chunks of text, even academic articles, in a style that closely resembles that of humans (Hutson, 2021; Thunström, 2022). While AI has not yet developed to the point whereby it can accurately carry out human functions, the aforementioned goal of machine learning could one day be achieved, leading to the creation of deep learning models which function on a level very similar to, or better yet indistinguishable from, humans.

AI: our helper or our competitor?

There has always been debate about how AI is unable to master human language, but what if the tables were turned and, instead, the reverse occurred? In the last few years, there have been examples of AI systems inventing their own languages, which even humans are unable to understand. As Wilson (2017) notes in his article on the creation of languages by AI which are not comprehensible by humans, AI models are able to 'drift off understandable language and invent codewords for themselves', and beyond the programming languages that humans have created, there is 'no way of truly understanding any divergent computer language' because of the lack of 'bilingual speakers of AI and human languages' and how 'we don't generally understand how complex AIs think because we can't really see inside their thought process'. An example of this invented AI language is the creation of unknown words by an AI system called DALLE-E2, which generated images with text in response to given prompts (Daras & Dimakis, 2022). DALLE-E2, when prompted with the sentence *Two farmers talking about vegetables, with subtitles*, generates an image with some unknown text on it, *Vicootes* and *Apoploe vesrreaitais*, which the researchers surmise mean 'vegetables' and 'birds' respectively (Daras & Dimakis, 2022, p. 3).

Could these 'secret language(s)' which are not easily deciphered by non-machines (that is to say, humans) potentially be a cost-effective way for machines to communicate with each other, analogous to the pragmatic information encoded in human language? Is our inability to understand this unique AI-produced language analogous to how machines do not easily comprehend us? Does this suggest that AI is perhaps developing its own form of intelligence, albeit one that operates differently from our own (because machines and humans do not have the same cognitive structure)?

By cost-effective, I mean that by directly communicating with one another in their own unique language(s) containing machine-specific linguistic features that are only fully understandable by machines, language interactions between machines are made more efficacious because their systems are attuned to the specific features present in these machine-specific languages. This is akin to how we would feel lost if asked to process linguistic information from a language that operates on a logic that is totally different from human language as our brains are simply not wired to comprehend such a different system directly. As a result, we would need to spend a lot more effort searching for alternative ways to attempt to understand it; this links to the idea of cost-efficiency. Be it for humans or machines, cost-efficiency is compromised when one (machines or humans regardless) is made to process entirely different linguistic systems.

That said, to what extent is AI-produced language under our control? Given developments such as the 'secret language(s)' discussed above, how long would it be until the question is less about AI catching up to humans, and rather more about how humans could have to catch up to AI? There are indeed similarities between human and machine language processing which allow the latter to help us in our everyday communication. Yet could there be a time when AI is no longer our linguistic helper but our *competitor*? We'll just have to wait and see.

The near future of language in an AI age

There are areas of human language which AI models are still unable to replicate because of their inability to process linguistic information at a level of cost-efficiency that is comparable to human beings, and to understand pragmatic information on a sophisticated level. At the same time, the rapid development of AI and its deep entanglement with our daily language use to the point where the boundary between human- and AI-produced language is sometimes unclear, casts doubt on the claims that AI is definitely incapable of developing an instinct for learning language and using language as efficiently as humans. For now, AI still has a lot of room for development, particularly in the realm of pragmatic sensitivity, but its increasingly undeniable influential role in our day-to-day human communication means that further investigation is required to make our understanding of linguistic competence more sensible. Although these AI models are still not yet able to fully grasp the meaning of the content they are generating, there is no reason to doubt that in the future, with sufficient training data and computing power, we might actually be able to produce models which can both understand and generate language data to a high level of cost-efficiency – a level that is virtually indistinguishable from humans, albeit doing so in a different way from humans. Should this come to pass, we are inevitably led to question the role of AI: is it our helper or our competitor?

8

Towards a Sensible Syntax

Quick reminders

Generative linguistics has a significant impact on how we understand languages. Yet since its inception, the status quo has shown a clear bias for English and European languages. As I have argued throughout this book, non-European languages and other varieties which deviate from the standard also warrant study. What's more, drawing from a wider range of languages, we need a balanced view of the theory and data, of induction and deduction. Due to the rapid pace at which technology develops, resulting in truly multimodal communication, as well as the ever-increasing role of AI, it becomes all the more evident that we should think beyond the traditional linguistic confines which seek to definitively separate competence and performance. Key to this is an understanding of the vital role of pragmatics. In order to achieve all of this, we need to open a discussion between syntacticians and those from other disciplines which allow for a more holistic and fresher perspective. In this chapter, I summarize the main takeaways from this book, which should help us all move towards a better, more sensible, syntax.

A multilingual world

It's undeniable – we live in a multilingual world. While it seems like I'm stating the obvious, it's an often-overlooked reality in linguistic theory. Multilingualism is very much the present, the future, and for a while now has been the past too, as people engage with multiple languages in their daily life. Indeed, most of the world population is multilingual, yet the theory seems static and stuck in a past in which we all inhabit an imaginary homogenous, monolingual community. However, this view is outdated and harmful to our understanding of human linguistic competence; it is unwelcoming to the inherent diversity of languages.

More needs to be done to combat the pervasive Eurocentrism, particularly Anglocentrism, and to account for marginalized languages and varieties across the world. What I argue then is for increased inclusivity as the primary agenda for achieving a more sensible theory and practice of syntax. After all, what good is the theory when the data is so limited?

Balancing data and theory

As has been discussed in several parts of this book, managing data and theory is a delicate yet important balancing act. It is simply not sensible to completely isolate the two as if they have nothing to do with each other, which appears to have been the case in linguistics for several decades. Rather, data should feed theory and theory should constantly develop based on data. The two should have an organic relationship in which one influences the other and vice versa, as they are not disparate and dysfunctional to one another. Both inductive and deductive approaches are needed to work together in order to build a more well-founded and convincing theory that can really encapsulate human linguistic competence.

Beyond the sentence and letter words

As I have shown, analysing only the single sentence in isolation is problematic. Everyday, we produce novel structures, such as through conversations with friends over text, in which a so-called linguistic 'chunk' may differ greatly from a traditional idea of the 'sentence'. Constantly, spontaneously and limitlessly, people around the world make use of this unorthodox unit but, due to its prevalence cross-linguistically, it demands understanding. In fact, we easily find these units in our digital communication on social media platforms, which many of us make use of on a daily basis. Such communication is inherently multimodal and our theory of syntax needs to account for this. For example, as discussed in Chapter 6, emoji competence is an emerging area of linguistics which deserves further investigation. In my upcoming book titled *Emoji Speak* (Kiaer, 2023), I explore emoji competence, such as how reacting to different text messages using emojis requires pragmatic understanding. In devoting serious study to this phenomenon – which didn't even exist sixty years ago but is now so important in our daily communication – we can learn more about the nature of human linguistic competence and close the chasm between what we actually do, that is to say what we produce in language, and what we study.

An AI age

As much as we inhabit a multilingual world, so do we also live in an AI age. AI is continuing to rapidly develop, as evidenced by the last five years during which increased human–computer interaction has meant that AI has come close to human language production. In addition, the era of big data and social media coincides with the AI age. Social media is very much a grassroots language practice which should be at the centre of the Chomskyan mindset for it aptly demonstrates how human language is becoming ever-increasingly generative due to its multilingual and multimodal nature. In a way, these technological innovations (amongst others) reveal how much our linguistic landscape has changed since Chomsky's seminal works. However, these changes need to be adequately accounted for in theoretical assumptions and discussions on syntax. In order to do so, innovation – in multiple meanings of the word – needs to be welcomed, understood and actively incorporated in an open and ongoing dialogue. A first step to this may very well be an exploration of the terminology used in syntactic theory and how it could do with some reform.

Pragmatic considerations

Without doubt, there is unique human linguistic competence, but as said in Chapter 6, what is unique to linguistic human competence and what is universal may be better understood through pragmatic considerations. As I propose in my 3-E Model, efficiency, expressivity and empathy are the key pragmatic motivators that all work together as we communicate with others. Rather than affirming the claim that 'This is syntax, that is pragmatics, and the two are separate,' we should rethink the relationship between the two – one that is so much more closely intertwined than perhaps initially thought. When looking at languages across the world (I underscore the necessity of looking at non-European languages as current theory is highly Eurocentric), in a way, the 3-Es are what really need to be looked at more; they are the driving forces, the real causes of syntactic variation. All the more in an AI age, we need to examine in closer detail the 3-Es and ecological factors in order to model a more sensible syntax and grammar that can encapsulate and explain human linguistic competence.

Bridging the gap

Chomskyan linguistics has created lots of chasms, whether intentionally or not. Very often, human language, how we speak and communicate with one another, can't simply be seen through a microscope – we require macro-level observations. Looking beyond a particular small aspect of linguistic phenomena has been discouraged during the past sixty or so years but a holistic approach is long overdue. We need to bridge the gaps and initiate dialogues between different opinions, thoughts, schools and frameworks to find common data and come to an appropriate consensus. Ideally, if the findings are already there, they can be shared – from this, conclusions can be drawn. In other words, based on common data, we can evaluate which theory best (or better) explains the data. The ways of evaluating theoretical relevance need to make sense, and it's sensible to have a common set of data that is reliable and could encapsulate the diversity and relevance of ecological factors. Following this, the theory can bring up alternatives and then one can decide which works better based on principles like the simplicity hypothesis. However, at present, even the data itself is not shared, meaning that common findings are in all sorts of opposition. What is needed is collaboration in the present and future to open a dialogue between linguists, language learners, cognitive psychologists and more. In fact, learnability is an important issue but somehow it has been altogether underrepresented and undermined; we therefore need to actively engage language learners and syntax students with the theory. In doing so, we can create room for a much-needed interdisciplinary approach – only then can we move towards a sensible syntax. After all, you can't see the wood for the trees.

Some final thoughts: syntax must evolve

Syntax must evolve, and theories must recognize the AI-driven reality we now inhabit. Ideal speakers don't exist; instead, we have ordinary speakers who don't function in a homogeneous language vacuum but rather within highly multilingual and hybrid linguistic environments. Key concepts on which generative linguists have built their theories, such as native speakers and grammaticality judgements, have become seriously outdated. Adhering to these views can prevent linguistic research from embracing inclusivity and diversity.

One of the key proposals of this book is to advocate for the concept of 'Asian languages from an Asian perspective'. Although this may seem natural, it has not been fully realized to date. Asian languages are often analysed through non-Asian lenses, primarily using English and Western European perspectives, resulting in less accurate understanding. I argue that to gain a more comprehensive understanding of these languages, Asian languages must be studied from Asian perspectives.

To address the problems we face, simple updates to our linguistic toolbox are inadequate, as the issues are deeply rooted in our syntactic architecture. What we truly need is a reset to establish a more sensible approach to syntax in the age of AI.

Notes

Preface

1 Note that this is now a debated term as it leads to a host of questions.

Chapter 3

1 The reaction of a speaker to a sentence has traditionally been considered as a grammaticality judgement. However, as grammar is a mental construct not accessible to conscious awareness, speakers do not link the status of a sentence to the grammar. Instead, speakers judge sentences based on how 'good' or 'bad' they sound to them. An acceptability judgement, in this framework, is an immediate, spontaneous response of the native speaker to strings of words, where acceptability is a percept that exists only within a participant's mind. As percepts are in nature difficult to measure, one common method is to ask participants to report their perceptions along a devised scale. In this way, an acceptability judgement is in fact a reported perception of acceptability (Chomsky, 1965; Schütze, 1996).
2 Global checking may be possible and done in reading and writing, but not in speaking and hearing. In speaking and hearing – which reflects the spontaneous use of language – checking is only done locally.

Chapter 4

1 Sorbian and Basque exhibit OV ordering. German and Dutch in the generative grammar framework are considered OV ordering – although the OV orderings observed in these languages are significantly different from what we observe in Asian languages.
2 Arabic is interesting, in that according to World Atlas of Language Structures (WALS), Egyptian, Gulf, Kuwait and Iraqi Arabic show SVO order as a preferred order, whereas Modern Standard Arabic prefers VSO order, and Syrian Arabic prefers no dominant order.

Chapter 5

1. Abkhaz, Afrikaans, Alawa, Alyawarra, Amharic, Arabic (Egyptian), Arabic (Tunisian), Armenian (Eastern), Atchin, Avokaya, Awa Pit, Awngi, Azerbaijani, Bandjalang, Bari, Basque, Beja, Bengali, Brahui, Bulgarian, Burushaksi, Daga, Diding, English, Evenki, Fijian, Finnish, French, Georgian, German, Gooniyandi, Greek (Modern), Guarani, Gugada, Hawaiian Creole, Hebrew (Modern), Hindi, Hungarian, Icelandic, Imonda, Japanese, Jivaro, Kanakuru, Kannada, Kanuri, Khalkha, Korean, Kriol (Fitzroy Crossing), Kui (in India), Kuku-Yalanji, Kurmanji, Latvian, Lezgian, Maithili, Maltese, Mangarrayi, Maori, Martuthunira, Maun, Montagnais, Nenets, Ngiyambaa, Oromo (Harar), Panjabi, Persian, Portuguese, Quechua (Cochabamba), Quechua (Imbabura), Rama, Rapanui, Rawang, Romanian, Rukai (Tanan), Russian, Somali, Spanish, Swahili, Swedish, Tahitian, Tamil, Tangga, Temne, Tenyer, Tigré, Tigrinya, Tiwi, Tok Pisin, Turkish, Warao, Wolof, Worora, Yaqui, Zoque (Copainalá), Zuni.
2. Alamblak, Amele, Asmat, Baluchi, Barasano, Bongu, Buriat, Canela, Cheyenne, Chinantec (Palantla), Cocama, Dani (Lower Grand Valley), Grebo, Hixkaryana, Inuktitut (Salluit), Kewa, Kikuyu, Koasati, Luganda, Luvale, Maidu (Northeast), Mwera, Nama, Ngäbere, Nimboran, Ono, O'odham, Sanuma, Sesotho, Slave, Suena, Supyire, Tucano, Udmurt, Uyghur, Wichí, Yessan-Mayo, Zulu.
3. Chácobo, Yagua.
4. Abipón, Acoma, Ainu, Akan, Apurinã, Araona, Arapesh (Mountain), Bagirmi, Berber (Middle Atlas), Buli (in Indonesia), Burmese, Cantonese, Cebuano, Chamorro, Chepang, Chukchi, Chuukese, Cree (Plains), Diola-Fogny, Engenni, Ewe, Garífuna, Greenlandic (West), Halia, Hausa, Hawaiian, Hmong Njua, Indonesian, Isekiri, Jakaltek, Javanese, Juǀ'hoan, Karok, Kayardild, Ket, Khmer, Khmu', Kiowa, Koyraboro Senni, Krongo, Kutenai, Lahu, Lai, Lakhota, Lango, Lao, Lavukaleve, Makah, Malagasy, Mandarin, Mano, Mapudungun, Margi, Maricopa, Maybrat, Meithei, Mixtec (Chalcatongo), Motu, Nakanai, Ngambay, Nicobarese (Car), Nivkh, Oneida, Paiwan, Palaung, Pangasinan, Pirahã, Qaget, Rendille, Sango, Semelai, Seneca, Shuswap, Sundanese, Tagalog, Tem, Thai, Tojolabal, Tuareg (Ahaggar), Tukang Besi, Vietnamese, Wari', Wichita, Wolaytta, Yagaria, Yoruba, Yucatec, Yukaghir (Kolyma).
5. Thanks to Prof. Jiyoung Shin for insightful discussion on this topic.
6. See Merchant (2001) and van Craenenbroeck and Temmerman (2019) for more.
7. Van Craenenbroeck and Temmerman (2019) offer a good discussion on the matter of ellipsis.

Chapter 7

1 Here is the complete list of Asian language supported on Google Translate: Arabic, Assamese, Azerbaijani, Bengali, Bhojpuri, Cebuano, Chinese (Traditional/Simplified), Dhivehi, Dogri, Filipino, Gujarati, Hebrew, Hindi, Hmong, Ilocano, Indonesian, Japanese, Javanese, Kannada, Kazakh, Khmer, Konkani, Korean, Kurdish (Kurmanji), Kurdish (Sorani), Kyrgyz, Lao, Maithili, Malay, Malayalam, Marathi, Meiteilon (Manipuri), Mizo, Mongolian, Burmese, Nepali, Odia (Oriya), Pashto, Persian, Punjabi, Sanskrit, Sindhi, Sinhala, Sundanese, Tajik, Tamil, Tatar, Telugu, Thai, Turkish, Turkmen, Urdu, Uyghur, Uzbek and Vietnamese.

References

Abarim Publications. (2021). *The amazing name Asia: Meaning and etymology*. Abarim Publications. Retrieved 21 July 2022, from https://www.abarim-publications.com/Meaning/Asia.html.

Abdullaeva, N. (2020). *Tertiary student migration from Central Asia to Germany: Cases of Kazakhstan, Kyrgyzstan and Uzbekistan*. Wiesbaden: Springer.

Abdulrahman, A., & Richards, D. (2022). Is natural necessary? Human voice versus synthetic voice for intelligent virtual agents. *Multimodal Technologies and Interaction*, 6(7), 1–17.

Achiri-Taboh, B. (2022). On pausing before and after the complementizer *that*: The cases of Cameroon Englishes and implications for the teaching of EFL and ESL. In A. Ngefac (Ed.), *Aspects of Cameroon Englishes* (pp. 190–216). Newcastle upon Tyne: Cambridge Scholars Publishing.

Adambekov, S., Askarova, S., Welburn, S. C., Goughnour, S. L., Konishi, A., LaPorte, R., & Linkov, F. (2016). Publication productivity in Central Asia and countries of the former Soviet Union. *Central Asian Journal of Global Health*, 5(1), 261.

Adeel, M. (2016). Big data virtualization and visualization: On the cloud. In R. Kannan, R. U. Rasool, H. Jin, & S. R. Balasundaram (Eds.), *Managing and processing big data in cloud computing* (pp. 168–184). Hershey: IGI Global.

Allison, R., & Chanen, B. (2012). *Oxford IB Diploma Programme: English A: Language and literature course companion*. Oxford: Oxford University Press.

Almahasees, Z. (2022). *Analysing English–Arabic machine translation: Google Translate, Microsoft Translator and Sakhr*. New York: Routledge.

Ammanath, B., & Firth-Butterfield, K. (2021, 11 November). Chatbots and other virtual assistants are here to stay – here's what that means. *World Economic Forum*. https://www.weforum.org/agenda/2021/11/chatbots-and-other-virtual-assistants-are-here-to-stay-for-good-or-bad/

Anderson, P. W. (1972). More is different. *Science*, 177(4047), 393–396. https://doi.org/10.1126/science.177.4047.393

Andrews, E. (2014). *Neuroscience and multilingualism*. Cambridge: Cambridge University Press.

Aoun, J., Benmamoun, E., & Choueiri, L. (2009). *The Syntax of Arabic*. Cambridge: Cambridge University Press.

Arnaiz, A. R. (1998). An overview of the main word order characteristics of Romance. In A. Siewierska (Ed.), *Constituent order in the languages of Europe* (pp. 47–74). Berlin: Mouton de Gruyter, doi:10.1515/9783110812206.47

Asudeh, A. (2011). Local grammaticality in syntactic production. In E. M. Bender & J. E. Arnold (Eds.), *Language from a cognitive perspective: Grammar, usage, and processing: Studies in honor of Thomas Wasow* (pp. 51–79). Stanford: CSLI Publications.

Austin, J. L. (1975). *How to do things with words* (2nd ed.). Oxford: Oxford University Press.

Azuelos-Atias, S. (2018). Making legal language clear to legal laypersons. In D. Kurzon & B. Kryk-Kastovsky (Eds.), *Legal pragmatics* (pp. 101–116). Amsterdam: John Benjamins Publishing Company.

Bahry, S. (2016). Language ecology: Understanding Central Asian multilingualism. In E. S. Ahn & J. Smagulova (Eds.), *Language change in Central Asia* (pp. 11–32). Boston: De Gruyter Mouton.

Baker, C., & Jones, S. P. (1998). *Encyclopedia of bilingualism and bilingual education*. Clevedon: Multilingual Matters.

Ball, P. (n.d.). *Nature's patterns: A tapestry in three parts*. https://www.philipball.co.uk/nature-s-patterns-a-tapestry-in-three-parts

Ballantine, J. H., & Roberts, K. A. (2011). *Our social world: Introduction to sociology* (3rd ed.). Thousand Oaks: Sage.

Balogh, K. (2013). Hungarian pre-verbal focus and exhaustivity. In Y. Motomura, A. Butler, & D. Bekki (Eds.), *New frontiers in artificial intelligence: JSAI-isAI 2012 Workshops, LENLS, JURISIN, MiMI, Miyazaki, Japan, 30 November and 1 December 2012, revised selected papers* (pp. 1–16). Berlin: Springer, doi:10.1007/978-3-642-39931-2_1

Bansal, A. (2021). *Advanced Natural Language Processing with TensorFlow 2: Build effective real-world NLP applications using NER, RNNs, seq2seq models, Transformers, and more*. Birmingham: Packt Publishing.

Barrett, R. (2014). The emergence of the unmarked: Queer theory, language ideology, and formal linguistics. In L. Zimman, J. L. Davis, & J. Raclaw (Eds.), *Queer excursions: Retheorizing binaries in language, gender, and sexuality* (pp. 195–223). New York: Oxford University Press.

Bartens, J. P. (2011). Substrate features in Nicaraguan, Providence and San Andrés Creole Englishes: A comparison with Twi. In C. Lefebvre (Ed.), *Creoles, their substrates, and language typology* (pp. 201–224). Amsterdam: John Benjamins Publishing Company.

Bateman, J. A. (2017). The place of systemic functional linguistics as a linguistic theory in the twenty-first century. In T. Bartlett & G. O'Grady (Eds.), *The Routledge handbook of systemic functional linguistics* (pp. 11–26). New York: Routledge.

Batsaikhan, U., & Dabrowski, M. (2017). Central Asia – twenty-five years after the breakup of the USSR. *Russian Journal of Economics*, 3(3), 296–320.

Battiste, M., & Henderson, J. Y. (2000). *Protecting indigenous knowledge and heritage: A global challenge*. Saskatoon: Purich Publishing.

Bauer, B. L. M. (2017). *Nominal apposition in Indo-European: Its forms and functions, and its evolution in Latin-Romance.* Boston: De Gruyter Mouton. doi:10.1515/9783110461756

Belpaeme, T. (2022). Human–robot interaction. In A. Cangelosi & M. Asada (Eds.), *Cognitive robotics* (pp. 379–394). Cambridge: MIT Press.

Bever, T. G. (1970). The influence of speech performance on linguistic structure. In G. B. Flores d'Arcais & W. J. M. Levelt (Eds.), *Advances in psycholinguistics* (pp. 4–30). Amsterdam: North-Holland.

Bierwald, J. (2014). *Specialization in online innovation communities: Understand and manage specialized members.* Wiesbaden: Springer.

Birch, B. M. (2014). *English grammar pedagogy: A global perspective.* New York: Routledge.

Birner, B. J. (2021). *Pragmatics: A slim guide.* New York: Oxford University Press.

Bloomfield, L. (1935). *Language.* London: Allen & Unwin.

Bock J. K. (1986). Syntactic persistence in language production. *Cognitive Psychology, 18*(3), 355–387.

Bock, K., & Ferreira, V. S. (2014). Syntactically speaking. In M. Goldrick, V. S. Ferreira, & M. Miozzo (Eds.), *The Oxford handbook of language production* (pp. 21–46). Oxford: Oxford University Press, doi:10.1093/oxfordhb/9780199735471.013.008

Bock, K., Loebell, H., & Morey, R. (1992). From conceptual roles to structural relations: Bridging the syntactic cleft. *Psychological Review, 99*(1), 150.

Bogost, I. (2022, 16 December). CHATGPT is dumber than you think. Retrieved 14 March 2023, from https://www.theatlantic.com/technology/archive/2022/12/chatgpt-openai-artificial-intelligence-writing-ethics/672386/

Bolinger, D. (1979). Meaning and memory. In G. Haydu (Ed.), *Experience forms: Their cultural and individual place and function* (pp. 95–112). New York: De Gruyter Mouton.

Branigan, H. P., Pickering, M. J., & McLean, J. F. (2005). Priming prepositional-phrase attachment during comprehension. *Journal of Experimental Psychology: Learning, Memory, and Cognition, 31*(3), 468–481. doi:10.1037/0278-7393.31.3.468

Bresnan, J. (1982). Control and complementation. *Linguistic Inquiry, 13*(3), 343–434.

Burkette, A. P. (2015). *Language and material culture.* Amsterdam: John Benjamins Publishing Company.

Buschfeld, S. (2013). *English in Cyprus or Cyprus English: An empirical investigation of variety status.* Philadelphia: John Benjamins Publishing Company.

Caplan, S. E. (2006). Problematic internet use in the workplace. In M. Anandarajan, T. S. H. Teo, & C. A. Simmers (Eds.), *The internet and workplace transformation* (pp. 63–79). London: M.E. Sharpe.

Carnie, A. (2002). *Syntax: A generative introduction* (1st ed.). Oxford: Blackwell Publishers.

Chao, Y. R. (1968). *A grammar of spoken Chinese.* Los Angeles: University of California Press.

Chapman, S. (2006). *Thinking about language: Theories of English*. Basingstoke: Palgrave Macmillan.

Chapman, S. (2011). *Pragmatics*. Basingstoke: Palgrave Macmillan.

Cheng, L. S., Burgess, D., Vernooij, N., Solís-Barroso, C., McDermott, A., & Namboodiripad, S. (2021). The problematic concept of native speaker in psycholinguistics: Replacing vague and harmful terminology with inclusive and accurate measures. *Frontiers in Psychology, 12*, 1–22.

Chérif, E., & Lemoine, J. F. (2019). Anthropomorphic virtual assistants and the reactions of Internet users: An experiment on the assistant's voice. *Recherche et Applications en Marketing* (English Edition), *34*(1), 28–47.

Chokobaeva, A., & Ninnis, D. (2021). Less attraction, more fear: The future of China's and Russia's soft power in Kyrgyzstan. In K. Nourzhanov & S. Peyrouse (Eds.), *Soft power in Central Asia: The politics of influence and seduction* (pp. 215–248). New York: Lexington Books.

Chomsky, N. (1957). *Syntactic structures* (Janua linguarum. Series minor; 4). The Hague: Mouton.

Chomsky, N. (1959). Review of *Verbal Behavior*, by B. F. Skinner. *Language, 35*(1), 26–58. doi:10.2307/411334

Chomsky, N. (1964). *Current issues in linguistic theory*. The Hague: Mouton.

Chomsky, N. (1965). *Aspects of the theory of syntax*. Cambridge: The MIT Press.

Chomsky, N. (1968). *Language and mind*. New York: Harcourt, Brace & World.

Chomsky, N. (1969). Linguistics and philosophy. In S. Hook (Ed.), *Language and philosophy: A symposium* (pp. 51–94). New York: New York University Press.

Chomsky, N. (1980). *Rules and representations*. New York: Columbia University Press.

Chomsky, N. (1981). *Lectures on government and binding*. Dordrecht: Foris.

Chomsky, N. (1986). *Knowledge of language: Its nature, origin, and use*. Westport: Praeger.

Chomsky, N. (1995). *The minimalist program*. Cambridge, MA: MIT Press.

Chomsky, N. (2002). *Syntactic structures* (2nd ed.). Berlin: Mouton de Gruyter.

Chomsky, N. (2007). Approaching UG from below. In Sauerland, U. & Gärtner, H. M. (eds.) *Interfaces + Recursion = Language?* New York: Mouton de Gruyter.

Chomsky, N. (2015). *Aspects of the theory of syntax* (50th Anniversary edition). Cambridge: The MIT Press.

Christian, E. (2011). History of social networks 1976–1999. In G. A. Barnett (Ed.), *Encyclopedia of social networks* (pp. 372–376). London: Sage.

Comrie, B. (1989). *Language universals and linguistic typology: Syntax and morphology*. Chicago: The University of Chicago Press.

Cook, M., & Lalijee, M. (1970). The interpretation of pauses by the listener. *British Journal of Social and Clinical Psychology, 9*(4), 375–376, doi:10.1111/j.2044-8260.1970.tb00988.x

Cook, V., & Newson, M. (2007). *Chomsky's Universal Grammar: An introduction*. Malden: Blackwell.

Cornelius, V. (2005, 25 January). *Ang Mo Kio*. National Library Board. Retrieved 16 June 2022, from https://eresources.nlb.gov.sg/infopedia/articles/SIP_230_2005-01-25.html#:~:text=The%20name%20Ang%20Mo%20Kio,red%2Dhaired%20man's%20bridge%E2%80%9D.&text=Ang%20Mo%20Kio%20was%20largely,result%20of%20the%20rubber%20boom

Coulmas, F. (2018). *An introduction to multilingualism: Language in a changing world.* Oxford: Oxford University Press.

Cowan, N. (2008). What are the differences between long-term, short-term, and working memory? *Progress in brain research, 169,* 323–338.

Craenenbroeck, J. van, & Temmerman, T. (2019). *The Oxford handbook of ellipsis.* Oxford: Oxford University Press.

Croft, W. A. (2006). The relevance of an evolutionary model to historical linguistics. In O. N. Thomsen (Ed.), *Competing models of linguistic change: Evolution and beyond* (pp. 91–132). Amsterdam: John Benjamins Publishing Company.

Crystal, D. (2003). *English as a global language.* Cambridge: Cambridge University Press.

Dadabaev, T. (2017). Introduction to survey research in post-Soviet Central Asia: Tasks, challenges and frontiers. In T. Dadabaev, M. Ismailov, & Y. Tsujinaka (Eds.), *Social capital construction and governance in Central Asia: Communities and NGOs in post-Soviet Uzbekistan* (pp. 29–55). New York: Palgrave Macmillan.

Dahl, Ö., & Velupillai, V. (2013). The past tense. In M. S. Dryer & M. Haspelmath (Eds.), *The world atlas of language structures online [WALS].* Leipzig: Max Planck Institute for Evolutionary Anthropology. Retrieved 14 June 2022, from http://wals.info/chapter/66

Daneman, M. (1991). Working memory as a predictor of verbal fluency. *Journal of Psycholinguistic Research, 20*(6), 445–464.

Daras, G., & Dimakis, A. G. (2022). Discovering the hidden vocabulary of DALLE-2. *arXiv preprint arXiv:2206.00169,* 1–6.

daryl76. (2021, 17 September). *this char siew is legendary.* Hardwarezone.com. Retrieved 16 June 2022, from https://forums.hardwarezone.com.sg/threads/this-char-siew-is-legendary.6600770/page-5

de Bot, K., & Makoni, S. (2005). *Language and aging in multilingual contexts.* Ontario: Multilingual Matters.

De Costa, P. I., Green-Eneix, C., Li, W., & Rawal, H. (2021). Interrogating race in the NEST/NNEST ideological dichotomy: Insights from raciolinguistics, culturally sustaining pedagogy and translanguaging. In R. Rubdy & R. Tupas (Eds.), *Bloomsbury World Englishes volume 2: Ideologies* (pp. 127–140). London: Bloomsbury Academic.

Derwing, B. L. (1979). Against autonomous linguistics. In T. A. Perry (Ed.), *Evidence and argumentation in linguistics* (pp. 163–189). Berlin: de Gruyter, doi:10.1515/9783110848854-010

Dickson, B. (2022, 3 May). What's the transformer machine learning model? And why should you care? *The Next Web.* https://thenextweb.com/news/whats-the-transformer-machine-learning-model

Dixon, R. M. W. (2012). *Basic linguistic theory volume 3: Further grammatical topics.* New York: Oxford University Press.

Doerr, N. M. (2009). Introduction. In N. N. Doerr (Ed.), *The native speaker concept: Ethnographic investigations of native speaker effects* (pp. 1–10). New York: Mouton de Gruyter.

Dover, S. (2012, 17 October). Study: Number of smartphone users tops 1 billion. *CBS News.* https://www.cbsnews.com/news/study-number-of-smartphone-users-tops-1-billion/

Dryer, M. S. (2013). *Feature 81A: Order of Subject, Object and Verb, WALS.* Retrieved 10 March 2023, from https://wals.info/feature/81A#2/18.0/152.9

Duarte, J., & Gogolin, I. (2013). Introduction: Linguistic superdiversity in educational institutions. In J. Duarte & I. Gogolin (Eds.), *Linguistic superdiversity in urban areas: Research approaches* (pp. 1–24). Philadelphia: John Benjamins Publishing Company.

dude123. (2022, 9 June). *Value dollar store made me realised how overcharged other shops are.* Hardwarezone.com. Retrieved 16 June 2022, from https://forums.hardwarezone.com.sg/threads/value-dollar-store-made-me-realised-how-overcharged-other-shops-are.6020067/page-1241

Duguine, M. (2017). Reversing the approach to null subjects: A perspective from language acquisition. *Frontiers in Psychology, 8*, 1–11, doi:10.3389/fpsyg.2017.00027

Eckert, P. (2012). Three waves of variation study: The emergence of meaning in the study of sociolinguistic variation. *Annual review of Anthropology, 41*, 87–100.

Einstein, A., & Infeld, L. (1938). *The evolution of physics: The riddle of motion.* New York, NY: Simon & Schuster. https://vinaire.files.wordpress.com/2014/02/evolution-of-physics-einstein-1938.pdf

Elkana, Y. (1982). The myth of simplicity. In G. Holton & Y. Elkana (Eds.), *Albert Einstein, historical and cultural perspectives: The centennial symposium in Jerusalem* (pp. 205–252). Princeton: Princeton University Press.

Ellis, R. (2003). *The study of second language acquisition.* Oxford: Oxford University Press.

Enfield, N. J. (2003). *Linguistic epidemiology: Semantics and grammar of language contact in Southeast Asia.* London: Routledge.

Enfield, N. J. (2007). *A grammar of Lao.* Boston: De Gruyter Mouton.

Ethnologue. (2022a). Asia. Retrieved 21 July 2022, from https://www.ethnologue.com/region/asia

Ethnologue. (2022b). English. Retrieved 19 June 2022, from https://www.ethnologue.com/language/eng

Ethnologue. (2022c). What is the most spoken language? Retrieved 19 June 2022, from https://www.ethnologue.com/guides/most-spoken-languages

Evans, N., & Levinson, S. C. (2009). The myth of language universals: Language diversity and its importance for cognitive science. *Behavioral and Brain Sciences, 32*(5), 429–448.

Eysenck, M. W., & Keane, M. T. (2020). *Cognitive psychology: A student's handbook* (8th ed.). London: Psychology Press.

Falk, J. S. (1999). *Women, language and linguistics: Three American stories from the first half of the twentieth century*. London: Routledge.

Fasold, R. W. (2013). The politics of language. In R. W. Fasold & J. Connor-Linton (Eds.), *An introduction to language and linguistics* (pp. 373–400). Cambridge: Cambridge University Press.

Ferreira, F., Foucart, A., & Engelhardt, P. E. (2013). Language processing in the visual world: Effects of preview, visual complexity, and prediction. *Journal of Memory and Language, 69*(3), 165–182.

Ferreira, V. S., & Bock, K. (2006). The functions of structural priming. *Language and Cognitive Processes, 21*(7–8), 1011–1029.

Fierman, W. (2015). Forty years of building and crossing bridges: Personal reflections. In N. Bakić-Mirić & D. E. Gaipov (Eds.), *Current trends and issues in higher education: An international dialogue* (pp. 5–18). Newcastle upon Tyne: Cambridge Scholars Publishing.

Fillmore, C. J. (1976). The need for a frame semantics within linguistics. *Statistical Methods in Linguistics, 12*, 5–29.

Fiorini, R. A. (2020). New CICT framework for deep learning and deep thinking application. In Information Resources Management Association (Ed.), *Deep learning and neural networks: Concepts, methodologies, tools, and applications* (pp. 330–352). Hershey: IGI Global.

Firth, A., & Wagner, J. (1997). On discourse, communication, and (some) fundamental concepts in SLA research. *The Modern Language Journal, 81*(3), 285–300.

Firth, A., & Wagner, J. (2007a). On discourse, communication, and (some) fundamental concepts in SLA research. *The Modern Language Journal, 91*, 757–772.

Firth, A., & Wagner, J. (2007b). Second/foreign language learning as a social accomplishment: Elaborations on a reconceptualized SLA. *The Modern Language Journal, 91*, 800–819.

Fischer, S., Gabriel, C., & Kireva, E. (2014). Towards a typological classification of Judeo-Spanish: Analyzing syntax and prosody of Bulgarian *judezmo*. In K. Braunmüller, S. Höder, & K. Kühl (Eds.), *Stability and divergence in language contact: Factors and mechanisms* (pp. 77–108). Philadelphia: John Benjamins Publishing Company, doi:10.1075/silv.16.05fis

Fodor, J. D. (2002). Prosodic disambiguation in silent reading. *Proceedings of the North East Linguistic Society, 32*, 113–132.

Fracchia, J. (2022). *Bodies and artefacts: Historical materialism as corporeal semiotics*. Boston: Brill.

Frajzyngier, Z., & Shay, E. (2016). *The role of functions in syntax: A unified approach to language theory, description, and typology*. Amsterdam: John Benjamins Publishing Company, doi:10.1075/tsl.111

Francis, W. S., Romo, L. F., & Gelman, R. (2002). Syntactic structure, grammatical accuracy, and content in second-language writing: An analysis of skill learning and on-line processing. In R. R. Heredia & J. Altarriba (Eds.), *Bilingual sentence processing* (pp. 317–337). Amsterdam: North-Holland.

Fröhlich, P., Baldauf, M., Meneweger, T., Tscheligi, M., de Ruyter, B., & Paternó, F. (2020). Everyday automation experience: A research agenda. *Personal and Ubiquitous Computing, 24*(6), 725–734.

Fromkin, V., Rodman, R., & Hyams, N. (2019). *An introduction to language* (11th ed.). Singapore: Cengage Learning.

ganster. (2013, 18 December). *Durian 2014*. Hardwarezone.com. Retrieved 16 June 2022, from https://forums.hardwarezone.com.sg/threads/durian-2014.4237300/page-18

Garcia, M. P., & Lopez, S. S. (2019). Exploring the uncanny valley theory in the constructs of a virtual assistant personality. In Y. Bi, R. Bhatia, & S. Kapoor (Eds.), *Intelligent systems and applications: Proceedings of the 2019 intelligent systems conference (IntelliSys) volume 1* (pp. 1017–1033). Cham: Springer.

Gargiulo, R. M. (2012). *Special education in contemporary society: An introduction to exceptionality*. Singapore: Sage.

Garten, J., Kennedy, B., Sagae, K., & Dehghani, M. (2019). Measuring the importance of context when modeling language comprehension. *Behavior Research Methods, 51*(2), 480–492.

Gaunt, John, Baĭarmandakh, L, & Chuluunbaatar, L. (2004). *Modern Mongolian: A course-book*. London: Routledge.

Gethin, A. (1990). *Antilinguistics: A critical assessment of modern linguistic theory and practice*. Oxford: Intellect.

Geveler, J., & Müller, N. (2016). Wh-fronting and Wh-in-situ in the acquisition of French: Really variants? In P. Guijarro-Fuentes, K. Schmitz, & N. Müller (Eds.), *The acquisition of French in multilingual contexts* (pp. 43–65). Bristol: Multilingual Matters.

Giacomini, A. (2021, 6 January). The past, present and future of messaging. *Forbes*. https://www.forbes.com/sites/forbestechcouncil/2021/01/06/the-past-present-and-future-of-messaging/?sh=5b62ee849f17

Gick, B., Wilson, I., & Derrick, D. (2012). *Articulatory phonetics*. Oxford: John Wiley & Sons.

Gil, D. (1994). The structure of Riau Indonesian. *Nordic Journal of Linguistics, 17*, 179–200.

Gil, D. (2001). Escaping Eurocentrism: Fieldwork as a process of unlearning. In P. Newman & M. Ratliff (Eds.), *Linguistic fieldwork* (pp. 102–132). Cambridge: Cambridge University Press.

Goddard, C. (2005). *The languages of East and Southeast Asia: An introduction*. Oxford: Oxford University Press.

Göksel, A., & Kerslake, C. (2005). *Turkish: A comprehensive grammar*. New York: Routledge.

Goldman-Eisler, F. (1968). *Psycholinguistics: Experiments in spontaneous speech*. London: Academic Press.

Goled, S. (2021a, 17 March). Why transformers are increasingly becoming as important as RNN and CNN? *Analytics India Magazine.* https://analyticsindiamag.com/why-transformers-are-increasingly-becoming-as-important-as-rnn-and-cnn/

Goled, S. (2021b, 6 July). Turing NLG, GPT-3 & Wu Dao 2.0: Meet The who's who of language models. *Analytics India Magazine.* https://analyticsindiamag.com/turing-nlg-gpt-3-wu-dao-2-0-meet-the-whos-who-of-language-models/

Gopalakrishnan, R., & Venkateswarlu, A. (2018). *Machine learning for mobile: Practical guide to building intelligent mobile applications powered by machine learning.* Birmingham: Packt Publishing.

Grenoble, L. A., & Whaley, L. J. (1998). Toward a typology of language endangerment. In L. A. Grenoble & L. J. Whaley (Eds.), *Endangered languages: Language loss and community response* (pp. 22–54). Cambridge: Cambridge University Press.

Gross, M. (1979). On the failure of generative grammar. *Language, 55*(4), 859–885.

Güneş, G., & Lipták, A. (2022). *The derivational timing of ellipsis.* Oxford: Oxford University Press.

Guy, G. R. (2011). Sociolinguistics and formal linguistics. In R. Wodak, B. Johnstone, & P. E. Kerswill (Eds.), *The SAGE handbook of sociolinguistics* (pp. 249–264). London: Sage Publications.

Halliday, M. A. K. (1964). Syntax and the consumer. In C. J. M. Stuart (Ed.), *Report of the Fifteenth Annual (First International) Round Table Meeting on Linguistics and Language Studies* (pp. 11–24). Washington: Georgetown University Press.

Hamada, Y. (2017). *Teaching EFL learners shadowing for listening: Developing learners' bottom-up skills.* London: Routledge.

Hankamer, J. (1979). *Deletion in coordinate structures.* New York: Garland.

Hanson, J. (2016). *The social media revolution: An economic encyclopedia of friending, following, texting, and connecting.* Santa Barbara: Greenwood.

Hao, K. (2021, 9 July). AI voice actors sound more human than ever – and they're ready to hire. *MIT Technology Review.* https://www.technologyreview.com/2021/07/09/1028140/ai-voice-actors-sound-human/

Harding, X. (2022, 18 March). Breaking bias – Diverse speech training? For virtual assistants, it's virtually non-existent. *Mozilla.* https://foundation.mozilla.org/en/blog/breaking-bias-diverse-speech-training-for-virtual-assistants-its-virtually-non-existent/

Harris, D. (2008). Transforming distance education: In whose interests? In T. Evans, M. Haughey, & D. Murphy (Eds.), *International handbook of distance education* (pp. 417–432). Bingley: Emerald Group Publishing.

Hawkins, J. (1994). *A performance theory of order and constituency.* Cambridge: Cambridge University Press.

Hawkins, J. (2004). *Efficiency and complexity in grammars.* Oxford: Oxford University Press.

Hawkins, J. (2014). *Cross-linguistic variation and efficiency.* Oxford: Oxford University Press.

Heaven, W. D. (2021, 24 February). Why GPT-3 is the best and worst of AI right now. *MIT Technology Review*. https://www.technologyreview.com/2021/02/24/1017797/gpt3-best-worst-ai-openai-natural-language/

Hebbar, P. (2017, 8 September). How predictive text analysis is changing communication. *Analytics India Magazine*. https://analyticsindiamag.com/predictive-text-analysis-changing-communication/

Hiramoto, M., & Sato, Y. (2012). *Got*-interrogatives and answers in Colloquial Singapore English. *World Englishes, 31*(2), 198–207.

Hobbs, J. J. (2012). *Fundamentals of world regional geography* (3rd ed.). Belmont: Brooks/Cole.

Hoffman, B. (1995). Integrating 'free' word order syntax and information structure. In *Proceedings of the Seventh Conference of the European Chapter of the Association for Computational Linguistics*. Association for Computational Linguistics.

Hoffmann, A. (1998). *Paradigms of artificial intelligence: A methodological and computational analysis*. Singapore: Springer-Verlag.

Holliday, A. (2018). Native-speakerism: Non-native English-speaking teachers (NNESTs). In J. I. Liontas (Ed.), *The TESOL encyclopedia of English language teaching* (pp. 1–7). Hoboken: Wiley Blackwell, doi:10.1002/9781118784235.eelt0027

hoz0r. (2010, 2 March). *chiong*. Urban Dictionary. Retrieved 16 June 2022, from https://www.urbandictionary.com/define.php?term=chiong

Huang, Y. (2000). *Anaphora: A cross-linguistic approach*. Oxford: Oxford University Press.

Hutson, M. (2021, 3 March). Robo-writers: The rise and risks of language-generating AI. *Nature*. https://www.nature.com/articles/d41586-021-00530-0

Hymes, D. H. (1962). The ethnography of speaking. In T. Gladwin & W. C. Sturtevant (Eds.), *Anthropology and human behavior* (pp. 13–53). Washington: The Anthropology Society of Washington.

Ish Skywaalker. (2022, 16 June). *Then mampos my fav Nasi Ayam goreng and Nasi Goreng Kampong and even prata's price will increase.* [Comment on a post.] Facebook. Retrieved 16 June 2022, from https://www.facebook.com/groups/348293689060800/permalink/1125614681328693/

Janenova, S. (2019). The boundaries of research in an authoritarian state. *International Journal of Qualitative Methods, 18*, 1–8.

Japan Advanced Institute of Science and Technology. (2022, 3 February). Mimicking the brain to realize 'human-like' virtual assistants. *Tech Xplore*. https://techxplore.com/news/2022-02-mimicking-brain-human-like-virtual.html

Jegerski, J. (2014). Self-paced reading. In J. Jegerski & B. VanPatten (Eds.), *Research methods in second language psycholinguistics* (pp. 20–49). New York: Routledge.

Jenny, M. & Tun, H. (2016). *Burmese: A comprehensive grammar*. London: Routledge.

Johnston, T., & Schembri, A. (2007). *Australian Sign Language (Auslan): An introduction to sign language linguistics*. New York: Cambridge University Press, doi:10.1017/CBO9780511607479

Kahng, J. (2022). Fluency. In T. M. Derwing, M. J. Munro, & R. I. Thomson (Eds.), *The Routledge handbook of second language acquisition and speaking* (pp. 188–200). New York: Routledge.

Kalan, A. (2016). *Who's afraid of multilingual education?: Conversations with Tove Skutnabb-Kangas, Jim Cummins, Ajit Mohanty and Stephen Bahry about the Iranian context and beyond*. Bristol: Multilingual Matters.

Kappala-Ramsamy, G. (2011, 24 July). Nim Chimpsky: The chimp they tried to turn into a human. *The Guardian*. https://www.theguardian.com/film/2011/jul/24/project-nim-chimpsky-chimpanzee-language

Karunakaran, D. (2018, 23 April). Deep learning series 1: Intro to deep learning. *Medium*. https://medium.com/intro-to-artificial-intelligence/deep-learning-series-1-intro-to-deep-learning-abb1780ee20

Kecskes, I. (2019). *English as a lingua franca: The pragmatic perspective*. Cambridge: Cambridge University Press.

Kennison, S. M. (2014). *Introduction to language development*. London: Sage Publications.

Kerr, P. (2014). *Translation and own-language activities*. Cambridge: Cambridge University Press.

Khalid, C., & Sekkappan, C. (2022, November 21). Common Singlish words you need to know to speak like a local. *TimeOut*. Retrieved 15 December 2022, from https://www.timeout.com/singapore/things-to-do/common-singlish-words-you-need-to-know-to-speak-like-a-local

Kiaer, J. (2007). *Processing and interfaces in syntactic theory: The case of Korean*. Unpublished doctoral dissertation, University of London, London.

Kiaer, J. (2014). *Pragmatic syntax*. London: Bloomsbury Academic.

Kiaer, J. (2017). Does a language have to be European to be modern? *Language on the move*. https://www.languageonthemove.com/does-a-language-have-to-be-european-to-be-modern/

Kiaer, J. (2021). *Pragmatic particles: Findings from Asian languages*. London: Bloomsbury Academic.

Kiaer, J. (2023). *Emoji speak: Communication and behaviours on social media pragmatic particles*. London: Bloomsbury Academic.

Kiaer, J., & Cagan, B. (2022). *Pragmatics in Korean and Japanese translation*. London: Routledge, doi:10.4324/9781003217466

Kim, S. (2010). *Hwupochwung kwumwunuy wunyulkwu hyengseng yangsang, 'A Prosodic Analysis on Post-verbal Expressions in Korean'*. Master's thesis, Korea University, Seoul.

Kirkpatrick, A. (2012). Theoretical issues. In E. Low & A. Hashim (Eds.), *English in Southeast Asia: Features, policy and language in use* (pp. 13–32). Philadelphia: John Benjamins Publishing Company.

Kirkpatrick, A. (2020). 'English as an ASEAN lingua franca'. In K. Bolton, W. Botha, & A. Kirkpatrick (Eds.), *The handbook of Asian Englishes* (pp. 725–740). Hoboken: John Wiley & Sons. doi.org/10.1002/9781118791882.ch32

Kirkpatrick, A., Deterding, D., & Wong, J. (2008). The international intelligibility of Hong Kong English. *World Englishes, 27*(3–4), 359–377.

Kluge, B. (2019). On translating pronominal and nominal terms of address: State of the art and future directions. In B. Kluge & M. I. Moyna (Eds.), *It's not all about you: New perspectives on address research* (pp. 47–74). Philadelphia: John Benjamins Publishing Company.

Kondo, M., Shiratori, T., Minai, N., Kogure, S., Konishi, T., & Itoh, Y. (2005). Detection and grammaticality judgment of forms in a language education system oriented for focus on form. In C. Looi, D. Jonassen, & M. Ikeda (Eds.), *Towards sustainable and scalable educational innovations informed by the learning sciences: Sharing good practices of research, experimentation and innovation* (pp. 203–210). Amsterdam: IOS Press.

Kubota, R., Corella, M., Lim, K., & Sah, P. K. (2021). 'Your English is so good': Linguistic experiences of racialized students and instructors of a Canadian university. *Ethnicities*, 1–21, doi:10.1177/14687968211055808

Kumar22. (2021, 18 October). *5 Indian sweets you should know and where to find them this Deepavali*. Hardwarezone.com. Retrieved 16 June 2022, from https://forums.hardwarezone.com.sg/threads/5-indian-sweets-you-should-know-and-where-to-find-them-this-deepavali.6624383/

Kuno, S. (1973). *The structure of the Japanese Language*. Cambridge, MA and London: MIT Press.

Kuteva, T., Heine, B., Hong, B., Long, H., Narrog, H., & Rhee, S. (2019). *World lexicon of grammaticalization* (2nd ed.). New York: Cambridge University Press.

Labov, W. (1972). *Sociolinguistic patterns*. Philadelphia: University of Philadelphia Press.

Lakoff, R. T. & Sutton, L. A. (2017). *Context counts: Papers on language, gender, and power*. Oxford: Oxford University Press.

Lamichhane, D. R., Read, J. C., & You, Z. (2021). Maybe I can help? Google as a translator and facilitator for an inter-lingual children's chat application. In C. Stephanidis, M. Antona, & S. Ntoa (Eds.), *HCI International 2021 – Posters 23rd HCI International Conference, HCII 2021, Virtual Event, July 24–29, 2021, Proceedings, Part I* (pp. 208–215). Cham: Springer.

Lee, J. (2004a). *buay song*. A Dictionary of Singlish and Singapore English. Retrieved 16 June 2022, from http://www.mysmu.edu/faculty/jacklee/singlish_B.htm#buay_song

Lee, J. (2004b). *Deepavali*. A Dictionary of Singlish and Singapore English. Retrieved 16 June 2022, from http://www.mysmu.edu/faculty/jacklee/singlish_D.htm#Deepavali

Lee, J. (2004c). *kena*. A Dictionary of Singlish and Singapore English. Retrieved 16 June 2022, from http://www.mysmu.edu/faculty/jacklee/singlish_K.htm#kena

Lee, J. (2004d). *kueh*. A Dictionary of Singlish and Singapore English. Retrieved 16 June 2022, from http://www.mysmu.edu/faculty/jacklee/singlish_K.htm#kueh

Lee, J. (2004e). *lagi*. A Dictionary of Singlish and Singapore English. Retrieved 16 June 2022, from http://www.mysmu.edu/faculty/jacklee/singlish_L.htm#lgi

Lee, J. (2004f). *sedap*. A Dictionary of Singlish and Singapore English. Retrieved 16 June 2022, from http://www.mysmu.edu/faculty/jacklee/singlish_S.htm#sedap

Lefebvre, C. (2004). *Issues in the study of pidgin and creole languages*. Amsterdam: John Benjamins Publishing Company.

Levelt, W. J. M. (1989). *Speaking: From intention to articulation*. Cambridge: The MIT Press.

Lexico. (n.d.). *mamak*. Retrieved 16 June 2022, from https://www.lexico.com/definition/mamak

Li, D. C. (2000). 'Hong Kong English': New variety of English or interlanguage? *EA Journal*, 18(1), 50–59.

Li, W., Tan, J., & Zhu, N. (2022). Double-x: Towards double-cross-based unlock mechanism on smartphones. In W. Meng, S. Fischer-Hübner, & C. D. Jensen (Eds.), *ICT systems security and privacy protection: 37th IFIP TC 11 International Conference, SEC 2022, Copenhagen, Denmark, June 13–15, 2022, Proceedings* (pp. 412–428). Cham: Springer.

Lim, L. (2007). Mergers and acquisitions: On the ages and origins of Singapore English particles 1. *World Englishes*, 26(4), 446–473.

Liu, M. Y. (2012). *Under Solomon's throne: Uzbek visions of renewal in Osh*. Pittsburgh: University of Pittsburgh Press.

Loewen, S., & Reinders, H. (2011). *Key concepts in second language acquisition*. Basingstoke: Palgrave Macmillan.

Loewenthal, R. (1957). *The Turkic languages and literatures of Central Asia: A bibliography*. Berlin: De Gruyter Mouton.

Luong, P. J. (2004). Politics in the periphery: Competing views of Central Asian states and societies. In P. J. Luong (Eds.), *The transformation of Central Asia: States and societies from Soviet rule to independence* (pp. 1–26). New York: Cornell University Press.

Lyons, J. (1972). Human language. In R. A. Hinde (Ed.), *Non-verbal communication* (pp. 49–85). London: Cambridge University Press.

MacRae, D. (2021). Toward benevolent AGI by integrating knowledge graphs for classical economics, education, and health: AI governed by ethics and trust-based social capital. In A. Hooke (Ed.), *Technological breakthroughs and future business opportunities in education, health, and outer space* (pp. 163–186). Hershey: IGI Global.

Marian, J. (n.d.). *European languages by number of native speakers*. https://jakubmarian.com/european-languages-by-number-of-native-speakers/

Marlina, R. (2017). The prospect of teaching English as an international language in a Chinese context: Student-teachers' reactions. In Z. Xu, D. He, & D. Deterding (Eds.), *Researching Chinese English: The state of the art* (pp. 173–188). Cham: Springer.

Marr, B. (2018, 1 October). What is deep learning AI? A simple guide with 8 practical examples. *Forbes*. https://www.forbes.com/sites/bernardmarr/2018/10/01/what-is-deep-learning-ai-a-simple-guide-with-8-practical-examples/?sh=776ce6bc8d4b

Masoom, K. (2014). *The entrepreneur's dictionary of business and financial terms*. Singapore: Partridge.

Matthewson, L. (2010). Cross-linguistic variation in modality systems: The role of mood. *Semantics and Pragmatics*, 3, 9–74.

McCarthy, A. (2019, 13 August). How 'smart' email could change the way we talk. *BBC*. https://www.bbc.com/future/article/20190812-how-ai-powered-predictive-text-affects-your-brain

McCulloch, G. (2019). *Because internet: Understanding the new rules of language*. New York: Riverhead Books.

Mendívil-Giró, J. (2019). How much data does linguistic theory need? On the tolerance principle of linguistic theorizing. *Frontiers in Communication*, 3, 1–6.

Merchant, J. (2001). *The syntax of silence: Sluicing, islands, and the theory of ellipsis* (Oxford studies in theoretical linguistics; 1). Oxford: Oxford University Press.

Mesthrie, R. (2006). Society and language: Overview. In K. Brown (Ed.), *Encyclopedia of Language and Linguistics* (vol. 11, pp. 472–484). Amsterdam: Elsevier.

Mesthrie, R. (2008). Pidgins/creoles and contact languages: An overview. In S. Kouwenberg & J. V. Singler (Eds.), *The handbook of pidgin and creole studies* (pp. 263–286). Malden: Wiley-Blackwell.

Micheuz, P. (2020). Approaches to artificial intelligence as a subject in school education. In T. Brinda, D. Passey, & T. Keane (Eds.), *Empowering teaching for digital equity and agency: IFIP TC 3 Open Conference on Computers in Education, OCCE 2020, Mumbai, India, January 6–8, 2020, Proceedings* (pp. 3–13). Cham: Springer.

Miller, D., Costa, E., Haynes, N., McDonald, T., Nicolescu, R., Sinanan, J., Spyer, J., Venkatraman, S., & Wang, X. (2016). *How the world changed social media*. London: UCL Press.

Miller, N. (2010). Motor speech disorders: An overview. In J. Gurd, U. Kischka, & J. Marshall (Eds.), *The handbook of clinical neuropsychology* (2nd ed., pp. 251–273). Oxford University Press.

Millman, R. (2022, 17 June). What is GPT-4 and what does it mean for businesses? *ITPro*. https://www.itpro.co.uk/technology/artificial-intelligence-ai/368288/what-is-gpt-4

Montgomery, D. W. (2022). Central Asia in context. In D. W. Montgomery (Ed.), *Central Asia: Contexts for understanding* (pp. xix–xxiii). Pittsburgh: University of Pittsburgh Press.

Moorkens, J. (2022). Ethics and machine translation. In D. Kenny (Ed.), *Machine translation for everyone: Empowering users in the age of artificial intelligence* (pp. 121–140). Berlin: Language Science Press.

mrbrown. (1998, 14 August). *this char siew is legendary*. mrbrown.com. Retrieved 16 June 2022, from https://www.mrbrown.com/blog/1998/08/the_great_singl.html#:~:text=Tok%20Kong,%3A%20%22No%20Lah...

Mufwene, S. (2001). *The Ecology of Language Evolution* (Cambridge Approaches to Language Contact). Cambridge: Cambridge University Press.

Muhamedowa, R. (2015). *Kazakh: Routledge Comprehensive Grammars*. London and New York: Routledge.

Muhamedowa, R. (2016). *Kazakh: A comprehensive grammar.* London: Routledge.
Murray, J. A. H. (1911). *Lectures I, II, and V to Oxford School of English.* Unpublished lectures. University of Oxford School of English (MP Box 27).
Murray, N. (2012). *Writing essays in English language and linguistics: Principles, tips and strategies for undergraduates.* New York: Cambridge University Press.
Musan, R., & Rathert, M. (2011). Tense across languages – An introduction. In R. Musan & M. Rathert (Eds.), *Tense across Languages* (pp. 1–7). Boston: Walter de Gruyter. https://doi.org/10.1515/9783110267020.1
Mycock, L. (2015). Syntax and its interfaces: An overview. In T. Kiss & A. Alexiadou (Eds.), *Syntax – theory and analysis: An international handbook*, volume 1 (pp. 24–69). Berlin: De Gruyter Mouton, doi:10.1515/9783110377408.24
Naftulin, J. (2016, 13 July). Here's how many times we touch our phones every day. *Insider.* https://www.businessinsider.com/dscout-research-people-touch-cell-phones-2617-times-a-day-2016-7
Nagao, M. (1989). New directions of machine translation. In J. E. Altais (Ed.), *Georgetown University Round Table on Languages and Linguistics (GURT) 1989: Language teaching, testing, and technology: Lessons from the past with a view toward the future* (pp. 378–384). Washington: Georgetown University Press.
Nelson, P., Urs, N. V., & Kasicheyanula, T. R. (2022). Progress in Natural Language Processing and language understanding. In M. V. Albert, L. Lin, M. J. Spector, & L. S. Dunn (Eds.), *Bridging human intelligence and artificial intelligence* (pp. 83–103). Cham: Springer.
Newmeyer, F. J. (1983). *Grammatical theory: Its limits and its possibilities.* Chicago: The University of Chicago Press.
Newmeyer, F. J. (2005). *Possible and probable languages: A generative perspective on linguistic typology.* Oxford: Oxford University Press.
Ng, M. Y. (2005). *Hong Kong English.* Hong Kong: The University of Hong Kong.
Ngo, B. (2020). *Vietnamese: An essential grammar.* London: Routledge.
Ngo, T. (2011). Meaning loss in translation: The what, why, and how. A case of Vietnamese-English translation. In A. Arnall & U. Ozolins (Eds.), *Proceedings of the 'Synergise!' Biennial National Conference of the Australian Institute of Interpreters and Translators: AUSIT 2010* (pp. 136–167). Newcastle: Cambridge Scholars Publishing.
Nordlinger, R., & Sadler, L. (2008). When is a temporal marker not a tense?: Reply to Tonhauser 2007. *Language, 84*(2), 325–331.
OED Online. (2022a, March). 'scramble, v.' Oxford University Press. Retrieved 24 May 2022.
OED Online. (2022b, June). 'linguist, n.' Oxford University Press. Retrieved 10 June 2022.
OED Online. (2022c). *wah, int.* Oxford University Press. Retrieved 16 June 2022, from https://www.oed.com /view/Entry/47085504?rskey=aYsqu8&result=2&isAdvanced= false#eid
Office for National Statistics (ONS), released 29 November 2022, ONS website, statistical bulletin, Ethnic group, England and Wales: Census 2021. https://www.ons.

gov.uk/peoplepopulationandcommunity/culturalidentity/ethnicity/bulletins/ethnicgroupenglandandwales/census2021#cite-this-statistical-bulletin

Oliphant, C. (2013). *Russia's role and interests in Central Asia*. London: Saferworld.

Osberger, M. J., & McGarr, N. S. (1982). Speech production characteristics of the hearing impaired. In N. J. Lass (Ed.), *Speech and language: Advances in basic research and practice volume 8* (pp. 221–283). New York: Academic Press.

Otwinowska, A. (2015). *Cognate vocabulary in language acquisition and use: Attitudes, awareness, activation*. Buffalo: Multilingual Matters.

Ouhalla, J. (1994). *Introducing transformational grammar: From rules to principles and parameters*. London: Edward Arnold.

Park, J., & Wilkins, K. (2005). 'Re-orienting the Orientalist gaze'. *Global Media Journal*, 4(6), 1–15.

Parker, R. S. (2012). *Concussive brain trauma: Neurobehavioral impairment and maladaptation* (2nd ed.). Boca Raton: CRC Press.

Patterson, B., & West, R. (2020). *Socio linguistics*. Essex: ED-Tech Press.

Pattie, C., & Johnston, R. J. (2011). Voting behaviors. In D. Southerton (Eds.), *Encyclopedia of consumer culture* (pp. 1511–1514). London: Sage.

Pederson, E. (2010). Linguistic relativity. In B. Heine & H. Narrog (Eds.), *The Oxford handbook of linguistic analysis* (pp. 663–678). Oxford: Oxford University Press.

Pennycook, A. (2016). Politics, power relationships and ELT. In G. Hall (Ed.), *The Routledge handbook of English language teaching* (pp. 26–37). New York: Routledge.

Pérez-Pereira, M., Peralbo, M., & Veleiro, A. (2017). Executive functions and language development in pre-term and full-term children. In A. A. Benavides & R. G. Schwartz (Eds.), *Language development and disorders in Spanish-speaking children* (pp. 91–112). Cham: Springer.

Perrigo, B. (2022, 5 December). Chatgpt says we should prepare for the impact of AI. Retrieved 14 March 2023, from https://time.com/6238781/chatbot-chatgpt-ai-interview/.

Phillip, G. (2017). Conventional and novel metaphors in language. In E. Semino & Z. Demjén (Eds.), *The Routledge handbook of metaphor and language* (pp. 219–232). London: Routledge.

Phillips, C. (1996). *Order and structure*. Unpublished doctoral dissertation, Massachusetts Institute of Technology.

Phillips, C. (2003). Linear order and constituency. *Linguistic Inquiry*, 34(1), 37–90.

Phillips, C. (2009). Should we impeach armchair linguists? In S. Iwasaki, H. Hoji, P. M. Clancy, & S.-O. Sohn (Eds.), *Japanese/Korean linguistics*, Volume 17 (pp. 49–64). Stanford: CSLI Publications.

Pinker, S. (1994). *The language instinct: How the mind creates language*. New York: Harper Perennial.

Plotkin, V. (2006). *The language system of English*. Boca Raton: BrownWalker Press.

Pym, A., & Turk, H. (2000). Translatability. In M. Baker & K. Malmkjær (Eds.), *Routledge encyclopedia of translation studies* (pp. 273–277). London: Routledge.

Quirk, R., & Svartvik, J. (1966). *Investigating linguistic acceptability*. The Hague: Mouton.
Railton, P. (2020). Ethical learning, natural and artificial. In S. M. Liao (Ed.), *Ethics of artificial intelligence* (pp. 45–78). New York: Oxford University Press.
Rasanayagam, J. (2010). Asia: Central. In A. Barnard & J. Spencer (Eds.), *The Routledge encyclopedia of social and cultural anthropology* (2nd ed., pp. 67–68). New York: Routledge.
Rha, H.-S., & Park S.-S. (2017). Korean 'exceptionally difficult languages to learn': US agency. *The Korea Times*. Retrieved 21 July 2022 from https://www.koreatimes.co.kr/www/nation/2017/12/181_240261.html
Richardson, W. J. (2018). Understanding Eurocentricism as a structural problem of undone science. In G. K. Bhambra, D. Gebrial, & K. Nişancıoğlu (Eds.), *Decolonizing the university* (pp. 231–247). London: Pluto Press.
Rizzi, L. (1994). The Chosmkyan program and linguistic typology. In C. Otero (Ed.), *Noam Chomsky: Critical assessments* (pp. 401–423). London: Routledge.
Ross, J. R. (1967). *Constraints on variables in syntax*. Unpublished doctoral dissertation, Massachusetts Institute of Technology. Published as Ross, J. R. (1986). *Infinite syntax!* Norwood, NJ: ABLEX.
Rothman, D. (2021). *Transformers for Natural Language Processing: Build innovative deep neural network architectures for NLP with Python, PyTorch, TensorFlow, BERT, RoBERTa, and more*. Birmingham: Packt Publishing.
Ryan, C. (2013). *Language Use in the United States: 2011* (Rep.). Retrieved 14 March 2023, from United Census Bureau website: https://www2.census.gov/library/publications/2013/acs/acs-22/acs-22.pdf
Sadler, L., & Nordlinger, R. (2006). Case stacking in realizational morphology. *Linguistics* 44(3), 459–487.
Sag, I. A. (1976). *Deletion and logical form*. Unpublished doctoral dissertation, Massachusetts Institute of Technology.
Sag, I. A. (2010). English filler-gap constructions. *Language*, 86(3), 486–545.
Saito, M. (1985). *Some asymmetries in Japanese and their theoretical implications*. Unpublished doctoral dissertation, Massachusetts Institute of Technology.
Sampson, G. (2015). *Evolutionary language understanding*. London: Bloomsbury.
Schlyter, B. N. (2001). Language policies in present-day Central Asia. *International Journal on Multicultural Societies*, 3(2), 127–136.
Schneider, E. W. (2007). *Postcolonial English: Varieties around the world*. Cambridge: Cambridge University Press.
Schoeberlein, J. (2009). Marginal centrality: Central Asian studies on the eve of a new millennium. In M. Juntunen & B. N. Schlyter (Eds.), *Return to the silk roads: Current Scandinavian research on Central Asia* (pp. 23–44). London: Routledge.
Schroeder, S. (2017). Grammar and grammatical statements. In H. Glock & J. Hyman (Eds.), *A companion to Wittgenstein* (pp. 252–268). Chichester: Wiley Blackwell.
Schütze, C. T. (1996). *The empirical base of linguistics: Grammaticality judgments and linguistic methodology*. Chicago: University of Chicago Press.

Schütze, C. T. (2006). Linguistic evidence, status of. In L. Nadel (Ed.), *Encyclopedia of cognitive science* (pp. 1–7). New York: Wiley, doi:10.1002/0470018860.s00291

Schwartz, O. *Can a computer write poetry?* (2016). *YouTube*. TED. Retrieved 10 March 2023, from https://www.youtube.com/watch?v=UpkAqPEcMyE

Scott, K. (1982). Soviet Central Asia: A religious limbo. In C. Caldarola (Ed.), *Religion and societies: Asia and the Middle East* (pp. 231–258). Berlin: De Gruyter Mouton.

Seikel, J. A., Drumright, D. G., & Hudock, D. J. (2021). *Anatomy & physiology for speech, language, and hearing* (6th ed.). San Diego: Plural Publishing.

Setter, J., Wong, C., & Chan, B. (2010). *Hong Kong English*. Edinburgh: Edinburgh University Press.

Sévigny, A. (2010). Kamo, an attitudinal pragmatic marker of Macedonian. In M. N. Dedaić & M. Mišković-Luković (Eds.), *South Slavic discourse particles* (pp. 45–63). Amsterdam: John Benjamins Publishing Company.

Shei, C. (2014). *Understanding the Chinese language: A comprehensive linguistic introduction*. London: Routledge.

Sherr-Ziarko, E., & Kiaer, J. (2019). A prosodic analysis of intervening objects in English phrasal verbs using the British National Corpus. In S. Calhoun, P. Escudero, M. Tabain & Paul Warren (eds), *Proceedings of the 19th International Congress of Phonetic Sciences. Melbourne, Australia 2019*, pp. 275–279. Canberra: Australia: Australasian Speech Science and Technology Association.

Shibatani, M. (2009). Honorifics, in *Concise Encyclopedia of Semantics*, ed. Keith Allan. Amsterdam: Elsevier, 381.

Shuck, G. (2006). Racializing the nonnative English speaker. *Journal of Language, Identity, and Education*, 5(4), 259–276.

Siewierska, A. (1988). *Word order rules*. London: Croom Helm.

Siewierska, A. (2011). Overlap and complementarity in reference impersonals: Man-constructions vs. third person plural-impersonals in the languages of Europe. In A. J. Malchukov & A. Siewierska (Eds.), *Impersonal constructions: A cross-linguistic perspective* (pp. 57–90). Amsterdam: John Benjamins Publishing Company, doi:10.1075/slcs.124.03sie

Silver, R. E., & Bokhorst-Heng, W. D. (2020). Concepts of globalization and English language teacher education in Singapore. In A. B. M. Tsui (Ed.), *English language teaching and teacher education in East Asia: Global challenges and local responses* (pp. 37–56). New York: Cambridge University Press.

Singaporean. (2017, 25 September). *jiak*. Singlish Dictionary. Retrieved 16 June 2022, from http://www.singlish.net/jiak/

Singaporean. (2018, 14 May). *7 early, 8 early (七早八早)*. Singlish Dictionary. Retrieved 16 June 2022, from http://www.singlish.net/7-early-8-early-%E4%B8%83%E6%97%A9%E5%85%AB%E6%97%A9/

Smagulova, J., & Ahn, E. S. (2016). Introduction. In E. S. Ahn & J. Smagulova (Eds.), *Language change in Central Asia* (pp. 1–10). Boston: De Gruyter Mouton.

Song, J. J. (2018). *Linguistic typology*. Oxford: Oxford University Press.

Squaredot. (2022a, 9 June). *Value dollar store made me realised how overcharged other shops are*. Hardwarezone.com. Retrieved 16 June 2022, from https://forums.hardwarezone.com.sg/threads/value-dollar-store-made-me-realised-how-overcharged-other-shops-are.6020067/page-1241

Squaredot. (2022b, 14 June). *Value dollar store made me realised how overcharged other shops are*. Hardwarezone.com. Retrieved 16 June 2022, from https://forums.hardwarezone.com.sg/threads/value-dollar-store-made-me-realised-how-overcharged-other-shops-are.6020067/page-1250

Staal, J. F. (1967). *Word order in Sanskrit and universal grammar*. Dordrecht: D. Reidel Publishing Company.

Statista Research Department. (2023, March 31). The most spoken languages worldwide in 2022 (by speakers in millions). *Statista*. Retrieved 14 April 2023, from https://www.statista.com/statistics/266808/the-most-spoken-languages-worldwide/

Stillings, N. A., Weisler, S. E., Chase, C. H., Feinstein, M. H., Garfield, J. L., & Rissland, E. L. (1995). *Cognitive science: An introduction* (2nd ed.). London: The MIT Press.

Stine-Morrow, E. A. L., Worm, T. W., Barbey, A. K., & Morrow, D. G. (2022). The potential for socially integrated and engaged lifestyles to support cognitive health with aging: Precursors and pathways. In G. Sedek, T. M. Hess, & D. R. Touron (Eds.), *Multiple pathways of cognitive aging: Motivational and contextual influences* (pp. 276–305). New York: Oxford University Press.

Stringer, A. (2003). Soviet development in Central Asia: The classic colonial syndrome? In T. Everett-Heath (Ed.), *Central Asia: Aspects of transition* (pp. 146–166). London: Routledge.

Stowe, L. A. (1986). Parsing WH-constructions: Evidence for on-line gap location. *Language and Cognitive Processes*, 1(3), 227–245, doi:10.1080/01690968608407062

Tabor, W., Galantucci, B., & Richardson, D. (2004). Effects of merely local syntactic coherence on sentence processing. *Journal of Memory and Language*, 50(4), 355–370, doi:10.1016/j.jml.2004.01.001

Takano, Y. (2002). Surprising constituents. *Journal of East Asian Linguistics*, 11, 243–301.

testerjp. (2022, 17 February). *Who here like to go Little India jiak Indian food*. Hardwarezone.com. Retrieved 16 June 2022, from https://forums.hardwarezone.com.sg/threads/who-here-like-to-go-little-india-jiak-indian-food.6699142/page-3

Tezgiden-Cakcak, Y. (2019). *Moving beyond technicism in English-language teacher education: A case study from Turkey*. London: Lexington Books.

Thagard, P. (2021). *Bots and beasts: What makes machines, animals, and people smart?* Cambridge: The MIT Press.

Tham, P. (2021, 4 November). *5 things to know about that awesome Indian snack Murukku*. Wonderwall. Retrieved 16 June 2022, from https://www.wonderwall.sg/food/5-things-to-know-about-that-awesome-indian-snack-murukku/

Thibault, H. (2018). *Transforming Tajikistan: State-building and Islam in post-Soviet Central Asia*. London: I.B. Tauris.

Thompson, H. R. (2012). *Bengali* (Vol. 18). Amsterdam: John Benjamins Publishing.

Thunström, A. O. (2022, 30 June). We asked GPT-3 to write an academic paper about itself – then we tried to get it published. *Scientific American.* https://www.scientificamerican.com/article/we-asked-gpt-3-to-write-an-academic-paper-about-itself-then-we-tried-to-get-it-published/

Toktomushev, K. (2017). *Kyrgyzstan – regime security and foreign policy.* London: Routledge.

Tsuda, Y. (2014). The hegemony of English and strategies for linguistic pluralism: Proposing the ecology of language paradigm. In M. K. Asante, Y. Miike, & J. Yin (Eds.), *The global intercultural communication reader* (pp. 445–456). New York: Routledge.

Tsujimura, N. (2005). *An introduction to Japanese linguistics.* Oxford: John Wiley & Sons.

Tsujimura, N. (2007). *Belpaeme* (2nd ed., Blackwell textbooks in linguistics). Malden, MA; Oxford: Blackwell.

Twilhaar, J. N., & van den Bogaerde, B. (2016). *Concise lexicon for sign linguistics.* Amsterdam: John Benjamins Publishing Company, doi:10.1075/z.201

Tyson, L. (2006). *Critical theory today: A user-friendly guide.* London: Routledge. doi:10.4324/9780203479698

Utomo, D. (2020, 25 April). *13 words that have a different meaning in Singapore than anywhere else.* TimeOut. Retrieved 16 June 2022, from https://www.timeout.com/singapore/things-to-do/words-that-have-a-different-meaning-in-singapore-than-anywhere-else

Vanderveken, D. (2002). Universal grammar and speech act theory. In D. Vanderveken & S. Kubo (Eds.), *Essays in speech act theory* (pp. 25–62). Amsterdam: John Benjamins Publishing.

Vaswani, A., Shazeer, N., Parmar, N., Uszkoreit, J., Jones, L., Gomez, A. N., ... & Polosukhin, I. (2017). Attention is all you need. In I. Guyon, U. Von Luxburg, S. Bengio, H. Wallach, R. Fergus, S. Vishwanathan, & R. Garnett (Eds.), *Advances in neural information processing systems 30 (NIPS 2017)* (pp. 1–15). La Jolla: Neural Information Processing Systems Foundation.

Velupillai, V. (2012). *An introduction to linguistic typology.* Amsterdam: John Benjamins Publishing Company, doi:10.1075/z.176

Vovin, A. (2010). *Koreo-Japonica: A Re-evaluation of a common genetic origin.* Honolulu: University of Hawaiʻi Press: Center for Korean Studies, University of Hawaiʻi.

Vulchanova, M., Vulchanov, V., Sorace, A., Suarez-Gomez, C., & Guijarro-Fuentes, P. (2022). Editorial: The notion of the native speaker put to the test: Recent research advances. *Frontiers in Psychology, 13,* 1–6.

Warren, D. E., Rubin, R., Shune, S., & Duff, M. C. (2018). Memory and language in aging: How their shared cognitive processes, neural correlates, and supporting mechanisms change with age. In M. Rizzo, S. Anderson, & B. Fritzsch (Eds.), *The Wiley handbook on the aging mind and brain* (pp. 270–295). Hoboken: John Wiley & Sons.

Wasow, T. (2002). *Postverbal behavior*. Stanford: CSLI.

Wheeler, G. (1977). The Turkic languages of Soviet Muslim Asia: Russian linguistic policy. *Middle Eastern Studies, 13*(2), 208–217.

White, E. (2012). Ethnicity and national identity in England and Wales: 2011. Retrieved 14 March 2023, from https://www.ons.gov.uk/peoplepopulationandcommunity/culturalidentity/ethnicity/articles/ethnicityandnationalidentityinenglandandwales/2012-12-11

Widdowson, D. (1990). Discourses of enquiry and conditions of relevance. In J. E. Alatis (Ed.), *Georgetown University Round Table on Languages and Linguistics (GURT) 1990: Linguistics, language teaching and language acquisition: The interdependence of theory, practice and research for the future* (pp. 37–48). Washington: Georgetown University Press.

Wiktionary. (2022a, 6 April). sama-sama. Retrieved 16 June 2022, from https://en.wiktionary.org/wiki/sama-sam

Wiktionary. (2022b, 9 June). prata. Retrieved 16 June 2022, from https://en.wiktionary.org/wiki/prata#English

Wilcox, S., & Morford, J. P. (2007). Empirical methods in signed language research. In M. Gonzalez-Marquez, I. Mittelberg, S. Coulson, & M. J. Spivey (Eds.), *Methods in cognitive linguistics* (pp. 171–200). Amsterdam: John Benjamins Publishing Company.

Wiley, T. G., & Lee, J. S. (2009). Introduction. In T. G. Wiley, J. S. Lee, & R. W. Rumberger (Eds.), *The education of language minority immigrants in the United States* (pp. 1–34). Blue Ridge Summit: Multilingual Matters. doi:10.21832/9781847692122-003

Wilkin, P. (2015). The myth of simplicity. In G. Holton & Y. Elkana (Eds.), *Albert Einstein, historical and cultural perspectives: The centennial symposium in Jerusalem* (pp. 205–252). Princeton: Princeton University Press.

Wilson, M. (2017, 14 July). AI is inventing languages humans can't understand. Should we stop it? *Fast Company*. https://www.fastcompany.com/90132632/ai-is-inventing-its-own-perfect-languages-should-we-let-it

Wilss, W. (1996). *Knowledge and skills in translator behavior*. Philadelphia: John Benjamins Publishing Company.

Wilton, A. (2009). Multilingualism and foreign language learning. In K. Knapp, B. Seidlhofer, & H. Widdowson (Eds.), *Handbook of foreign language communication and learning* (pp. 45–78). Berlin: Mouton de Gruyter.

Wiltschko, M. (2014). *The universal structure of categories: Towards a formal typology*. Cambridge: Cambridge University Press.

Wittgenstein, L. (1953). *Philosophical investigations* (3rd ed., G. E. M. Anscombe, Trans.). New York: Macmillan.

Wittgenstein, L., & Anscombe, G. E. M. (1963). *Philosophical investigations* (2nd ed.) Oxford: Basil Blackwell.

Wong, J. O. (2014). *The culture of Singapore English*. Cambridge: Cambridge University Press.

Wong, J., Nerva, C., & Ang, J. (2022, 25 January). *34 Singlish phrases to know before visiting Singapore*. TripZilla. Retrieved 16 June 2022, from https://www.tripzilla.com/singlish-phrases-singapore/95014

Wooden, A. E., Aitieva, M., & Epkenhans, T. (2009). Revealing order in the chaos: Field experiences and methodologies of political and social research on Central Eurasia. In A. E. Wooden & C. H. Stefes (Eds.), *The politics of transition in Central Asia and the Caucasus: Enduring legacies and emerging challenges* (pp. 30–71). London: Routledge.

Xu, Z., John, D., & Boucouvalas, A. C. (2006). Fuzzy logic usage in emotion communication of human machine interaction. In C. Ghaoui (Ed.), *Encyclopedia of human computer interaction* (pp. 227–233). Hershey: Idea Group Reference.

Yang, Charles D. (2016). *The price of linguistic productivity*. Cambridge, MA: The MIT Press.

Ye, J. C. (2022). *Geometry of deep learning: A signal processing perspective*. Singapore: Springer Nature.

Yeoh, G. (2019, 16 March). *Look, can we please learn how to spell Malay words properly before using them???* Rice Media. Retrieved 16 June 2022, from https://www.ricemedia.co/culture-life-commonly-misspelt-malay-words-jelak/

Yip, M. (2002). *Tone*. Cambridge: Cambridge University Press.

Yoon, D., & McGrenere, J. (2021, 7 June). Making virtual assistants sound human poses a challenge for designers. *The Conversation*. https://theconversation.com/making-virtual-assistants-sound-human-poses-a-challenge-for-designers-161240

Yu, F. T. S., Yu, E. H., & Yu, A. G. (2019). *The art of learning: Neural networks and education*. London: CRC Press.

Zdorenko, T. (2010). Subject omission in Russian: A study of the Russian National Corpus. In S. T. Gries, S. Wulff, & M. Davies (Eds.), *Corpus-linguistic applications: Current studies, new directions* (pp. 119–133). Amsterdam: Rodopi, doi:10.1163/9789042028012_009

Zhou, F. (2020). *Models of the human in twentieth-century linguistic theories: System, order, creativity*. Singapore: Springer.

Zui. (2017, 19 May). *Adventures in Colloquial Singaporean English (Singlish) – The curious case of 'already'*. The Language Closet. Retrieved 16 June 2022, from https://thelanguagecloset.com/2017/05/19/adventures-in-colloquial-singaporean-english-singlish-the-curious-case-of-already/#:~:text=The%20former%20draws%20influence%20from,used%20in%20positive%20situations%2C%20however.

Zwartjes, O. (2011). *Portuguese missionary grammars in Asia, Africa and Brazil, 1550–1800*. Philadelphia: John Benjamins Publishing Company.

Index

Page numbers followed by 'n' indicate a note.

3-E Model 139, 173–4
    in artificial intelligence age 143–4
    efficiency 140–1
    empathy 143
    expressivity 141–3

Abarim Publications 72
Abdulrahman, A. 137
acceptability judgement 44, 50, 177n1
Ahn, E. S. 83
AI. *See* artificial intelligence
Allison, R. 118
American English 57, 61–3, 65
Anatolia 72–3
Anderson, Philip W. 145
Andrews, E. 29
Anglocentrism 37, 71, 91, 172
    Asian languages in 103
    in syntactic architecture 124–6
ANN. *See* artificial neural networks
Apple 136
applied linguists 9
arbitrary PF (phonetic form) deletion 102
Arnaiz, A. R. 107
articulation 36, 122, 134
    definition 135
    in human language 136
    memory and 134, 138, 140
    in speech production 135
artificial intelligence (AI) x, 1, 16, 22–3, 67, 68, 69, 145, 164
    3-E Model in 143–4
    age 146, 170, 173
    AI-backed deep learning language models 16
    bots xiv
    deep learning 146–7
    developments in 146–8
    generation 134, 137, 142
    generative 142, 146
    human languages and 169
    language models 16–17
    language translation programs and 6
    linguistic habits and 167
    linguistic lines between humans and 166–8
    models 164, 168–9, 170
    natives xiii, xiv
    smart devices and 166–7
    transformer-based language models 147
    translations 142, 145, 151, 163
    voice actors 136
artificial neural networks (ANN) 146, 147
Asia
    cultural diversity in 74
    origin of term 72–3
Asian languages ix, xiii, 14, 19, 37, 81, 87, 104, 151, 175
    Anglocentric analysis 103
    Central Asian languages 82–6
    classification of 75–8
    Eurocentrism in side-lining of 87
    European languages *vs.* 79–80
    flexible word order 88–9
    glossing difficulties 97–100
    Google Translate 149
    grammaticality of 42–3, 52–5
    grammatical properties of 92–3
    Korean speech corpora expressions 54
    linguistic characteristics 73
    as minority languages 78–9
    as modern languages 75–8
    noun-and-particle sequence in 91
    Pacific Island languages and 79
    particles, rich use of 89–91
    'pick-and-choose' approach 91–2
    plethora of particles 94–5

pragmatic principle 96
pro-drop 101–2
pronoun omission 101
realization of subjects 100
second-person pronoun 100–1
simplicity hypothesis 102–3
as socio-pragmatically rich 88
socio-pragmatic features of 73–4
socio-pragmatic sensitivity 53
'square pegs into round holes' 92–3
syntactic fluidity in 89
syntactic freedom 93–4
in syntax 71–2
underrepresentation of 79–82
verb-finality for SOV 54
verb-final languages 95–6
verbs in 126–7
Aspects of the Theory of Syntax (Chomsky) (1965) viii, 1, 19, 22, 26, 36, 67, 71, 93, 105, 117
Assuwa 72
Aṣṭādhyāyī (Pāṇini) 87
asterisk (*) symbol 45, 48
Asudeh, A. 51
Australia
  Aboriginal languages, flexible word order in 108–9
  foreign languages in 79
autocorrect software, for spelling and grammar 25

Baker, C. 78
Balogh, K. 108
Bateman, J. A. 7, 8
Batsaikhan, U. 84
Battiste, M. 92
BERT model 145, 147, 148
Bever, T. G. 53
big data 23, 122, 173
  language patterns and 25–6
  machine learning and 26
Birch, B. M. 31
Bloomfield, L. 25, 87
Bock, K. 112, 125
Bogost, I. 160
Bokhorst-Heng, W. D. 30
Bolinger, D. 137
Branigan, H. P. 112
British English 30, 57, 61–3, 65

British National Corpus 47, 122
Buddhism 73
Bulgarian, flexible word order in 110–11
Buschfeld, S. 34

Canada, foreign languages in 79
Carnie, A. 45
CCG. *See* Combinatory Categorial Grammar
Central Asia
  geographical region of 82
  multilingualism in 83
Central Asian languages 82–6
  lack of research on 84
  major 85–6
  paucity of studies on 85
  underrepresentation of 83
Chanen, B. 118
ChatGPT xiv, 23, 134, 142, 145, 147, 150
  future of pragmatic translation 162–3
  generative abilities of 163
  Google *vs.* 148–50
  for Indonesian 158–9
  for Japanese 153–4
  for Korean 152–3
  for Mandarin 154–6
  mistranslations of Kazakh in 160–1
  mistranslations of Mongolian in 161–2
  for Mongolian 161–2
  one output *vs.* many outputs 152
  for pragmatic translation 151
  for Russian 157–8
  for translating sentence 151
  for Turkish 159–60
  for Vietnamese 156–7
Cheng, L. S. 29
Cherif, E. 136–7
Chinese languages 13, 79. *See also* classical Chinese 154–5; linguistic hybridity, in Singlish
Chomskyan linguistics 1–2, 15, 105, 134, 174
  learning in language acquisition 33
  linguistic competence in 15, 34
  study of language 8
Chomsky, N. viii, x, 1, 17, 19, 23, 24, 26, 52, 55, 65, 67, 81, 87, 101, 105, 111, 117, 124, 128, 130, 133, 140, 143, 173
  Chomskyan Minimalist Program 81

formalisms 6
generative theory 2
on grammaticality 41, 43–4, 45
ideal speaker-listener 21–2, 36
on language acquisition 33–4
native *vs.* non-native speakers 32
tradition of generative linguistics 22
view on language ability 17–18
classical Chinese 154–5
Classical Greek, pro-drop in 112–13
classical languages, labelling of 76
CNN. *See* convolutional neural networks
Combinatory Categorial Grammar (CCG) 121
communities of practice 65, 67
Comrie, B. 8
Confucianism 73
constituency conflict phenomena 120
contemporary linguistics 7, 10, 21, 22, 72, 87, 106
contemporary syntax 22, 25
convolutional neural networks (CNN) 147
Cook, M. 118
core *vs.* periphery phenomena 105–6
cost-efficiency principle 140, 141
Craenenbroeck, J. van 178n7
cross-linguistic variation 23, 24
Crystal, D. 62, 64

Dabrowski, M. 84
DALLE-E2 169
Daneman, M. 138
De Costa, P. I. 21
deep learning 146–7, 168
DeepL Translator 152
dichotomies, possible/impossible 10
digital native xiii
disfluencies
 at core or periphery 117–19
 in speech 117–18
Dryer, M. S. 95
Duarte, J. 28
Duguine, M. 113

East Asian languages 13, 112
Eckert, P. 65
EFL. *See* English as a foreign language
Einstein, A. 3, 5–6, 103
ellipsis 43, 126

derivational timing of 125
PF-deletion accounts of 125
PF-non-realization of 124
elliptical phenomena 124, 125
Ellis, R. 52
emoji competence 66–7, 172
emojis x, 26, 66–7, 172
Emoji Speak (Kiaer) 172
Enfield, N. J. 81–2, 92
English 71–2. *See also* American English; British English; Hong Kong English; linguistic hybridity, in Singlish; Singlish
finite sentence in 8
grammaticality of other 61–5
language tests 31
non-standard varieties of 62
particles role in 91
social media and 63–4
in tense marking 117
varieties of 30
as world language 32, 64
English as a foreign language (EFL) 18
learners 31–5
ESL. *See* English as a second language
Ethnologue 31, 61
Eurocentrism 15, 71, 86, 91, 104, 172
in classification of languages 75–7
East Asian languages and 13
non-European languages and 11
problem of 10–13
in side-lining of Asian languages 87
Southeast Asian languages and 11–12
European languages 12, 15, 72, 75, 77–8, 82, 97
Asian languages *vs.* 79–80
contemporary linguistics 10–11
non-European languages and 80–1
pro-drop in 113, 115
Evans, N. 11
experimental syntax 54

Ferreira, F. 125
Fierman, W. 84
Filled-Gap Effect 46–7
Fillmore, C. J. 137
Finnish, flexible word order in 110
Firth, A. 28, 32
Fischer, S. 110

Index

flexible ordering 93, 96
flexible word order viii, 14, 93, 107, 127
   in Asian languages 88–9, 96
   in Australian Aboriginal languages 108–9
   in Bulgarian 110–11
   in Finnish 110
   in Hungarian 108
   in Nhanda 109
   in Polish 108
   in Slovene 110
Fodor, J. D. 123
Foreign Service Institute (FSI) 74
Fracchia, J. 167
Frajzyngier, Z. 108
Francis, W. S. 138
frequency asymmetry 121–4
   domain-efficient structures 122
   minimized domain (MiD) 123
   syntactic and prosodic structures 123
Fromkin, V. 117–18
FSI. *See* Foreign Service Institute
'The Future of Modern Foreign Languages in Higher Education' 75

Gabriel, C. 110
Garcia, M. P. 137
Garten, J. 16
Gelman, R. 138
generative grammars 1, 9, 24, 35, 39, 47, 51
   Chomskyan tradition of 87
   computational efficiency in 130
   grammaticality and 42, 43
   independently motivated rules 130
   intuitions in 52, 53
   PF-deletion approach 124, 125
   syntactic operations and 105, 106
   syntactic structure 125
generative linguistics 27, 37, 38, 55, 101, 143, 171
   Chomskyan 10, 22
   syntactic categories in 12
generative theory 2, 130
Geveler, J. 52
Gil, D. 10, 11, 12, 13
glossing difficulties 7–100
glossing pragmatic particles 97, 100
Goddard, C. 88
Gogolin, I. 28

Göksel, A. 129
Goldman-Eisler, F. 117
Google 19, 69, 151, 162
   Alexa 136
   ChatGPT *vs.* 148–50
Google Scholar 85
Google Translate 142, 145, 148–50, 157
   Asian languages 149, 179n1
   feedback about translations 151
   human language 149–50
   for Indonesian 158
   translation resources 149
   for Vietnamese 157
Google Trends 19
GPT. *See* ChatGPT
grammaticality 41, 47, 51, 55, 64, 69, 121. *See also* grammaticality judgement
   acceptability notion 48
   for Asian languages 42–3, 52–5
   checking, globally 50–1
   as core criterion 43–4
   efficiency and frequency in 42, 46–8
   felicity notion 48
   from historical perspective 43
   of hybrid varieties 55–6
   knowledge as purely syntactic 48–9
   limitations 42
   methods used to determine 51–2
   of other Englishes 61–5
   socio-pragmatic awkwardness 49–50
grammaticality judgement x, 22, 42, 54, 55, 69, 177n1
   criteria 48, 56
   limitations of 44–6
   on linguistic forms 51–2
   prosody in 49
grammaticality test 44, 52
Gross, M. 37

Halliday, M. A. K. 8
Hamada, Y. 33
Harris, D. 167
hash sign (#) symbol 45, 48
Hawkins, J. 47, 96, 123, 140
HCI. *See* human–computer interaction
heavy NP Shift 47
Henderson, J. Y. 92
Herodotus 72
Hindi. *See* linguistic hybridity, in Singlish

Hiramoto, M. 60
Hittites 72
Hokkien. *See* linguistic hybridity, in Singlish
Hoffmann, A. 168
Holliday, A. 28
Hong Kong English 63
Huang, Y. 113, 114
human articulation 135
human brain 10, 145, 146, 148
human–computer interaction (HCI) 3, 6, 66, 67, 144, 166, 173
human language 3, 174
   animals learning 17
   creativity and 142–3
   processing 16
human(s)
   AI generation *vs.* 137
   synthetic voices *vs.* 136–7
   use of language 35
Hungarian, flexible word order in 108
hybrid varieties, grammaticality of 55–6
Hymes, D. H. 137

ideal native speaker 2, 6, 26, 31, 43, 52, 67
ideal speaker-listeners 2, 21–2, 32, 130, 133
incrementality hypothesis 120, 121
Indian English 62
Indonesian 116
   ChatGPT for 158–9
   Riau 11–12
Infeld, L. 5
injustices, of syntactic terminology/architecture 105
   Anglocentrism in decision-making 124–6
   core *vs.* periphery 105–6
   disfluencies 117–19
   frequency asymmetry 121–4
   independently motivated rules 130
   operational injustice 119–31
   output-only syntax (no procedural syntax) 120–1
   pragmatic/ecological insensitivity 130–1
   pro-drop 111–17
   scrambling 106–11
   tense marking 115–17

   terminal injustice 106–19
   verb-centred architecture 126–9
internet language 64
intuition tests 52, 53

Jakobson, R. 87
Janenova, S. 85
Japanese 4, 25, 39, 55, 73, 91
   ChatGPT for 153–4
   linguistics 55, 94
   use of particles in 90
Jelinek, F. xiv
Jenny, M. 129
Johnston, T. 108
Jones, S. P. 78
Journal of Linguistics 80

Kazakh mistranslations, in ChatGPT 160–1
Kecskes, I. 137
Kennison, S. M. 110
Kerslake, C. 129
Kiaer, J. 51, 77, 95, 100, 127, 139, 143
Kim, S. 54
Kireva, E. 110
Kirkpatrick, A. 63
Kluge, B. 12
Kondo, M. 51
Korean 25, 50, 54, 73, 74, 79, 95, 99
   ChatGPT for 152–3
   linguistics 4, 55, 94
   second-person pronoun in 89
   as super-hard language 153
The Korea Times 74
K-pop tweets 55
Kubota, R. 30
Kuno, S. 90

Labov, W. 52
Lakoff, R. T. 5, 9
Lalijee, M. 118
LaMDA ('language model for dialogue applications') 69
The Language Instinct (Pinker) 168
language modelling 147
languages. *See also specific entries*
   ability 17–18
   acquisition 17, 31, 33, 34, 118, 138
   categories 76

208 Index

deductive perspective 8–9
inductive perspective 8–9
tenses in 115–17
use 2, 4, 5, 9, 14, 15, 23, 133, 139
Lao 81–2
descriptive grammars of 92
large language model (LLM) 150
Latin 73, 76, 108, 126
pro-drop in 112–13
Lefebvre, C. 52
Leipzig Glossing Rules 90, 95, 97, 98
Lemoine, J. F. 136–7
Levelt, W. J. M. 36
Levinson, S. C. 11
lexical expressions 102
lexical functional grammar (LFG) 101
LFG. *See* lexical functional grammar
linguistic ability 4, 17, 27, 34
linguistic competence 10, 15, 19, 27, 32, 64, 122
human 68, 69, 138, 171, 172, 173–4
studies into 36
symbols and 67–8
linguistic forms, grammaticality judgements on 51–2
linguistic hybridity, in Singlish 56
English 57
English + Hokkien + Chinese (literal translation) 60
English + Malay 57–8
English + Malay + Chinese + Southern Chinese languages 60
English + Malay + Hokkien 59
English + Malay + Hokkien + Southern Chinese languages 61
English + Malay + Tamil/Hindi 58–9
linguistics xi
collaborations of different fields in 7–8
competence 19
curriculums 4
descriptive 9
Eurocentric perspectives in 87
independently motivated principles 14–15
performance 19
pragmatic principles 36–7
rules 14–15
linguistic theories xi, xiii, 2, 3, 14, 23, 33, 93, 130

artificial intelligence and 6
deductive approach 7
on deriving rules 5
formalism 6
functionalism 6
inclusivity in 31
inductive approach 6–7
language use and 5
weakness of 15
linguistic variations 33, 53, 141–2
Liu, M. Y. 83
LLM. *See* large language model
Loewenthal, R. 84
long short-term memory (LSTM) networks 147
Lopez, S. S. 137
LSTM. *See* long short-term memory
Luong, P. J. 83
Lyons, J. 117

Macedonian, pragmatic markers in 98–9
machine learning 26, 146, 168
Mandarin 56, 79, 129, 151
ChatGPT for 154–6
Mao Zedong 154
Matthewson, L. 98
memory 50, 54, 123–4, 137, 140, 141
interplay between prosody and 138
limitations 2, 10, 21, 22, 36, 41, 130, 133
in verbal abilities 138
Mendivil-Giro, J. 6, 7
Mesthrie, R. 27, 28, 56
MiD. *See* minimized domain
Miller, N. 135
Minimal Link Condition 130
minimized domain (MiD) 123
Modern Foreign Languages 75
modern language 75–7
Mongolian, ChatGPT for 161–2
monolingualism 27–8
Montgomery, D. W. 82
'more is different' concept 145–6
Morford, J. P. 97
morpho-syntactic variation 53, 140, 143
Mufwene, S. 104
Muhamedowa, R. 129
Muller, N. 52
multilingualism 29–30, 32, 64, 83, 171–2
Murray, J. A. H. 62

Murray, N. 98
Mycock, L. 110

Nagao, M. 15
native language 27, 29, 30
native speakerism
  harmfulness of 28–9
  linguistic discrimination and 30
native speakers (NS) 29
  definition 27
  generative tradition 27
  in language use 33
  negative consequences 28
  non-native speakers *vs.* 32, 33
  notion of 29
natural language 26, 95, 133, 137, 146, 167, 168
Naver 151
Newmeyer, F. J. 8
Ng, M. Y. 63
Nhanda, flexible word order in 109
NNS. *See* non-native speakers
non-European languages 11, 13, 55, 76, 80–1, 171, 173
non-native speakers (NNS) 29, 30, 31, 33
  issue of 28
  native speakers *vs.* 32, 33
non-pro-drop languages 112, 113
Nordlinger, R. 99, 129
NS. *See* native speakers

ordinary language, importance of 24–5
Orientalism 75
oriental language 76–7
Ouhalla, J. 23
output-only syntax 120–1
OV (object–verb) ordering 95–6, 177n1

Pāṇini 87
Papago Translator 151–2
particles
  constructive 94, 95
  expressive 94, 95
  plethora of 94–5
  rich use of 89–91
Pederson, E. 97
Perez-Pereira, M. 138
PF-deletion approaches 124, 125
Phillips, C. 37–8, 44, 54, 55, 120, 121, 140

phonation 135
phrasal verbs 122
'pick-and-choose' approach 91–2
Pinker, Steven 168
Plotkin, V. 107
Polish, flexible word order in 108
pragmatic/ecological insensitivity 130–1
pragmatics 116, 133, 163
  3-E model 139–44
  AI models 164–5
  considerations 173–4
  human articulation 135
  human languages and 142
  human *vs.* synthetic voices 136–7
  memory 138
  motivations 139
  particles 60, 61, 97, 100
  processing 1
  prosodic balance 134
  resource-sensitivity 133–4
  synthetic voices 136
  translation, ChatGPT in 162–3
pre-minimalist X-bar theory 91
Prensky, Marc xiii
pro-drop 106, 111, 124, 131
  in Classical Greek and Latin 112–13
  definition 111
  in European languages 113, 115
  null objects and 113–14
  phenomenon 101–2
  in Russian 115
  in Sign Language of the Netherlands 114–15
  in Spanish 114–15
pronoun omission phenomenon 101, 111
prosody 41, 42, 48, 73, 88, 123, 134
  in grammaticality judgements 49
  interplay between memory and 138
  prosodic balance 134
  prosodic proximity 140, 141
  prosodic structures 123–4

rational choice theory (RCT) 165–6
RCT. *See* rational choice theory
recurrent neural networks (RNN) 147
Reid, T. R. 73
Review of Verbal Behavior (Skinner) 65
Riau Indonesian 11–12
Richards, D. 137

Richardson, W. J. 10
Rizzi, L. 8
RNN. *See* recurrent neural networks
Romance languages 107
Romo, L. F. 138
Ross, J. R. 47, 130
Rules and Representations (Chomsky) 33
Russian 82, 84, 107
    ChatGPT for 157–8
    pro-drop in 115
    second-person pronoun 158

Sadler, L. 99, 129
Sag, I. A. 105
Sampson, G. 163
Sapir, E. 13
Sapir-Whorf hypothesis 73
Sato, Y. 60
Saussure, F. 87
Schembri, A. 108
Schroeder, S. 14
Schneider's Dynamic Model 29
Schutze, C. T. 44, 45, 52, 53
scrambling viii, 71, 94, 101, 103, 106, 111, 130, 131
    at core or periphery 106–11
    definition 106
    flexible word order 107–11
    languages 106–7, 112
    in syntactic theory 107
    in Turkish 88–9
second-person pronoun
    English 100–1
    Indonesian 158–9
    Japanese 154
    Mongolian 161, 162
    Russian 158
    Turkish 159
    Vietnamese 157
Seikel, J. A. 135
semantically abnormal sentence 48
semiotic repertoires 26, 68
Shay, E. 108
Shei, C. 129
Shuck, G. 30
Siewierska, A. 107, 115
Sign Language of the Netherlands, pro-drop in 114–15
Silver, R. E. 30

simplicity hypothesis 39, 72, 102–3, 122, 130, 174
Singlish (Singaporean English)
    linguistic hybridity in (*see* linguistic hybridity, in Singlish)
    as mix of multiple languages 56
Siri 136
Skinner, B. F. 65, 143
Slovene, flexible word order in 110
Smagulova, J. 83
smart devices 1, 6, 166
social grammars 65–6
social media 19, 22, 23, 43, 63–4, 173
Song, J. J. 107
Southeast Asian languages 11, 57–8, 78, 96, 116
    context dependency 12
    multilingualism in 29–30
Soviet Union 82–3
Spanish, pro-drop in 114–15
speaker inconsistency 52
speech production 135, 138
split intransitivity hypothesis 4
Staal, J. F. 87
Stillings, N. A. 113
Stowe, L. A. 46, 47
Stringer, A. 84
structure building 47, 48, 89, 90, 96, 116, 120
subject pronoun omission 112
superficial differences 23–4
Sutton, L. A. 5, 9
symbolic competence 67–8
syntactically abnormal sentence 48
syntactic architecture 10, 16, 53, 81, 93, 175
    constituency conflict 120
    in generative grammar 42–3
    incrementality hypothesis 120–1
syntactic architecture injustice 119
    Anglocentrism in decision-making 124–6
    frequency asymmetry 121–4
    independently motivated rules 130
    output-only syntax (no procedural syntax) 120–1
    pragmatic/ecological insensitivity 130–1
    verb-centred architecture 126–9
syntactic competence 1, 68, 134, 146

syntactic flexibility 93, 112, 117, 119, 130, 131
syntactic freedom 71, 93–4, 124, 133
syntactic operations 105–6, 164
syntactic representations 9–10, 91, 120, 124
syntactic structure 10, 18, 47, 88, 95, 115, 120, 123–5, 135
Syntactic Structures (Chomsky) xiii, 1, 2, 19, 43, 44, 81
syntactic terminology injustices 105–6
   disfluency 117–19
   pro-drop 111–17
   scrambling 106–11
   tense marking 115–17
syntactic variation 10, 14, 36, 128, 139, 143
syntax 5, 13, 19, 24, 26, 94, 126, 174–5
   Asian languages in 71–2
   contemporary 25
   generative 115, 134, 141
   output-only 120–1
   pragmatics in 133
   sensible 3–4, 171, 174–5
synthetic voices 136–7

Tabor, W. 51
Takano, Y. 94
Tamil. *See* linguistic hybridity, in Singlish
Temmerman, T. 178n7
tense marking 111, 115–17
Thagard, P. 149, 150
theoretical linguistic 2, 3, 13, 15, 23, 64, 103
theory of language 24
Thibault, H. 85
Thompson, H. R. 81
Toktomushev, K. 84, 85
transformer-based language models
   BERT to GPT-3 147
   cost-efficiency 147–8
transformer model 147
Tsujimura, N. 89, 92
Tun, H. 129
Turkish
   ChatGPT for 159–60
   scrambling in 88–9
Twilhaar, J. N. 114
Twitter 19

UG. *See* Universal Grammar
ungrammaticality 25, 48, 50
Universal Grammar (UG) viii, 6, 10–11, 13, 17, 23, 24, 34, 53, 71

van den Bogaerde, B. 114
Vanderveken, D. 164
Vaswani, A. 147
Velupillai, V. 109
verb-centred architecture 126–9
   verb-finality 54, 127
   verb-less structures 128–9
verb-final languages 37, 50, 93, 121
   Asian languages 95–6
   sidelining of 13–14
Vietnamese, ChatGPT for 156–7
virtual assistants 136, 137
virtual reality (VR) xiv, 22–3
VO (verb–object) ordering 96
Vovin, A. 73
VR. *See* virtual reality
Vulchanova, M. 29

Wagner, J. 28, 32
WALS. *See* World Atlas of Language Structures
Wasow, T. 46, 47
Western European languages 7, 14, 37, 81, 87, 104, 126, 127
Westminster Education Forum 75
Wheeler, G. 83
Widdowson, D. 137
Wilcox, S. 97
Wilkin, P. 17
Wilson, M. 168
Wilss, W. 17
Wiltschko, M. 97
Wittgenstein, L. xi, 14, 119
World Atlas of Language Structures (WALS) 88, 90, 95–6, 101, 107, 113, 116, 131, 177n2
The World Atlas of Language Structures Online (WALS) 37

Yuen Ren Chao 13
Yu, F. T. S. 164

Zdorenko, T. 113, 115

www.ingramcontent.com/pod-product-compliance
Lightning Source LLC
Chambersburg PA
CBHW052109300426
44116CB00010B/1593